More Praise for *Point, Click & Wow!*

"Stands out. It's a real roadmap for organizing and creating better communications. It guides us step by step in building powerful PowerPoint presentations. But it does much more. It impresses on us how we build our own careers by projecting real executive presence when we make presentations. It's not just what we say . . . it's how we say it. I've already started to use some of Claudyne's suggestions."

—Michael D. Jeans, president, New Directions, Inc.

"Please don't buy this book. If you do, that will be one less person committing Death by PowerPoint, and one less person who might need to seek my services or attend my conference. One less person boring an audience with gratuitous animation or over laden text slides. Does the world really need one less person committing presentation blunders in public?

Well, the world needs about 15,000,000 less people doing those things, and Claudyne is the person to be singing that message. I particularly like how she advocates in Chapter 4 for templates that actually contain content instead of just a slide master or two. And a few pages later when she writes, 'refuse to give up white space'—yes! And do you own a wireless remote, as she recommends? No? That's like a carpenter not owning a hammer!

So please don't buy this book . . . but if you insist, I am sure that you will master your inner monologue (Chapter 7) and become the magic in your own presentation (Chapter 9)."

—Rick Altman, The PowerPoint Live User Conference,
www.powerpointlive.com

"This book is an essential resource for all professionals whose success depends greatly on how effectively they communicate with their many audiences, whether these be corporate clients, public-policy analysts, university academics, the public at large, or graduate students. In this book readers will find the insider knowledge of public speaking that we all need but were never taught."

—Estela Mara Bensimon, professor and director, Center for
Urban Education, University of Southern California

"My presentations persuade my audiences better than ever before! Claudyne's first book saved me hours of time by turning the formerly intimidating PowerPoint menu and templates into manageable, helpful tools to deliver appealing slides. Her latest guide helps me infuse these slides with coherent, compelling narrative threads."

—Dave Fink, sales and profit training consultant

"Effective communication is *essential* for success. The truth is most people have not learned *how* to communicate. Fortunately, Claudyne is here as your personal coach throughout this comprehensive guide to preparing and delivering a successful presentation. She will teach you how to focus your message, how to connect with your audience and how to communicate with confidence."

—Julie Terberg, presentation designer,
author and consultant, Terberg Design

"Talk about WOW, this book is not just another 'how to create and present effective PowerPoints'; it's about living, working and communicating in a community where people actually meet face to face and interact. This powerful book is full of practical tools and effective techniques that teach a complete presentation style where communicating shades of meaning and listening are balanced with a clear understanding how to create the perfect visual. I know my presentations skills just got a big boost!"

—John Kalb, futurist and founder of Home Preferred

"Even the most polished speaker will find new tactics and even small but so thoughtful tips about using PowerPoint and organizing slide shows. Given the importance of making persuasive presentations, this should be required reading for every manager. I would particularly recommend it for university speech classes and MBA students."

—Martin Kenney, professor, Department of Human and
Community Development and senior fellow, Center for
Entrepreneurship, University of California, Davis

"I've just finished reading *Point, Click & Wow!* and now I know what to do to improve my next couples workshop. I'll be giving new information right away, looking at the right people when I answer questions, and using facts, opinions and emotions in their proper order. I'll be more confident because I practiced my opening talk the way Ms. Wilder recommends, and I'll have practiced daily to overcome my tendency to be a nervous pleaser when I first meet a new couples workshop group. And my PowerPoint slides will rock! Thank you, Claudyne, for an excellent book."

—Mona Barbera, Ph.D., author, *Bring Yourself to Love:
How Couples Can Turn Disconnection into Intimacy*

"Claudyne has provided us with all of the tools and know how to create powerful presentations for any situation and any audience. Her real-world experience in coaching clients of all types comes through clearly in her practical recommendations. This book is one that you should read through from cover to cover—in an emergency, the easy to use format also lets you dive into it a section at a time to find last minute help for an ailing presentation. Her checklists and templates work wonders!"

—Lynne Richer, director, Learning & Development, Avid Technology

"This book is worth its weight in gold. Once you buy it, you'll have, in one place, a fantastic resource that can unlock for you all the secrets of the greatest presenters. It not only covers the 3 Ts (presentation tips, techniques and technologies), it also helps you to understand and connect with your audience so that you can be a much more successful and relaxed presenter than you may have ever thought possible. And, thanks to Claudyne's enthusiasm for the subject, you'll find *Point, Click & Wow!* to be a fun read, as well!"

—Dennis Ricks, president and CEO, CrystalGraphics, Inc.

"Presentation software can be a visual aid or a visual distraction. *Point, Click & Wow!* has all the elements to provide those with a point the power to present, with clarity and conviction. No other book provides so much practical help for presenters."

—Stephen J. Resch, associate professor, Indiana Wesleyan University, College of Adult and Professional Studies.

"*Point, Click & Wow!* distills Claudyne's wisdom about making your presentation clean, clear, and concise, to get the outcome you want. A 'must read' for any presenter, from the factory floor to the boardroom."

—Tom Caldwell, Summit Associates of Bedford LLC

"A first rate guide with tons of practical tips to improve and fine tune your presentations. Organized to the 'T' and easy to digest. Applied learning at its best!"

—Jon Rosen, president, Impact Communications, Greenwich, CT

"It may be rare that an endorsement is provided by a former trainee, but this is the case. Without a doubt this is a book that will keep you the presenter from running yourself ragged because of an unorganized approach to developing your presentation. Claudyne Wilder, using clear language, practical suggestions and field-tested trainee advice, coaches the reader through each phase of a presentation. This thoughtful updated version is rich with all of the coaching support a busy executive or academic leader will need. After reading this book, you will never approach developing your presentation as before, because all of the practical approaches are at your fingertips."

—Leonard C. Beckum, Ph.D., associate vice president for Academic Affairs and professor, The Pacific Graduate School of Psychology, Stanford, Palo Alto, CA

"*Point, Click & Wow!* is a great resource for presenters and is chock full of great tips and techniques. The book offers many great suggestions that will take any presentation from good to great. Anyone who has to give presentations must have a copy of this book and refer to it frequently. If you are not using Claudyne's suggestions, then you are probably not giving a good presentation!"

—Steve Mandel, founder, Mandel Communications, Inc.,
and author, *Effective Presentation Skills*

"Whether you are a novice or seasoned presenter, *Point, Click & Wow!* has critical insights for you to look, sound and feel like a winner. Claudyne is clearly the 'John Wooden' in the world of successful presentations."

—Gary A. Williams, co-author, *The 5 Paths to Persuasion.*

"This powerful book covers everything that's needed to deliver influential presentations. I'll keep near me at *all* times when I'm working, on the road and in the office. It's fast and easy to find the essential wisdom and practical tips that will draw your audience in and hold their attention."

—Stephanie Wu, senior vice president of Program Development, City Year

"Claudyne Wilder is one of the most articulate and organized presenters out there today. This book served as a wake-up call for me, not just as a refresher, but a revitalizer. Claudyne gives us what we all need in order to produce our best presentations."

—Jim Tull, International Conflict Resolution Specialist

"*Point, Click & Wow* is a resource that all must have if giving presentations. This practical and easy-to-read book provides the novice as well as the seasoned presenter with the tools and techniques to be successful. I recommend this book to everyone I coach on presentation skills!"

—Marci Bloch, director of learning & development,
Fresenius Medical Care - North America

About This Book

Why is the topic important?

You present every day of your life, maybe not formally but informally. If you have a job in a corporation, you will present in meetings in front of your peers or to the executives in the company. If you are like most people, you have never really learned the skills and art of how to create and deliver an effective presentation. But your future depends on your ability to speak confidently and coherently in front of people. Your promotions depend on your ability to make a point or state a concise argument in a meeting. Your desire to receive more resources for one of your key projects depends on your ability to convince upper management. Let's face it; you should invest time in studying the key ingredients to looking and sounding extremely confident in front of an audience. This book will help you find the magic in your presentations, the magic of creating an effective presentation and connecting to your audience.

What can you achieve with this book?

This book is a compilation of all the seminars and individual coaching sessions I have done over the past years. When you actually go through this book, use the worksheets, and follow the guidelines, I guarantee you will have success. I know, because I see my clients achieve more success than they imagined possible. But you have to do the work. I am giving you all the necessary information and PowerPoint ideas. All you have to do is carry out my suggestions. You will be able to create a fabulous, results-oriented presentation in much less time and with better outcomes.

How is this book organized?

This book is organized in the way I work with my clients. I'm pretending you are my client and I am coaching you. I open with a discussion about content and focusing your message, move on to considering your audience's interests, offer several chapters on creating effective slides, give pointers on technology issues, rehearsing your presentation, and finally how to demonstrate confidence and professionalism when you present. Each chapter opens with a problem/solution format, presents a story to illustrate the issue, and then goes on to explore the issue in detail, providing many examples and tips. Each chapter also includes at least one checklist to help ensure that your presentations stay on track.

What additional training materials are available with this book?

The accompanying CD-ROM includes copies of the checklists and PowerPoint slide samples, some bonus PowerPoint designs, plus added PowerPoint resources for you to use. This book can also be used as a text for teaching presentation training at colleges and universities. If you are an instructor, use the URL below to access the course outline and extra materials that are available online for free.

www.pfeiffer.com/go/pcw3e

Consider this book your own personal coaching session with me. I look forward to hearing from you and receiving e-mails about your successes. Contact me at: claudyne@wilderpresentations.com.

About Pfeiffer

Pfeiffer serves the professional development and hands-on resource needs of training and human resource practitioners and gives them products to do their jobs better. We deliver proven ideas and solutions from experts in HR development and HR management, and we offer effective and customizable tools to improve workplace performance. From novice to seasoned professional, Pfeiffer is the source you can trust to make yourself and your organization more successful.

Essential Knowledge Pfeiffer produces insightful, practical, and comprehensive materials on topics that matter the most to training and HR professionals. Our Essential Knowledge resources translate the expertise of seasoned professionals into practical, how-to guidance on critical workplace issues and problems. These resources are supported by case studies, worksheets, and job aids and are frequently supplemented with CD-ROMs, websites, and other means of making the content easier to read, understand, and use.

Essential Tools Pfeiffer's Essential Tools resources save time and expense by offering proven, ready-to-use materials—including exercises, activities, games, instruments, and assessments—for use during a training or team-learning event. These resources are frequently offered in looseleaf or CD-ROM format to facilitate copying and customization of the material.

Pfeiffer also recognizes the remarkable power of new technologies in expanding the reach and effectiveness of training. While e-hype has often created whizbang solutions in search of a problem, we are dedicated to bringing convenience and enhancements to proven training solutions. All our e-tools comply with rigorous functionality standards. The most appropriate technology wrapped around essential content yields the perfect solution for today's on-the-go trainers and human resource professionals.

Essential resources for training and HR professionals

www.pfeiffer.com

Point, Click & Wow!

THE TECHNIQUES AND HABITS OF SUCCESSFUL PRESENTERS

Third Edition

Claudyne Wilder

Pfeiffer

A Wiley Imprint

www.pfeiffer.com

Published by Pfeiffer An Imprint of Wiley.
989 Market Street, San Francisco, CA 94103-1741
www.pfeiffer.com

For additional copies/bulk purchases of this book in the U.S. please contact 800-274-4434.

Pfeiffer books and products are available through most bookstores. To contact Pfeiffer directly call our Customer Care Department within the U.S. at 800-274-4434, outside the U.S. at 317-572-3985, fax 317-572-4002, or visit www.pfeiffer.com.

Pfeiffer also publishes its books in a variety of electronic formats. Some content that appears in print may not be available in electronic books.

Library of Congress Cataloging-in-Publication Data:

Wilder, Claudyne.
    Point, click & wow! : the techniques and habits of successful presenters / Claudyne Wilder.—3rd ed.
      p. cm.
    Includes bibliographical references and index.
    ISBN 978-0-7879-9745-8 (paper/cd)
      1. Business presentations—Graphic methods. 2. Multimedia systems in business presentations.
      I. Title.
    HF5718.22.W55   2008
    658.4'5—dc22

                                                          2008016490

Acquiring Editor: Marisa Kelley	Production Editor: Michael Kay
Marketing Manager: Brian Grimm	Editor: Rebecca Taff
Director of Development: Kathleen Dolan Davies	Manufacturing Supervisor: Becky Morgan
Developmental Editor: Susan Rachmeler	

Printed in the United States of America

Printing   10 9 8 7 6 5 4

To my husband, whose love, support, and joy of life enabled me to write this book. Tad dances me through life—literally with Argentine Tango and figuratively every day.

CONTENTS

CONTENTS OF THE CD-ROM

CD Summary and Use Statement

CHAPTER 1: FOCUS ON YOUR KEY MESSAGES

Exhibit 1.1: The Presentation Overview
Exhibit 1.3: Mini-Talk Meeting Overview
Exhibit 1.5: Presentation Checklist
Figures 1.1 to 1.30: Formats and Executive Summaries

CHAPTER 2: CONNECT TO YOUR AUDIENCE

Exhibit 2.2: Connect Checklist
Figure 2.1: The Communication Pyramid
Figure 2.2: Sample Quiz Game Slide
Figure 2.3: Your Priorities: Additions and Comments
Figure 2.4: Agenda Slide

CHAPTER 3: USE SPECIFIC POWERPOINT FEATURES

Exhibit 3.1: Using PowerPoint Checklist
Figure 3.1: Ten Steps to Your Success
Figure 3.1: Ten Steps to Your Success with Hyperlinks

CHAPTER 4: DESIGN PROFESSIONAL SLIDE LOOKS

Figures 4.13 to 4.29: Professionally Designed "Empty" Content Slides
Exhibit 4.1: Slide Looks for Your Library Checklist

ACKNOWLEDGMENTS

So many people offered suggestions and ideas for this basically new book. Geetesh Bajaj offered his expertise on PowerPoint 2007, and was my partner in doing our presentation survey. Steve Zwickel gave his advice on giving technical, academic, and poster presentations. Joan Babinski clarified the finer points about on-demand presentations. Ellen Finkelstein gave me her web presentation ideas. Joe Giglio gave me the idea to discuss academic presentations and then added his own invaluable ideas to that section. Thank you to Terry Williams for sharing his Bluefield's project with us. Sally Iles shared her process work at Massachusetts General Hospital. Colin Purrington provided some really excellent information on giving a poster presentation. Cheryl Hubbard from Senture let us show her slides. Amanda Pullen graciously let us show Harvard Medical International overview slides. Ginger Burr provided her expertise on dressing for a presentation. Gary Williams graciously edited my information from his *5 Paths to Persuasion* book.

Then there were the designers who helped. Julie Terberg graciously let me show the slides she designed for Harvard Medical International. She crafted fabulous professional visual concepts for Harvard Medical International's presentations. Kelly Ellis was a jewel. She was ready to redo slides at a moment's notice. Kelly was indispensable to helping me with this book. She also contributed some of the before and after slides. Jennifer Root, my assistant, provided support and help throughout this effort. Neil Gray let us redo his slides and show them.

My husband read this whole book three times. His comments and edits were invaluable in making the book come together and added levity and spice. He now deserves many free weekends. My sister Nanci La Rue offered many useful ideas based on her work in business. David Fink read chapters and then edited them with wonderful comments. Nancy Vescuso read several chapters at the last moment. Danielle Thompson read several chapters and offered very specific suggestions on how to clarify key points. Taylor La Rue, Carly Turpel, and Corey Turpel keep reminding me how well children show their enthusiasm and exuberance for a subject. Adults need to keep encouraging this part of themselves. Dan Drop of ADTech gave his ideas about the future of technology.

Thank you to these executives who offered their suggestions on demonstrating executive presence: Ross Elkin, Drew Staniar, Tad Jankowski, Philippe Dauman, Mitch Rubenstein, Mike Jeans, and Shari Redstone. And to all those executives who have shared with me their expectations of how they desire their employees to present. All of these people added their ideas to my book, and I thank them for their time and very useful suggestions: John Kalb, Marion and Peter London, Stephanie Wu, Peter Butterfield, Judie Knoerle, James Creutz, Marilyn Smith, Donna Harr, Carol Rosener, Martha Miller, Sarah Murdock, Ann Riding, Sandra Barnes, Bonnie Sandberg, Rae Drysdale, Sally Iles, Dave Poulin, Cindy Yates, Tim Dees, Heather Stefl, Susan Arb, Henry Mora, Neil Gray, Fernando Quintero, Barry Mirrer, Nina Coil, Michele McNamara, Anne Camille, Jon Rosen, Graciela Pineiro, Nick Miller, Greg Rocco, Don Lambert, Frank Campagna, Richard Armstrong, Jeffrey Maxwell, Estela Bensimon, Steven Zwickel, Holly Vogel, Daniel Gonzalez, Nadja Krylov, Michele McNamara, and Dave Hogan. My sense of gratitude goes out to all the participants in my classes who willingly shared themselves so that all of us could learn from their failures and successes.

Thank you to all my colleagues and clients over the years. You have taught me that the ability to make effective and confident presentations in one's professional as well as personal life is one of the most important skills that we, as constantly communicating human beings, will ever learn.

I also thank Michael Kay, the production editor, who took such care with so many details. Adrian Morgan, senior art director, helped design the cover just right. Marisa Kelley, senior assistant editor, kept everything moving on schedule. Susan Rachmeler provided excellent editorial ideas.

This book is your presentation coach to advise you how to look and sound confident and credible when speaking. Since chances are that I will never have the pleasure of meeting you or have the opportunity of seeing you, my readers, in my classes, I have taken the opportunity to organize the contents of this book so that the ideas and concepts are presented in much the same way they are when I personally consult with or teach my clients. You will be reading and doing exactly what my clients do when we work together. As I write this book, I imagine that you have come to me asking for help in putting together a very important presentation. And you have just told me, "This has got to be the best presentation of my career." This is your personalized coaching book. I guarantee that when you follow the advice in this book and really do the key tasks and utilize the skills I suggest, you will be seen as a credible and confident person when you make your presentations. Since these two traits are universally recognized as being invaluable in business and social contexts, this will put you well on your way to being very successful in whatever endeavor you choose to follow.

This is the third edition of *Point, Click & Wow!* The first version came out in 1996, in color, no less. The subtitle was "*A Quick Guide to Brilliant Laptop*

Presentations" and on the cover was a beautiful graphic of a laptop and all kinds of chart-like images. The "Wow" in the title at that point meant the graphics you showed. But since that time everyone is showing fancy graphics—or at least trying to. Indeed, we are inundated on a daily basis with incredible graphic images, whether watching television, surfing the web, or perusing magazines. And quite honestly, people are tired of eye-hurting animations, grating sounds that don't fit the talk, slide after slide of unreadable text, non-understandable charts, and/ or five unrecognizable pictures on one slide. I would say that the advice that I give these days is, "Cut, cut, cut. Use fewer animations (and never the fly animations) and fewer slides. No one wants to sit through all this."

Today the "Wow" stands for YOU! You must be the Wow. The Wow is you talking. Why? Because no matter how fancy you make your slides, how many new images, animations, and colors you use, you still have to explain what your audience is seeing. And you will create the Wow with your explanations and stories. If you don't do that, your presentation becomes something the audience has to sit through and look interested when in fact they are bored and daydreaming or—even worse—sleeping with their eyes open.

Geetesh Bajaj and I did a survey on the Internet, where 750 professionals shared their successes and frustrations with developing, designing, and giving presentations. In this study, participants identified many barriers to effective presentations. You will read more about this survey in different parts of this book. Here are a few of the results:

- *Only* 22 percent of respondents are very satisfied with their presentations.
- 42 percent said 10 to 20 percent of their presentations were a waste of time.
- 58 percent of presenters spend over three hours organizing content for each thirty-minute presentation.
- 52 percent said they could save from forty-five minutes to three hours if given outlines for specific types of presentations.
- 67 percent are not provided these outlines by their companies.

This book is about how to set up and create the Wow. There is, of course, information about slides, but more in the context of how to organize the content on the slides. This is not a book about using PowerPoint, although I give you some ideas that I see my clients do not know. You will be able to use this book to put together any type of speech; it is not just focused on people who give PowerPoint presentations.

Over the years I have found that the need to make a good presentation is not limited to business, but pervades our daily lives. In the last year I stood up in front of two hundred people at a funeral service and read a poem about a much-loved friend. Believe me, all the skills I talk about in this book I used at that moment. Because, you see, not only did I have to read the poem, which I had practiced, but I had to speak extemporaneously—all the while seeing my dear friend's wife right in front of me.

One of my clients speaks on controversial subjects at town meetings. She said, "I am amazed at myself. Now when I use the executive summary and speak, people listen." You too will find these skills invaluable as you live your life.

For those of you who already feel that you are experts at presenting and for all of you who want to explore some of the unlimited possibilities of personalizing your talk and aiming for more success, especially read Chapter 8, Demonstrate Executive Presence.

WHAT'S NEW IN THIS EDITION?

I rewrote this book to share with you all the experience I have had since I wrote the second edition. I also wrote it for those of you who will come to my classes and want a book to refresh your memory about all the learnings you took away from the seminar.

You have to do much more than put together a "deck" of slides. In fact, the term "deck" is fast disappearing from people's vocabulary. Now, more than ever, the "personal" or Wow factor has become what tips the balance between a successful presentation and one that fails. It has been a personal delight to see that, when people from all walks of life can find the Wow in themselves and communicate it to others effectively, they undergo transformations. And it is for that transformational experience that I have rewritten this book.

Here is what is new and/or expanded in this third edition:

• A chapter on demonstrating executive presence

• Almost all the images in the book, that is, all the PowerPoint slides

• Information on giving cross-cultural presentations

- Slides you can copy and use

- Storytelling tips and ideas for structuring your story

- Updated checklists from my two-day Winning Presentations seminar taught in corporations and non-profits

- Explanations of the differences between PowerPoint 2007 and PowerPoint 2003

- Several professionally designed presentation formats you can use to create concise, good-looking presentations—in less time and with better results

- Tips and examples on redesigning PowerPoint text slides

- Executive summary slides you can copy and use

- Examples of a slide image library you can create

- Details on giving successful on-demand and webinar presentations

- Sample add-on programs for PowerPoint

- Key recommendations for persuading executives

HOW TO READ THIS BOOK

Every chapter opens with a situation, problem, solution, and story related to the topic of that chapter. Then you'll read the chapter motto, the table of contents for the chapter, and an introduction. The end of the chapter has a conclusion and then a checklist.

This book is designed for you to read in many different ways.

If you have a presentation to give in the near future: Start with Chapter 1 and fill out the worksheets. You will have an excellent beginning to creating your talk. Then, depending on your talk, read Chapter 2 on connecting with your audience. After that chapter, see what chapter fits your needs for that particular presentation. Print out the "rehearsal checklist" in Chapter 7 and go about practicing those behaviors.

The situation and solution read: Most chapters begin with a sort of executive summary. I present the situation with regard to that particular chapter topic. I discuss the problems and then offer solutions. Then there is a short story sharing what can be different. So you can read all the beginnings of the chapters.

Read or print out the checklists and start using them: If you don't have time now to read the book, then you can read all the checklists at the end of the chapters.

They will tell you how to carry out the suggestions in each chapter. You can then print out the checklists, which are included on the CD that comes with the book.

The PowerPoint read: If you are interested in PowerPoint hints, you can go through the whole book and only read the PowerPoint Tips. This information is set off in each chapter.

The full book read: You can read the book cover-to-cover, sitting in your office or on vacation. For more interest and examples, you can open the CD and look at the color slides on the CD while reading about them at the same time.

The idea boxes: These are ideas for you to think about as you develop, design, or deliver your presentation.

HOW THIS BOOK IS ORGANIZED

When you have a presentation to give, your work consists of three parts. First, you develop and organize the content. Chapters 1 and 2 cover content issues. Second, you design the slides. Chapters 3, 4, and 5 cover different issues related to slide design. Third, you have to deliver the talk. Chapters 6, 7, and 8 present material related to presentation delivery.

Following is more detail about each chapter.

Chapter 1, Focus on Your Key Messages, takes you through the process I use when my clients are organizing the content for a talk. You may say you don't have time for this and will skip to the chapter on making effective slides, but first you really do need to figure out your key messages. This chapter provides you with methods, worksheets, and guidelines to influence others through your storytelling and logic.

Chapter 2, Connect to Your Audience, gives ideas on how to keep your audience engaged. This information is based on what my clients tell me as they listen to people's presentations. It is also based on my own experience of presenting to different types of groups. There is information on the differences between a selling versus a technical presentation. For those of you presenting globally, there are tips on giving cross-cultural presentations. You can also read about web conferences as well as on-demand presentations.

Chapter 3, Use Specific PowerPoint Features, covers those key elements that most presenters need to know in order to use PowerPoint productively. There are also some pointers about the differences between PowerPoint 2003 and 2007. And there are ideas on how to effectively use some of the PowerPoint features when customizing a presentation to an audience. Geetesh Bajaj, author of *Cutting Edge PowerPoint 2007 for Dummies,* provided the PowerPoint 2007 information.

Chapter 4, Design Professional Slide Looks, provides you with ideas on what to put in a library of images that you can use over and over again. This chapter gives you ideas on how to put something on your slides besides line after line of text. It also shows you how to "chunk" or arrange your information into meaningful bites so that it can be shown in a more organized manner. As much as I always tell my clients to avoid putting text on every slide, I realize some will keep doing that. This chapter provides ideas on how to more effectively show content on the screen. I have Julie Terberg of Terberg Designs to thank for letting me show some of her work here.

Chapter 5, Increase Your Credibility with Effective Slides, shows you how to take a slide with text and convert it into a slide that can do more for you. Remember, when people look at your slides, they will be associating their experience with you. How your slides look is definitely important. You will see many examples and gain ideas on how to change your slides into more visually appealing images. Examples of the slides I use when I teach and coach can be found on the accompanying CD. I have Kelly Ellis of Design Endeavors, Inc., to thank for creating many of these slides.

Chapter 6, Prepare for Technology Success, goes over the kinds of problems you can have with technology and how to prevent or anticipate and plan for them. Even though the equipment for making presentations has come a long way, there are no end of things that can go wrong with your laptop, the software, the pointer, the cables, and the projector. If you have been presenting a while, you no doubt have your own stories.

Chapter 7, Rehearse Like It's the Real Thing, asks you to rehearse. After all the work you have done on creating an incredible presentation, you should not practice it for the first time in front of your real audience. Remember, we are working on the Wow factor here. How you look and sound is critical to your presentation and your success. There are checklists and wonderful ideas that will assist and prepare you to look and sound like the professional you are.

Chapter 8, Demonstrate Executive Presence, tells those of you who are moving up in your particular organization the differences you need to be aware of when speaking to executives. This information is based on my own coaching of clients and their experiences, as well as wonderful ideas from executives who listen to presentations on a daily basis. The comments by these executives will motivate you to focus on enhancing your presentation skill set. You will learn a lot.

The accompanying CD has all the checklists in the book, plus lots of example slides and valuable information.

Focus on Your Key Messages

Situation today: You sit down to make PowerPoint slides or write your speech. When done, you go back over the presentation, trying to put it into some meaningful order. Before you realize it, you've worked for hours, reorganized the content, tried to cut it down (and discovered it grew instead)! Next, you review it with people who will be at the session, and even ask your boss to look over the outline. These people all say, "Shorten it!" or "It's over our heads!" Worse yet, they spend time trying to figure out the structure of your talk and what information should be included or excluded, instead of helping you check the content for accuracy and key messages.

Key problems: Many people are creating haphazard, disorganized presentations of data slides. People spend hours redoing presentations—time they really don't have. The key content of the subject is sometimes not even mentioned. The presentation is not convincing to the audience.

    Key opportunities: Save hours of time. Motivate your audience to listen. Look and sound professional. Gain credibility.

    Solution: Do not make a slide until you organize your information. Here is how to go about organizing your talk.

    First, create your presentation overview. This overview targets the key information that your audience will be interested in hearing and establishes the criteria by which you will exclude or include content. When given to your boss or others, the overview enables everyone to suggest how to put together the content before you spend time creating your talk. It is much easier for someone to critique and change the one-page overview than to have to review twenty slides in order to understand the talk.

Second, choose a format or outline with which to organize the content in the most effective manner for the audience to follow. Later in this chapter we will cover several different types of organizational structures that you will be able to use to achieve your particular purpose.

Third, write up an executive summary that really targets the overview of your entire talk before creating any slides or a written speech.

Fourth, plan to tell several stories so that the presentation becomes more memorable for the audience.

Story: In one of my classes, Clive, the manager of his company's intranet, brought a presentation about his company's new intranet site for us to discuss. His team had spent hours putting together a presentation they planned to give to hundreds of people in the company. The objective of the talk was to motivate people to look at and use the information on the new site. However, when we looked at the slides, it appeared that the presentation was almost exclusively about how they created the intranet site. They used a lot of jargon and included information no non-technical person would have cared about. Moreover, the presentation contained slide after slide of text with seven to nine phrases (almost sentences) on each slide. The key message derived from this talk seemed to be "Look how difficult this was to do, and since we worked so hard, we suggest you go look at it." After Clive prepared a presentation overview and made a one-slide executive summary, he redid the slides to focus on his audience. Specifically, he explained three benefits that people using this new site could gain. He removed the confusing jargon. When he practiced giving the talk, he sounded excited and enthusiastic. Without having done the necessary preparation, he never would have realized how his presentation actually discouraged people from wanting to go look at the company's new intranet site.

Chapter Motto: *If you take more time preparing before creating all your slides, your success will come easier.*

FOCUS ON YOUR KEY MESSAGES

- Fill Out the Presentation Overview
- Choose or Create a Format
- Create an Executive Summary
- Write Your Opening and Closing
- Identify and Plot Stories to Tell
- Plan Your Notes
- Decide on Your Handouts

There are seven steps to focusing on your key messages. This step-by-step process will guide you from filling out a presentation overview to deciding on your handouts. The Presentation Overview forces you to plan your messages and to think about how you want your audience to respond during your talk. When you use a format to lay out your content, you will save hours of time attempting to reorganize the content after the slides are created. The executive summary is just that, a one-slide summary for people who don't have the time or desire to listen to the details. By writing out your opening and closing, you will be much more relaxed as you start the talk and sound much more confident when you conclude. Stories will add spice and variety to your talk. You may need some notes for your talk, and this section tells you how to use them. Finally, by being clear about the use of your handouts, you can create a presentation that provides the audience materials they may actually find useful to look at during or after the talk.

FILL OUT THE PRESENTATION OVERVIEW

As noted in the opening solution, the first task you should do when preparing a presentation is to create an overview. Exhibit 1.1 provides a specific outline you can use.

Following are descriptions of each of the sections of the Presentation Overview.

Title: There are titles and then there are *titles*. Think about one that will engage your audience and get their attention.

Objective: You should have only one clear, concise objective for a presentation. You may have other underlying objectives you wish to accomplish, but you

Exhibit 1.1
The Presentation Overview

FOCUS	EXPLANATION OF FOCUS
Title	Title of the presentation.
Objective	One-sentence objective.
Theme	Underlying theme or storyline that will weave through the presentation.
Three Key Messages	List the three key messages you want to get across and either the type of story or data that will go with each message.
Audience Reaction	Write down what you want your audience to . . . Say after your talk: Do after your talk: Feel after your talk:
Two Stories	List two stories you can tell to make your messages connect emotionally to the audience.
How to Ask for What You Want	What will you say or do to obtain a "yes" on your recommendation?
Best Way to Reach Your Objectives	Will you only use PowerPoint? Will you talk and maybe show several images but not make PowerPoint the whole talk? Will you hand out a document and go through it?

need to specify one overall objective before you start making the presentation. This objective answers these two questions:

• What does my audience want from my speech?

• What do I want from my audience?

By analyzing the answers to these questions, you can write down the objective of your talk. Some objectives might be:

• Sell them my product today

• Convince the vice president to give me resources for a project

- Show that I am in charge and in control of the project
- Increase my credibility by presenting the analysis in a logical, focused manner.

Theme: There is an overall mood that goes through a talk. Here are some theme ideas:

- *"Stay tuned into the company; check out the intranet."* This can be highlighted throughout the talk with certain types of images.
- *"We deliver what we promise."* Many kinds of examples can be given about how customers have been provided the products they requested.
- *"We're ahead of the changes coming to the industry."* This presentation could show examples of how a company adapted with new products as the industry evolved, illustrating for potential investors that the company is always on the cutting edge in developing new and successful products.

Three key messages: I know you sometimes have a difficult time deciphering the key messages in other people's presentations. The presenter may have started with an agenda, but that usually does not include the key messages of the talk. Motivate your audience to listen. Make it easy for them to follow your talk. Start with your key messages. Here's one example of an opening:

> "In considering what you want to achieve with your presentations, there are three key points. You want to look and sound credible and confident. You want to gain commitment. And you want to do all this in the least amount of time possible. This talk will tell you how to do these three things."

These key messages will then be repeated throughout the talk.

Audience reaction: You are usually giving a talk to achieve some type of reaction from your audience. Now is the time to specifically write it down. For example, you could write, "I want the chief information technology officer to say that the product we are proposing is up-to-date. I want her to call us for a demo of our product. I want her to feel excited about seeing what we have to offer."

Two stories: Why tell a story? My clients say, "I don't have time to tell stories. I have so much information." Consider this: Most of us remember stories long after the information has left our consciousness. We like to go home and tell someone, "I heard an interesting story today about. . . ." There are wonderful books about how to tell a story. These are listed in the Resources section of this book.

How to ask for what you want: Usually a presentation is used to obtain some type of approval. Don't leave that to chance. Decide now on the words you will use and when you will ask for what you want. Plan every move, stage every prop, prepare every syllable; this is the most important moment in your talk. Think of how carefully a young man prepares before asking someone to marry him. The talk should revolve around this. Find that perfect moment to "pop the question."

Best way to reach your objective: Some of you reading this book go fishing. When you go fishing you usually want to catch a fish. You select the bait you are going to use depending on what you want to catch. Well, why don't you do the same when you give a talk?

- Who is your audience?
- What do they like?
- What will make them bite?
- What will make them ignore your offer?
- What will make them want to fight once they become interested?

If you want your audience to make an engineering decision based on what you will present, you probably need to show comparison charts, tables, and images so that your audience can make a decision. This information frequently needs to be in the form of handouts. Why? The charts, tables, and images may contain so many details that are impossible to read on the screen. Showing PowerPoint slides with text on them may not be the best way to reach your objective.

In summary, the reason you fill out the Presentation Overview is so that you have an overview of your talk before you create slides and/or other visuals such as storyboards. The more focused you are, the easier it will be for you to create the most appropriate visuals in order to achieve your objective. Exhibit 1.2 is an example of a Presentation Overview filled out by Terry Williams for the Bluefields project. See how much you can learn about the project from just this overview.

Exhibit 1.2
Bluefields Presentation Overview

FOCUS	EXPLANATION OF FOCUS
Title	*Bluefields: Achieve a Sustainable Community by 2020*
Objective	To secure the commitment—in cash and kind—of key influential individuals on which the Bluefields' campaign will be based.
Theme	Establish Bluefields as the model of sustainable development efforts in the Caribbean.
Three Key Messages	1. **Jobs for All:** Target people's entrepreneurial instincts to create gainful employment opportunities. 2. **Food Security for All:** Develop and launch a Farmers and Fishers General Stores business concept that can be franchised to community-owned and operated enterprises. 3. **Education for All:** Improve local schools' infrastructure and create adult education infrastructure
Audience Reaction	Say after your talk: "This is a great plan." Do after your talk: Commit to help in cash or kind. Feel after your talk: Excited enough about the possibilities that they want to participate.
Two Stories	1. My own evolution of thinking that convinced me that the approach of focusing on people's entrepreneurial tendencies is the right one. 2. How one of the current leaders came to us unable to read or write. Nearly twenty years later he's running the fisherman's co-op as well as his own business, employing five community members.
How to Ask for What You Want	We can't do this alone: How can you help us?
Best Way to Reach Your Objective	Use PowerPoint some, but not all the time. Tell stories without showing slides.

In the next section, we'll look at two specific presentation situations: presenting technical information and presenting at a meeting.

Preparing Technical Information

Tan is an expert in water filtration, having studied it for years. He has been asked by a salesperson, Jim, to give a talk to one of Jim's potential customers. However, Jim and Tan have not discussed what the objective of the talk is to be. Tan starts to prepare his speech and makes fancy graphs and charts to show the filtration system. He has worked on this system for years and prides himself on being a technical expert. He actually builds a water filtration system on the screen and includes all the small technical details he personally considers important. The slides look impressive!

One would think, from looking at all Tan's slides, that the objective is to share all the nitty-gritty details of the water filtration system. Unfortunately, that is not the objective Jim has in mind. Jim's objective for Tan's speech is to sell the benefits of water filtration. Naturally, a little bit of technical information that supports the benefits would be convincing. Jim wanted Tan to emphasize the key messages about saving money, ease of use, and up-to-date technology. Tan would have made a very different presentation if he had spent some time discussing the objective and messages with Jim. This type of situation happens all the time between salespeople and technical experts. It is solvable when they agree on the objective and the presentation is then created around that objective. Much of the drill-down technical information can be placed on a notes page so that the speaker has it to refer to, if necessary, and the attendees can read it in the handouts.

Sharing too much technical information also occurs when salespeople are brought in from the field to learn about new products. They are usually told all the technical information about the product, with very little emphasis on benefits for the customer. Since they have been told this information, naturally, they expect that this is the information that they are expected to present to their customers! Your true objective—whether it is a product update, new software release, or brand extension—is to prepare those salespeople to sell it, not build it. Your presentation should model what you want these salespeople to tell their customers. Do not tell them every bit of product knowledge that exists. They should be given the presentation that they are expected to give to their customers. Then other slides can be added to give them more technical knowledge.

Preparing for a Meeting

For those of you who have ten minutes before a meeting and have been told you need to give a brief talk, here is a quick, two-sentence presentation overview. To do this, finish the two sentences shown in Exhibit 1.3.

Now, you have the beginnings of the organization for your talk. You can use this information as criteria for what needs to be included and what is extraneous. As you create and organize your presentation and make decisions regarding the content of your talk, ask yourself:

- Will this content help me explain my message?
- Will this content or image encourage the audience to do what I would like them to do after the talk?
- Will this content help me reach my objective?

Exhibit 1.3
Mini-Talk Meeting Overview

FIRST SENTENCE	SECOND SENTENCE
During my talk I plan to [a verb and noun] so that [a noun and verb].	By the end of my speech, my audience will . . .
Example 1 *During my talk* I plan to present my company's new product so that my audience decides to buy it.	*By the end of my speech, the audience will* be convinced that there are three reasons why my product will help run their company intranet.
Example 2 *During my talk* I will motivate my manager so that she sees the absolute necessity of hiring three more people.	*By the end of my speech, my manager will* have the information and presentation visuals necessary to convince her boss to let her hire three more people. She will be able to tell her boss how the department can achieve its goals on time with the addition of these three new hires.

CHOOSE OR CREATE A FORMAT

Now that you have written up your overview and the key messages of your talk, you want to put your content in some logical sequence. Don't create the slides in a stream-of-consciousness manner and then try to organize them. That is backwards. Plus, it is a lot of extra work. Most importantly, your audience will know what you did. A systematic flow is invaluable for audience comprehension. If you skip from one unrelated point to another, the audience will wonder in frustration, "How does this fit together?" And, a warning: when some audiences become frustrated they start interrogating you. Sophisticated technology loses its value when the presentation slide content is not organized in a logical sequence with just the right amount of detail.

In his book, *Blink,* Malcolm Gladwell tells about a research project to discover the most accurate way for emergency room doctors to determine whether someone has had, or is about to have, a heart attack. Lee Goldman, a cardiologist, developed a decision tree of three urgent risk factors. He wanted to see whether this decision-tree way of determining heart attacks was more effective than the doctors asking many questions to gather as much information as possible about the person's health before making a decision. For two years Cook County Hospital used Goldman's algorithm. "It was a whopping 70 percent better than the old method of recognizing the patients who weren't actually having a heart attack" (Gladwell, 2005, p. 135). The lesson was that sometimes having too much information resulted in a decision that was not as good as one made with less information focused on the most important issues. What is important is not the quantity of information but the quality. This same advice applies to so many presentations in the world today. Your job as a presenter is to figure out what is the most useful information needed to achieve your presentation's goal. So, how does one go about determining what is the right information to include in order to make the most accurate decision? One way to help you in making that decision is to use an organizational format.

A format is an invaluable tool in helping you organize your presentation. For my work, I have co-authored twenty-six professionally designed presentation "shells" for PowerPoint. Each shell offers a detailed outline, numerous tips for creating effective content, and carefully chosen sophisticated visual elements. I created them because people were losing their productivity. In this book, two of these formats are included in this chapter and on the accompanying CD for your use.

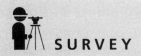
Unless you have several formats, such as are provided on the CD, you are wasting a tremendous amount of time whenever you create a presentation. How do I know this? I have individual clients and participants in my classes who use these formats and I see how much quicker they can put together talks. And I have clients who make their own formats. When they have a presentation to give, all they have to do is open the format and insert their information. They may add other slides, but the logical structure of the talk is already created.

Formats, or outlines, need to be created for the specific type of presentations given most frequently. Companies need formats that help their employees organize and craft the content. Here are several formats many companies could use:

- Product launch
- Company overview
- Product sales
- Strategy recommendation
- Project update
- Technical update

These formats need to be created and tested by the people who will be using them. Many companies take my formats and customize them for specific situations. These formats will help you organize your information so that you have more time to plan your stories and anecdotes. You can use them to write a white paper, to give a PowerPoint talk, or to write a speech not using slides.

Following are examples of formats for selling a product, service, or idea and convincing an audience that a problem exists. Both examples can be found (in color) on the accompanying CD.

Sell a Product, Idea, or Service

The selling format forces you to think abut the benefits of your product or service for your audience and not just information about the product. Following are some of the slides for the selling format. This will give you an idea of how to organize your thoughts. Notice that there is a question slide that encourages the audience to speak. Notice also that there is a slide after the question period that encourages the presenter to give a second conclusion after the last question. See Figures 1.1 through 1.13.

**Figure 1.1
Presentation Title**

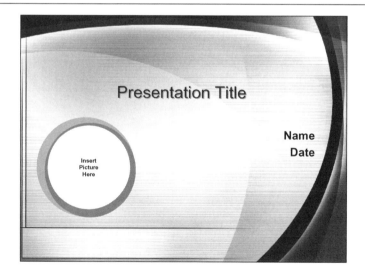

Figure 1.2
Executive Summary
This is the whole summary of your presentation in one slide.

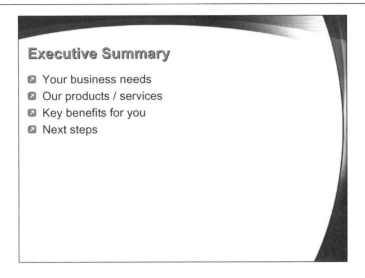

Figure 1.3
Your Needs
Here is where you talk about the needs of your audience. You do this before you talk about your company and its products. You want to be sure you are accurate in your assessment of your audience because you are only going to talk about the information that relates to their needs.

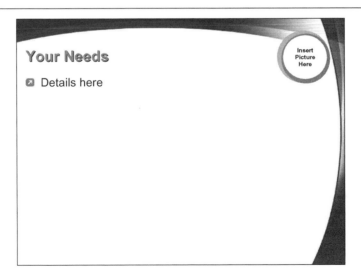

Figure 1.4
Questions to Ask the Audience

Now you ask your audience questions to listen to their other concerns you may not have mentioned or to hear them elaborate on their interests in your product or service.

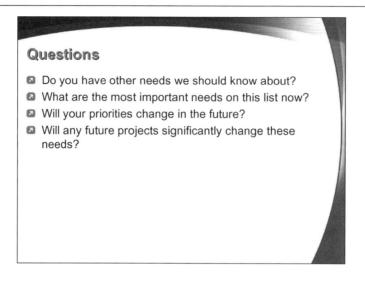

Questions

- Do you have other needs we should know about?
- What are the most important needs on this list now?
- Will your priorities change in the future?
- Will any future projects significantly change these needs?

Figure 1.5
State a Product That Meets Prospect Needs

After you have heard their interests, you are better able to talk about the specifics of what they desire.

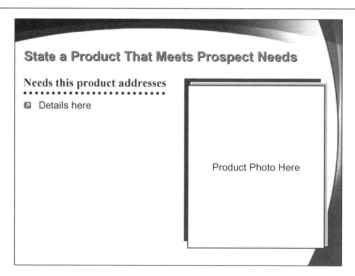

State a Product That Meets Prospect Needs

Needs this product addresses

- Details here

Product Photo Here

Figure 1.6
Product Features

As you show this, you can speak about some of the features. This slide may be optional to show depending on the audience.

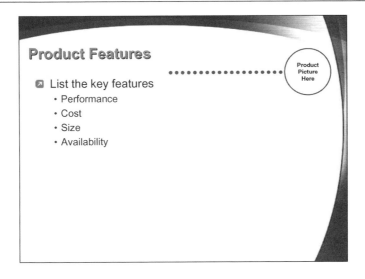

Figure 1.7
List the Key Benefits of the Product Here

As you have already heard them talk about their reasons for wanting to speak with you, you can now discuss only the benefits that will interest them.

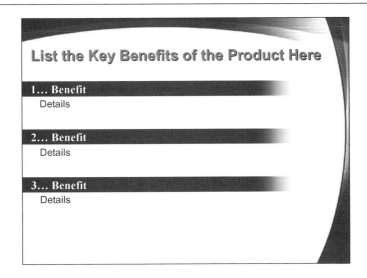

Figure 1.8
Competitive Advantages

This is to frame their decision-making process so they will consider certain advantages when deciding whether to purchase from your company. Generally, never say the competition's name out loud. A company that publishes competitive strength ratings is www.wratings.com.

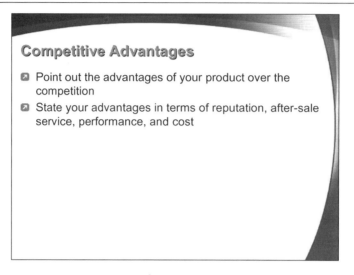

Figure 1.9
Customer Comments

Here you demonstrate that you do have people who like your product. Make the testimonials short. Sometimes companies include the logos of their clients, but you need to obtain permission from your clients before using their logos.

Figure 1.10
Achieving Your Business Objectives

Now you are again talking about your audience's business objectives. You are demonstrating that you know about their business and have thought about their objectives.

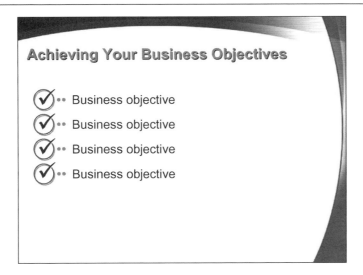

Figure 1.11
Recommended Next Steps

You've spent time with the potential customer to discover what type of match exists between your product and their needs. Don't leave without some next steps.

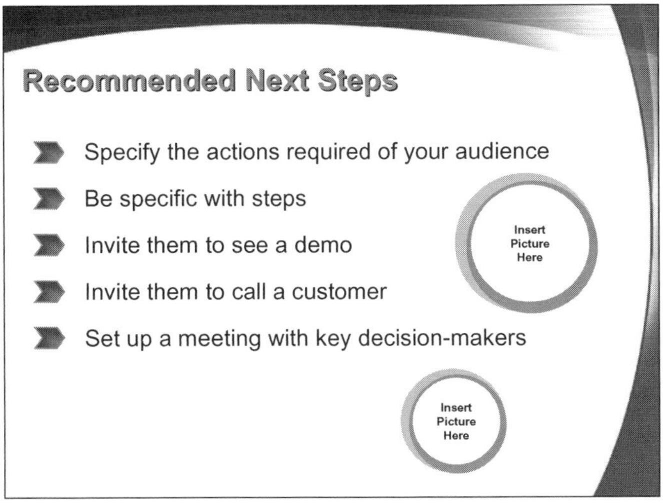

Figure 1.12
Your Questions and Comments

Notice I just don't put the word "questions" on this slide. People should be encouraged to make comments as well as ask questions. You want to know a potential prospect's views on what you have said.

Your Questions & Comments

Put pictures here of product

Figure 1.13
Our Vision for You

This is the slide you show after the question period. You are wrapping up the meeting the way you choose. You don't want your presentation to be the victim of the last question or comment. You set the tone and energy as you end the session.

Our Vision for You

- Show pictures or list 3 key points about your vision for your prospect's business after using your products
- Describe the solution your product provides for the prospect's problems

Convince People of a Problem

This format helps you explain the overarching problem you want to fix. You are laying out all the other problems that stem from this one overarching problem. It shows you how to discuss the situation in a convincing, detailed manner so you can obtain agreement on some solutions. See Figures 1.14 through 1.26.

Figure 1.14
Presentation Title

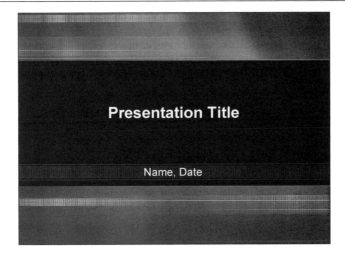

Figure 1.15
Executive Summary

Here again you have the overall key points of your total presentation. As you will read over and over in this book, people do not always want to listen to a lot of data. They just want the key points, at least, before you explain the details.

Figure 1.16
Present Situation

You are now explaining the situation today. You are doing this to share information as well as gain agreement that this is how your audience sees the situation.

Present Situation

▸▸ Describe how we operate today to set the purpose of the presentation

Figure 1.17
Problems with the Present Situation

Now you are listing some of the key problems with this situation. Don't list as many as you can think of. Your job is to sort out the critical few from the many and to tell your readers about those few.

Problems with the Present Situation

☑ Problem
☑ Problem
☑ Problem
☑ Problem

Figure 1.18
Are There Any Other Problems

You are asking your audience how they see the situation. This should encourage people to start talking, which is what you want.

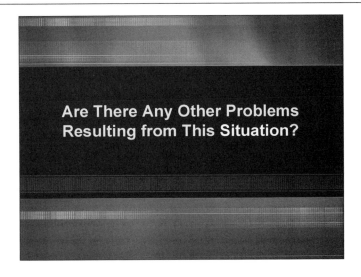

Figure 1.19
Areas Affected by the Situation

You may elect to use this slide in lieu of the slide in Figure 1.17. You are broadening the problem into certain areas and will talk about those areas.

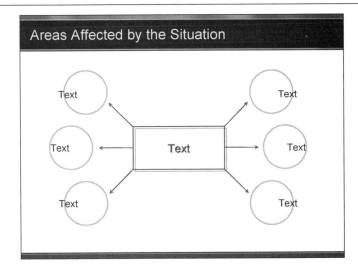

Figure 1.20
Why Solve the Problems

Some people may say, "Well, it has always been like this. This isn't a problem." This slide helps them see the advantages of changing the way things have always been done.

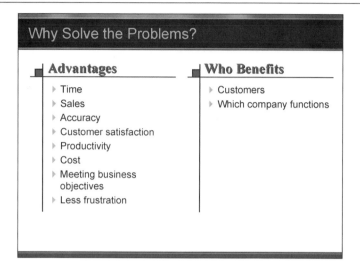

Why Solve the Problems?

Advantages	**Who Benefits**
▹ Time	▹ Customers
▹ Sales	▹ Which company functions
▹ Accuracy	
▹ Customer satisfaction	
▹ Productivity	
▹ Cost	
▹ Meeting business objectives	
▹ Less frustration	

Figure 1.21
Ideas to Solve the Problems

You are offering choices on how to solve the problems. You may believe there is one best choice, but in certain situations your audience may want an opportunity to discuss these various choices. They want time to reach their own conclusions.

Ideas to Solve the Problems

Idea 1
▹ Advantage
▹ Disadvantage

Idea 2
▹ Advantage
▹ Disadvantage

Idea 3
▹ Advantage
▹ Disadvantage

Figure 1.22
Recommendations to Begin
This illustrates that you know how to start making the changes.

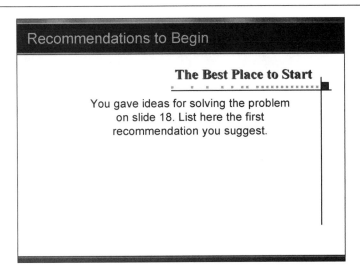

Figure 1.23
Requirements
This shows you know what resources will be needed.

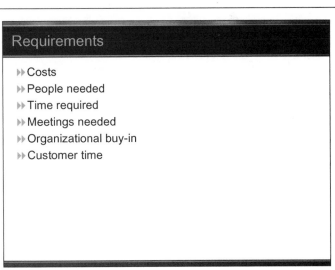

Figure 1.24
Next Steps

Now you are getting more specific so that the resources can be agreed on. You may decide this is the right time to present this or that the next steps are for a separate presentation.

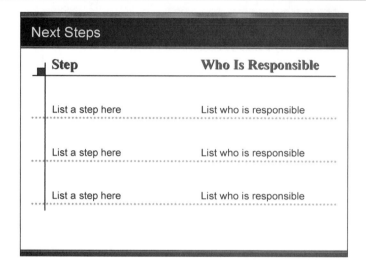

Figure 1.25
Your Questions and Comments

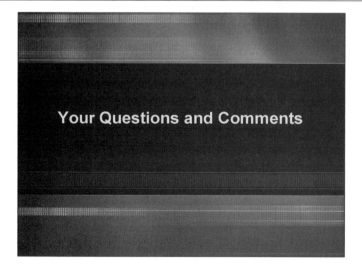

Figure 1.26
Key Benefits in a Year

You end after the questions and comments with a vision of what can be different in the future.

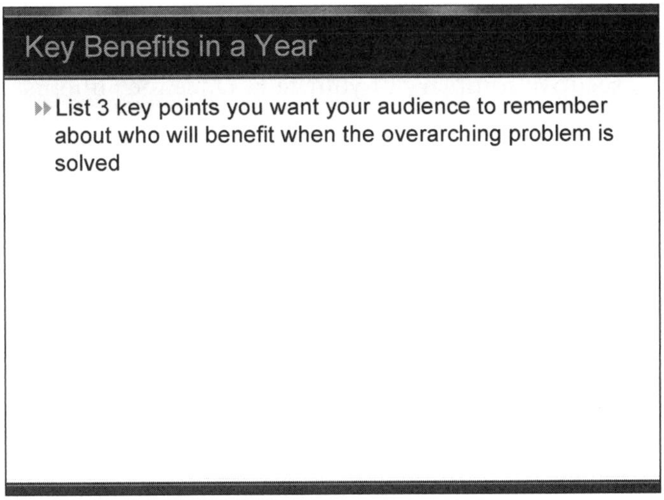

Key Benefits in a Year

▸▸ List 3 key points you want your audience to remember about who will benefit when the overarching problem is solved

CREATE AN EXECUTIVE SUMMARY

At this point, you want to sit down and make your slides. You just can't stand it any more. You think this is way too much preparation, but it is not. You still have a few more things to do! First and foremost, you need to create an executive summary. The executive summary will be given at the opening of your talk to provide the overview of your talk or at the end to close.

Presenting to executives: In most situations when speaking to the president, vice president, or executives in a company, you should provide an executive summary when you start your talk. They want to know the bottom line first.

Executives spend their days sorting through information. Before a presentation, they hope that you have sorted through and chosen the best information to give to them so they can either make a decision, agree with the decision you have proposed, or suggest what else is needed before a decision can be made. You do them and yourself no favor when you start by presenting slide after slide of information. You will have the executives on your side if you first give them an executive summary of your talk. Once they understand the decision that needs to be made, the answer you have selected, and its benefits, then they are ready to listen to more of the details. If you have put together a good executive summary, you may frequently discover that they may have heard enough.

Another reason to start with an executive summary is that it helps you to sound interesting and intelligent as you begin. No one is going to appear brilliant when going over the agenda for the talk. You need to start in such a way that you sound in charge, confident, and in control of your information. Remember, the executive summary is not the agenda. It is a summary of the talk—including only the most salient points.

Using an executive summary is not limited to when you are presenting to executives. You can also use one in the following situations.

Technical and non-technical audience: An executive summary can be used to give non-technical people an overview when you are speaking to a combined technical and non-technical audience. Start with a summary that everyone can understand. You want your non-technical audience to grasp the overall messages of your talk before you get into the details and technical jargon. It will give them a basis or context from which to understand the remainder of the talk, and it will make them feel like experts themselves.

Many functions: An executive summary can be used to get everyone on board with your talk when you are speaking to people from different functional areas. This situation might occur for a management update, a problem-solving talk, or a cross-functional team meeting. Make sure your executive summary has something for all members of your audience. For example, the finance people will want to know the cost ramifications of whatever you are suggesting. Tell them right at the beginning of your talk.

Selling: Let's consider that you will be speaking to the people making the purchasing decisions as well as those who will install your product. First, give an executive summary to your decision makers. They really don't care to hear about the installation process. You can talk about that later. Perhaps they will even leave at that point.

Research: When presenting a project update of your research, a one-slide executive summary may provide just enough information to your audience. If not, you can use other images or tables for illustrating such points as past and future projections and expected or unexpected results.

The best way to explain an executive summary is by illustration. Figures 1.27 through 1.30 are examples of executive summary slides. All of these slides can be found on the accompanying CD, and you can edit them as necessary to fit your particular situation.

Figure 1.27
The Business Overview

This is a way to provide an overview of your business in one slide. You must be able to do this in a way that allows your audience to understand the essence of your business. This is your "elevator pitch" (an explanation short enough that you could give it to someone during an elevator ride).

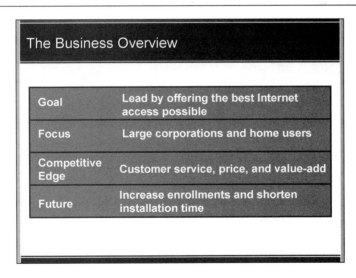

The Business Overview

Goal	Lead by offering the best Internet access possible
Focus	Large corporations and home users
Competitive Edge	Customer service, price, and value-add
Future	Increase enrollments and shorten installation time

Figure 1.28
Question and Answer Opening

You can also do an executive summary in question form.

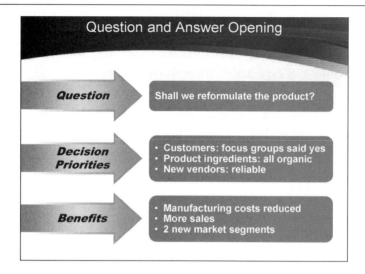

Figure 1.29
Conditioning Exercise for Kids

Here is a summary of a program being offered. This is done using the strategy recommendation format.

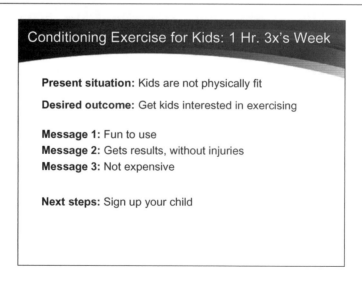

Figure 1.30
Resellers Are Not Getting Higher Incentives

Here is an example of selling an idea to upper management. The issue is in the title and then you learn why this is happening and what can be done. The person who put this together said she didn't need many slides after organizing this summary.

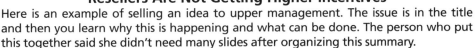

Resellers Are Not Getting Higher Incentives

- **Why**
  - Don't receive information at the right time
  - Don't have time to check status of sales numbers
  - Don't know how close they are to a higher % incentive
- **Solution**
  - Send them a monthly spreadsheet with their information
- **Benefits for them…**
  - Higher incentives
  - More motivated
  - Purchase and sell more of our products

Everyone is more satisfied: They sell and we sell!

WRITE YOUR OPENING AND CLOSING

Your executive summary is done. You can now write the opening and closing. You will then have the structure of your talk and an even better sense of what to leave in or take out. Some of you will say, "But I can't write them yet. I don't know how this talk is going to turn out." I say to you, "OK, wait. But be careful. You may wait so long you do not have time to truly think about your opening and closing. You miss two important opportunities to capture your audience."

Opening Ideas

First, what are some opening ideas? Here are some options depending on your audience and the purpose of your talk.

1. You immediately start with a story that ties into your content.

2. You start with your executive summary. This is excellent to do when you are presenting to an audience that is overworked, a bit impatient, and wants the point quickly.

3. You say a few words before discussing your executive summary. For example, "This year's company conference is focused on our relationship with the customer. We are taking our 'account relationships' to a new level. You are about to hear my executive summary of our vision for this coming year."

4. You tell the audience the benefits of listening to your talk. For example: "There are three benefits you will take away from our talk today. You will know how to access our new company intranet. You will see all the fabulous courses that you can take for free and how in two clicks you can sign up for them. You will see short resumes of all our employees so you can get to know some of your colleagues better."

5. You speak to the audience's interests. For example: "As salespeople in this field I am sure that you want to learn the best way in which to deal with rejections, how to keep yourself motivated, and how to make your calls and schedule appointments in ways that enable you to save time. You will leave with all that information today."

6. You give them a "wake-up" message. Here are two examples: "Company X is the best company I have seen in years in this area. I know we should invest in it" or "After this training, your work will never be the same. Your telephone calls will be shorter and you will schedule more sales leads. Your work life will be easier, more fun, and much more productive."

Closing Ideas

When you have finished your talk, how can you close? Here we are really talking about two closes. One close is at the end of your talk before you take questions. The other is after the questions. After you have answered the questions, let's assume the last one was a bit hostile and your answer did not provide the best way to end your talk. You ask, "Are there more questions?" No one responds. Don't then just say thank you and sit down. You want to close again so you set the tone and message that you want your audience to remember. The ideas below can be used for either of these closes.

1. Go over the executive summary.

2. Tell a vision story. "Just imagine when . . . " You tell a vision about what will happen in the future when your recommendation is carried out. You are

describing a mini-movie of what the future could be. You are getting your audience excited by the vision you create.

3. Give someone a piece of paper and ask him or her to sign it. If your presentation is for a project approval, hand people a project approval form and get them to approve it so there is no ambiguity at all about what you have all agreed to.

IDENTIFY AND PLOT STORIES TO TELL

Getting your key points told again: John is sitting down to lunch with a colleague, Harvey, and begins to tell him a story he just heard in a presentation. He remembers all of it. He even remembers the punch line and the point of the story. That afternoon, Harvey tells the story to two people during a meeting. Obviously, the presenter's story emotionally captured her audience. The story has been told to three people during the day, maybe more. The presenter is getting her message disseminated via her excellent story.

You are almost set, but you want some way to really capture your audience and give them something they can tell others. You need to add some stories and examples. Ahead of time choose and practice the stories you will use in your presentation; otherwise you may run out of time and really miss an incredible opportunity to motivate and engage your audience. Yes, you did list a couple of ideas for stories in the Presentation Overview, but that is not enough. Before you create one slide, really work on your stories. You will probably discover that with your executive summary and your stories, you may need many fewer slides to share your key messages and reach your objective. Stories are a wonderful way for you to connect with your audience. Stories are also a way for your audience to take your message to many others. The more your stories emotionally engage your audience, the better chance someone in your audience will relate the story to a colleague that day or the next day. Don't miss out on this opportunity to spread your message.

The stories should engage the audience's interest so that they want to hear the whole presentation. Most importantly, they should emotionally connect with the audience. Many people make decisions based on emotion and then rationalize that decision with the facts. Executives often talk about making a decision from the gut.

Stories need to be told with emotion and finesse. Don't just tell them as you would when talking about numbers. Following are two examples: One is a presentation just dealing with data and the other is a presentation based on a story that contains some data. Now there is nothing wrong with presenting data that is all information, but unless the audience is already familiar with the subject matter (in this coming example, the physical exercises), stating what the exercises are called means nothing to them. When comparing the two, note how the story scenario follows a certain order—that is, the story develops through plot points to an ending.

Data Presentation

A kettlebell is a cast iron weight that is shaped somewhat like a basketball but with a handle. Kettlebells come in many weight sizes. The Russians have been using them for over one hundred years. When weightlifting with kettlebells, the exercises include kettlebell snatch, kettlebell squat, and kettlebell swing. You can make amazing strength gains and get in excellent physical condition by using kettlebells.

Story Scenario

Before: Joe came to a class at the gym. He was one hundred pounds overweight. He hadn't exercised in years. He couldn't jump rope because he was too heavy. He had a lot of trouble feeling which muscles to use in the different exercises. He became discouraged when he couldn't do what the other people were doing.

Plot point: One day, about two weeks after he began to come to class, a student took him aside and said, "You know Joe, I used to look like you. Stop complaining. You will look like me sooner if you just do the exercises and not spend time making excuses."

After: After that conversation, Joe started to change his attitude. I remember the day he lifted a twenty-pound kettlebell over his head and walked around the room. His face was beaming. Then there was the day he swung a forty-pound kettlebell thirty times. He was ecstatic. Imagine this—he reached the point where he could jump rope for five minutes at a time. After that day, he bought himself a jump rope and a kettlebell to use at home. So what is this kettlebell that kept Joe going?

The speaker would then go on to present data about kettlebells, having first piqued the audience's interest with a story.

Notice that in the story scenario of the kettlebells, there is a plot point that changes the character or the scene in some manner. This plot point wakes up the audience and captures their attention. You can change your way of storytelling just by making sure you emphasize the plot points.

What are plot points? They are the pivotal moments in a television or film script. In a film, Plot Point One usually occurs twenty to thirty minutes into the film and starts the major action of the movie. Something unexpected occurs to the hero and galvanizes him or her toward a goal. Plot Point Two occurs about seventy minutes into the film when it appears that the hero is beaten. At this point an event occurs that causes everything to change with the hero. The hero's goal becomes reachable. These plot points keep re-engaging the audience so their eyes stayed glued to the screen. In your case as a presenter, those using their BlackBerries start to pay attention.

Sally Iles at Massachusetts General Hospital's Leadership Academy in Boston, Massachusetts, spearheaded an effort to streamline the process for scheduling flu shots. The story chart in Exhibit 1.4 illustrates what happened. You can use it to give you ideas and help you on your way. Even if you did one story in your talk this way, you would be way ahead of most presenters in business today.

The example in Exhibit 1.4 is one way to organize your story. You can also start with the results. This is the "start with the end" way to approach telling a story. If the result is surprising to your audience, you have captured their attention and they want to hear how you achieved the result. Then you go back and share what happened to get to this result.

POWERPOINT TIP

Don't show your PowerPoint slides during the whole talk. Anything, even when done well, gets boring and puts us to sleep after a while. Plan part of a talk without showing PowerPoint.

Exhibit 1.4
The Flu Shot Success Story

Opening	Is it possible to make the yearly "fitting five hundred flu shot appointments in an already packed schedule" a pleasant experience for patients and our staff of doctors and assistants?
What Happened Before	First round of flu shots: 6.1 flu shots administered per hour of staff time
Plot Points	Some changes we made: Front desk prepared forms the night before Clinical staff does part of check-in such as asking patients about allergies by pointing to the posted question written in five languages RN periodically delivers batches of forms to front desk Desk puts in form information when not busy
What Happened After	Third round of flu shots: 30.2 flu shots administered per hour of staff time
Closing and Tie Back to Presentation's Message	Twenty small changes in process design increased productivity five-fold. The cumulative impact of all these little changes significantly improved the overall efficiency and quality of life within the practice.

Creating Your Plot

Several years ago I had the privilege of helping a friend who was trying to meet a Hollywood producer to have one of her stories made into a movie. She has had many fabulous life experiences that made for wonderful storytelling moments. She could make her audiences cry or laugh. Each story had its own plot, drama, and outcome. At the time, I read several books about writing a screenplay, and many of the authors discussed the importance of a clear plotline throughout the whole movie. Robert McKee's (1997) *Story* is a fascinating book about writing movie scripts, in which he discusses all the different types of movie plots. I'm not suggesting you make your presentation into a movie, but I am suggesting that you consider the idea of turning your stories into plots. For our purposes, a plot can be compared to the theme you listed in your Presentation Overview. Following are some business plots you might consider.

1. **Growth plot:** This signifies how your company grew its business during the last few years. Each product has its own growth curve, issues that made it easy or difficult to increase profits, and a path for the future. For example, a company's plot may be: we are constantly reinventing our business as the market changes.

2. **Failure plot:** A researcher explains how a particular test failed.

3. **From-failure-to-success plot:** A researcher explains how a failed test led him to try something else that produced the desired results.

4. **Consequences plot:** Rather than just share information on how to do certain processes, the speaker creates stories. He presents a positive-consequence story of using the correct process as well as a negative-consequence story.

5. **Visionary plot:** Help your audience envision the future you are creating with words, images, and emotional-impact examples. This can be a positive or negative vision.

There are many ways one can develop business plots. Let's say you want to recommend a specific strategy to a group of people that involves your sharing certain data. If you can create a plot within which to weave the data, rather than just read the data from the screen, your story will capture your audience's attention and make it easier for them to listen. Plus, if appropriate, it will be easier for you to smile with sincerity.

Next, be sure the story is related to your topic and makes a point. And, just to be sure, start with a transitional sentence that clarifies the connection between your topic and the story you are about to tell. Make it your own story. Chances are, if you steal a story from another speaker and claim it as your own, someone in your audience may have heard it. That will be very embarrassing! Make sure your story includes these elements:

1. A visual image, either on the screen or a vivid description

2. Feelings, shown through body language and the tone of your voice

3. Auditory interest (for example, giving both sides of a dialogue can make the story come alive).

Most importantly, practice telling the story to several people before you tell it to a live audience. And finally, keep it short. Make most of your business stories one to three minutes. That's enough to engage the audience and make your point. If needed, use a transition sentence after the story to tie it back to your presentation's message. Here is one example of a story using transitional elements:

> "I was making a software product presentation to an important prospect. 'Familiar and easy to use' was a key phrase point on a slide. I asked the prospect several questions. Audiences like to be asked about their own experiences. First, I questioned, 'Do any of you ever travel?' Most said, 'Yes.' Then I asked, 'Do you ever rent a car?' 'Of course,' they said. I told them that when I rent a car I can always count on knowing exactly how to start the car and drive it. The gas pedal, ignition, steering wheel, and brake are always in the same place. I am familiar with the user interface. It doesn't matter what kind of car I get, all the user interfaces are basically the same. Our product is designed the same way. Users will not have to learn a new way to surf the Web. The toolbar looks exactly like what they are familiar with in Windows. Since they will be able to use our product without any training or fear of something new, this is a huge advantage in getting them to start and then continue to use it."

When you are telling a story and talking about what someone else said, don't talk about it. Make the dialogue come alive. For example, you can say:

"Jose said this, 'I can't do that project. I never did it before.' I told him, 'Yes, you can. I'll coach you.' Six months later with the project complete, here is what he said, 'I can't believe it. I really did that project. I'm ready to do another one.' What started out as a negative, with coaching, ended as a big plus."

The above dialogue is a much better way to capture the words stated and to change the pace of your talk.

Even when you tell a story, you may sometimes need to summarize its major point or points in order to tie the story to your objective. You may say something like, "What this story points out is . . . " or "This story once again reminds us about how important our clients are to us."

Another way to summarize the objective of a story is to use a formula. The following is a "formula" from Nick Miller, president of Clarity Advantage Company. In his sales consulting, Nick reminds salespeople to focus on what is important to the client and says: "Nick Miller, president of Clarity Advantage, helps companies generate more sales, faster, more efficiently."

As with any formula, you may choose to say the words a bit differently. Here are some examples of how formulas are used.

- Formula 1: Your goal is . . . : "Your goal is to increase your market share." "Your goal is to revitalize your mature business."

- Formula 2: We are going to provide you with . . . : "We are going to provide you with an ad in *Woman's Day* magazine." "We will provide trends analysis of your marketplace."

- Formula 3: This will enable you to . . . : "This will enable you to send people to your website." "This analysis will enable you to decide which areas to expand into."

- Formula 4: You will gain . . . : "You will gain more sales." "You will be able to gain more customers."

Use a Mini Mini-Story to Tell Your Audience About Yourself

You may be delivering a scientific paper, explaining to the salespeople how the new system will change the way they place orders, or reporting on a project that no one really understands. When you stand up in front of an audience with people who have no idea who you are, you need to let them in on you as a person. Tell them a "secret" about yourself so they feel connected to you. Of course, share an appropriate secret that does not embarrass you or your audience. Decide whether to tell this mini mini-story as soon as you start talking, or perhaps after you present your executive summary.

How are you, as a person, different? Find something interesting about yourself that you can share, and relate it to your topic. For example, a presenter with twin sons could say, "You think it's hard to balance the company business, well, you haven't had twins. My twins are now ten years old and they have taught me a lot about setting priorities" or "Now that I am in charge of business operations, I can put to good use all that I've learned by having twins. Now that's an operation to manage!" One or two sentences say a lot about who you are and make you more human to your audience.

Here is how a scuba diver worked her passion into her presentation on a problematic new project plan that needed some hard work to resolve:

> "I'm a scuba diver by passion. What's really interesting in scuba diving is that the water can be very rough on the surface, but once I've gone down even forty feet, it becomes clear and the scenery is gorgeous. From my experience, just as in diving, we have some treacherous waters to navigate here before we can move forward in implementing this plan, but I guarantee you, it will be worth it once we get past the difficult areas."

This tells your audience something about yourself, indicates where you think you are now in the plan, and expresses the confidence that it is totally possible to reach a satisfactory conclusion.

Put Your Audience in the Stories

How do you get your audience to emotionally connect to your presentation? This is very important when your objective is to persuade them. You may want them to use a particular process in the research lab, donate money for a cause, or increase funding for a certain project.

One way to influence your audience is to explain the situation through their eyes. Here are some ideas:

Computer system: I see that many of you are feeling pressured with all the work you have to do. I have seen how you have to constantly redo the project forms. You have called me with questions, and I sense your aggravation. I wish I could wave a wand and have all those forms go away. Unfortunately, due to regulations, we have to fill them out. Today, I want to show you how much easier it will be when you use this computer system. But rather than explain it myself, let me ask Joe in our audience to help me. Joe, is that OK? So, Joe, I am going to take you through this process as if you were doing it right now. At any point, please stop me and tell me to slow down or ask questions. First Joe, you open this screen. You'll see with one click you are on the screen with the key form. . . .

Preserving the land: Everyone, imagine you are sitting on the hill here above this beautiful valley. The day is warm, as you see here in this photo. The sun is shining down on you. You feel peaceful and it is very quiet. You hear the birds singing and feel a slight breeze on your back. You say to yourself, "How lovely it is to be looking over this gorgeous highland meadow with luscious trees and flowers." This experience I am describing is one we want to preserve for all of us and our children for many years. That's why I'm here to explain what we need to do in order to protect this incredible spot.

PLAN YOUR NOTES

Finally, you may think that you are now ready to create your slides! Yes, you are, but as you create them consider what is needed for your own particular notes. Also, what will you give to your audience? Will you give them paper handouts? Will you send them an electronic file of your presentation? Will you provide them with all the information you presented or just with a summary of the major points? When you have this in mind, you will create the type of slides you need . . . and not have to redo them.

First, decide on the type of notes you need. If you are giving a formal speech, you may want them written out. But if you do write out your talk, start every sentence on the left side of the page. That way, there is less chance that you will lose your place. And, of course, make your notes big enough to easily read.

There is technology available for you to see your notes on your laptop and have your actual slides projected on the screen at the same time. I never suggest my clients use it. With effective slides, you should not need more notes. With notes to see on the screen, you will be even less likely to make eye contact with your audience. When you want to use paper notes, here are some tips.

Imagine this: You had your slides all set for your presentation but wanted some extra notes to remind you of a particular point. You jotted your thoughts down on a piece of paper and planned to use those notes when you got to a certain point in your speech. When you came to that point, you looked at your notes but couldn't read them. Your handwriting was too small and somewhat illegible. Because you couldn't stop, find your glasses, read the notes, and then speak, you continued without them. *But,* at that point, you were a little flustered and upset with yourself. Maybe the audience noticed or maybe they didn't—but you felt uneasy for the rest of your speech.

Rule number one: Make sure any notes you plan to use when speaking in front of a group are readable. "Readable" means you are able to read the notes when standing with the paper on a desk in front of you. You can see each word with a quick downward glance. Print your notes; don't write them by hand. Use at least twenty-four-point type size.

POWERPOINT TIP

To use speaker notes go to *View>Note Pages.* You can just type in your notes in the space below the slide. If you want to make the text bigger go to *View>Master>Notes Pages.* You can increase the size of the text for your notes.

2007: *View>Notes Pages.* To change the size of the text on the notes pages go to *View>Notes Master.*

Now that your notes are literally readable, make sure they are concise and make sense to you. Don't use complete sentences. You just want some phrases that remind you of what you want to say.

Rule number two: Do not write out your whole speech in speaker notes. Here's one presenter's comments about rule number two: "The only way I use speaker notes is when I am creating my speech and I have an idea or story I think of. I put that in speaker notes. Then I go back and look at them and remember them. I never read from the speaker notes pages. But that's because I know my subject."

You cannot possibly use speaker notes for every slide. Have as few extra notes as possible. You should spend most of your time connecting to your audience, not reading your notes. And always end your sentences looking at someone, not at your notes. Here's what you can put in your speaker notes:

- Opening sentence to make the slide's point
- Information you need in case you are asked certain questions
- Transition sentence to the next slide

If you write speaker notes for others, here are some ideas to include:

- **Speaker to do.** What the speaker can do at this point in the presentation, such as ask questions, show the products, etc.
- **Audience interaction.** How to involve the audience, for example, ask them to discuss in pairs the information just covered
- **Personalize.** What the presenter needs to add to customize the presentation to a specific audience

Ideas from Other Presenters

Below are ideas from other presenters. You will find them useful as you consider how to enhance your presentations.

- I make up speaker notes if someone else is giving my talk. Many times someone else presents the slides. I want it to be clear what the message is behind the slide. Frequently, I know the presenter is reading the slides for the first time the night before the talk. I make the notes concise, and I limit the number. I write them in order of the points on the slide.

- If I am the one who is actually going to click through the slides for the presenter, I get a copy of the speaker notes in order to follow along.

- I like to print the outline view of the presentation and have it handy when speaking. That way, if I am interrupted for any reason, I can quickly find my way back (or move to any other slide) by finding the number of the slide in the outline.

- I use very few notes if I am doing a PowerPoint presentation. I like them for my openings and closings. Since I never show a PowerPoint slide to open or close my talk, I will take a piece of paper and put three points on it for my opening. I put that paper near me to use when presenting. If I need to see my points, I can look down. I do the same thing for the closing. The key is that I can glance down and see the words without bending over. And no one really notices that I am looking. In reality, I rarely look, but I like to know that my notes are available if I want them.

DECIDE ON YOUR HANDOUTS

The question today is: Are you giving out paper handouts or are you sending an electronic file after your talk? First, let's assume that you are providing a paper handout. Think about when you want to give it out. If you hand it out ahead of time, you take away the element of surprise. Wherever possible, it is preferable to distribute handouts after the presentation. This keeps the audience's attention focused on you. But if they are the type of audience that likes to take notes about the slides, then give them the handout before your speech.

Whether the handout is paper or electronic, think about how much information your audience really wants and needs. Will your audience really look through the information at some future time? Do they only need specific key data and recommendations? I challenge you to do an anonymous survey and ask your audience what level of detail they want to have for future reference. Then you will really know what is important for you to spend your time creating as some type of handout.

Whether you hand out your slides in paper or send electronically, create a table of contents at the beginning of the talk. This way someone can easily find certain information. Salespeople tell me they receive a PowerPoint file for a new product with sixty slides and are told to find the answers in it. Who wants to look through sixty slides? Or, if on paper, who wants to page through a binder with hundreds of PowerPoint slides? If your handout is sent as a PowerPoint presentation, link each item in your table of contents to the appropriate slide. All the reader has to do is click the information and the slide comes up. To really help your reader navigate through the slides, set up a hyperlink on every slide that goes back to the table of contents. Put this hyperlink on the Slide Masters.

CONCLUSION

This first chapter encourages you to not start a presentation by sitting down and creating PowerPoint slides. This chapter starts with the motto: If you take more time preparing before creating all your slides, your success will come easier. You now have the foundation of a talk that has all the pieces of success: organization, executive summary brevity, focus, interest, audience-focused opening and motivational closing with next steps. The next chapter will provide you with some specific ideas for connecting with an audience. You will also learn what particular types of audiences appreciate and expect during a presentation.

Use the Presentation Checklist in Exhibit 1.5 to ensure that you have focused on your key messages.

Exhibit 1.5
Presentation Checklist

	Yes	Not Necessary or Appropriate
1. I have filled out the Presentation Overview and asked several people to go over it with me to be sure I have the most appropriate focus.		
2. I have a format for organizing my information. I've shown it to two people and they agree this is the best structure to logically use to make my points.		
3. My Executive Summary is done and people really understand it.		
4. I add value to what is on the screen and tell the audience information not on the slide.		
5. I practiced my stories with my colleagues and they agree these will be interesting to hear and useful for making my points.		
6. I have some notes for certain slides. I made them 24-point size so I can look down quickly and see my points.		
7. I know what is expected for handouts and have made them.		

Connect to Your Audience

Situation today: Most people prepare a presentation by first making PowerPoint slides or writing the talk. Then after a first draft, they spend many hours reorganizing the content, mostly cutting it down. However, they have not yet put themselves into the shoes of their intended audience. They have only put together a talk from their own experience and all the information they have.

Key problems: The presentation is not effective because it does not properly address the needs of the intended audience. The audience is not persuaded.

Key opportunities: Motivate the audience to listen. Capture their attention because you are speaking in a way that they find intellectually stimulating, easy to follow, and/or that helps them relax and enjoy the experience.

Solution: Tailor your presentation to your intended audiences.

Story: Suzanne, vice president of legal affairs, gives a quarterly update to her board via teleconference. She has been doing this for a year. The board has been complaining about her presentations and has become very frustrated with her. Some of their comments include, "She just does not get to the point," "Sometimes we can't even figure out from a legal perspective what she is suggesting," and "She goes on about points we do not care to even discuss." The president of the company realized that Suzanne had to change her manner of presenting so I was asked to work with her. Suzanne and I worked together for about six hours. First, we picked a particular subject the board complained about in terms of how she presented it. We asked several people what they thought the board wanted to know. They said, "They just want to know the end result based on your legal expertise. They don't care how you got there." So that's what we did.

We worked on how she could connect to that particular audience by immediately giving them the bottom line. She practiced giving them the bottom line about all the key outstanding issues. She created a mini executive summary for each outstanding issue. She also stopped showing slides. Her slides had been full of sentences and details. Consequently, her talk was half the length. What happened? She received compliments from the board. She still received some questions, but fewer than when she told the board more. They were nicer to her and didn't interrogate her the same way they used to. She relaxed and consequently spoke more slowly and louder.

Chapter Motto: *"First and always I establish and keep rapport with the audience by following their cues."*

CONNECT TO YOUR AUDIENCE

- Seven Ways to Connect to Your Audience
  - Tell them something they do not know
  - Set up a dialogue, not a monologue
  - Provide chunks of information, not an avalanche of details
  - Interpret the data, don't just read it
  - Know your audience and speak to their interests.
  - Ask questions
  - Have some fun
- Connecting Based on Specific Presentations
  - The Selling Presentation
  - The Technical Presentation
  - The Financial Presentation
  - The Cross-Cultural Presentation
  - The Audio or Web Conference

- The Academic Presentation

- The On-Demand Presentation

- The Poster Presentation

In this chapter you will learn several ways to connect with your audience as well as many tips on how to give certain types of presentations, such as a selling or technical presentation. Here are several short general guidelines that give you an advantage over most presenters. Show less, speak less, and stop speaking sooner. Some presenters are even more specific. They will only use eight slides and never speak for more than fifteen to twenty minutes. By the end of this chapter you will have begun to create your own personal guidelines for connecting to and engaging your audience.

SEVEN WAYS TO CONNECT TO YOUR AUDIENCE

The title of this book is *Point, Click, & Wow!* The "Wow!" is not because your audience is looking at your slides. The "Wow!" is because your audience is listening to you explain relevant information and share appropriate stories. In order to succeed, your audience should feel your connection to them . . . and more often than not as a result, they will seriously consider what you have said. Today there needs to be more human connection and fewer technological "Let me show you the latest feature" presentations. The technology features should be used to enhance the connection with your audience. If they don't, refrain from using them. Presentation slides don't connect, people do. I have clients who have been told, "Please don't bring a presentation. We'd like you to come and speak." This is due to the fact that people are no longer connecting to their audience. They spend more time looking and talking to the slides than to the audience. Make sure you connect with your audience not only with logic, but more importantly, with emotion. Be spontaneous; don't program every moment. Let your audience's reactions determine your presentation's moment-by-moment experience.

You need to be a living and breathing person up there in front of everyone. Show your humanity, and your audience will like you. When you think of your audience first, your preparation and delivery will be authentic. Your audience will react favorably if they sense that you have put some thought into caring about their interests.

First, let's look at some general "connecting" skills and behaviors that will help you in most presentation situations.

Tell Them Something They Do Not Know

What makes it interesting to listen to a speaker? Usually audiences stay interested when the speaker is telling them something new. That information can be surprising, upsetting, encouraging, have a direct effect on them, and/or be something they will go and tell someone outside the meeting. Most of us don't like to sit through a meeting and listen to something we already know. That becomes tedious and we have to pretend that we are listening, which also becomes tedious. Provide some new information to your audience. With this new information, the people in your audience are either going to make a decision, learn from it for future reference, or leave and think they learned something that they will probably never use. But at least you told them something they didn't know. I ask my clients to go through their presentations and be sure that there is new information for the audience.

Set Up a Dialogue, Not a Monologue

Generally speaking, an audience prefers to interact with the speaker. Even speakers who talk to five hundred or one thousand people find ways to motivate and engage the audience. When you engage your audience at the beginning of your talk, in the first three to five minutes, then they listen more attentively. Exhibit 2.1 differentiates between dialogue and monologue and provides some ideas for engaging your audience, not just talking to them.

Exhibit 2.1
Dialogue or Monologue

Dialogue	Monologue
Ask questions right at the beginning.	Talk very fast and don't stop for questions.
Tell stories that relate to their lives.	Don't check with audience whether the story rings true for them.
Set up hyperlinks so you can move around the presentation.	Start at the beginning of the talk that sounds and looks like a talk you gave yesterday to a different type of audience and go through it without stopping.

Put questions on the slides that you can ask when you begin.	Don't ask the audience anything when you start the talk.
Show the agenda and say one or two sentences about it and move on.	Explain the agenda in great detail using phrases such as, "Later, I'm going to show you. . . ." or "You'll hear more about this soon." The audience is thinking, "just start now, please. . . ."
Put frequently asked questions on a slide and then answer them—but don't have your answers on the slides.	Never acknowledge that your audience might have questions.
Show the agenda and ask what they would like to know about each item. Ask them what they hope to achieve by attending the meeting.	Don't check with the audience about your agenda. Just assume they want to know everything you have listed.
Once you have agreement on the agenda and objectives, decide as a group where you should start. This is important, as someone may have to leave early and you want to be sure you have covered his or her interests.	Don't find out who has what interests in the group. Don't even find out why each of them is attending the meeting.
Leave time for silence so that people feel they have time to ask a question. Cultivate a bi-directional exchange of ideas that will address the needs and wants of the client.	Talk very fast and give the impression you have to hurry through the talk.
Confirm how much time you have. State out loud how long the presentation or meeting will last. Ask whether anyone has to leave early. Between the time you set up the presentation/meeting and the time you arrive, another event may have been scheduled around the same time as your visit.	Don't mention the time. And don't even tell them how long you plan to talk.

Provide Chunks of Information, Not an Avalanche of Details

Your audience wants to follow what you are saying. They want to know the right amount of information at the right time so they can make a reasoned decision. Too many details will either lose them or bore them, especially details that are not explained in the right place. You can use a format and create an executive summary, but be sure you have the right information at the appropriate place geared toward your specific audience. Think about information as an outline. Rarely do you want to put the top level of your outline points and the next four levels down on the same slide.

Let's look at what happens when someone "dives" down into the details during a discussion on making bread. You bring some delicious bread to work and someone asks you how to make it. You give the basic ingredients interspersed with where to get the best flour, the difference between free range and regular eggs, the many kinds of liquids that can be used, the types of flour and what kind of consistency they provide to the bread, and finally the best butter and where to get it. Then you give directions to the person on how to get to the store that has the butter. While all this sounds helpful, the person may think twice about asking you for another recipe. Your conversation took twenty minutes and the person is walking away a bit overwhelmed, thinking, "Maybe making bread is too much work." Think about the times when you may have been subject to an overzealous salesperson telling you facts that you don't care about.

Continually ask yourself whether you are diving down too deeply in the information as you talk to your audience. Here are some questions to consider.

1. Have I chunked my information?
2. Have I gone too far down into my outline?
3. What level of information will most people in my audience understand?
4. What level will the decision-makers want to know?

When the speaker just talks on and on in more and more detail, the audience stops listening. It is almost impossible to listen to someone for very long when the person is speaking too fast trying to cover all the data. This attempt on the speaker's part usually results in many "ums" and a monotone voice, which is the best way to put your audience to sleep.

Interpret the Data, Don't Just Read It

Imagine that your ten-year-old son comes home from school and tells you he scored 82 percent on his math test. How do you react? Do you congratulate him enthusiastically or do you ask why he did not receive a 95 percent?

Although your son has shared some raw data, it is not useful information on which to base a decision. If he goes on to tell you that the class average was 89 percent and that only three kids got less than 85 percent, the information starts to become useful. If he adds that he studied extensively for the test but was feeling ill on the day it was given, this information adds a whole new perspective to the situation. What if he says he usually gets 75 percent and he has gone up to 82 percent? You are now emotionally involved and even moved by his story. His interpretation of the initial data point provides a perspective that is qualitatively different than just saying 82 percent and stopping there. He has provided extra information that allows the listener to understand the context in which to give the data meaning.

Quite frequently we see presentations with fancy screens used to glorify the communication of raw data, such as the 82 percent math score. After seeing tables filled with numbers, people walk out of such presentations asking, "What did all that mean? Should I worry about what is going on with manufacturing costs?" And some people are wondering deep down inside, "Why is this person overwhelming us with data? What is he hiding?"

Salespeople are constantly presenting raw data to their potential customers with no thought of interpreting what the numbers mean. Jim thought he had a winning presentation, but he was in for a surprise. Jim spent days putting together a presentation for a prospective customer. He worked with the multi-media group in his company and added some video clips. He was very proud of his colorful screens and fancy pie charts. As he was giving his talk, he began to notice the prospects' lack of enthusiasm and interest. He wanted them to be impressed by the statistics and the pictures of the product. Plus, one of the audience members began asking aggressive, in-depth questions about his statistics. What was happening?

On first glance, the presentation screens looked fine: the information was clear, there was lots of space on the screens, the numbers were large enough to read. But the screens mostly conveyed raw data. The people asking questions just wanted to find out what this information meant for their business decision. Jim's mistake, which is one which many presenters make, is that, to him, the raw data looks spectacular because he already knows what it means. He overlooks the fact that to others who do not have Jim's particular experience, the data may be meaningless without an explanation and interpretation. Jim has to add value by telling his audience more than is seen on the screen.

The Communication Pyramid (shown in Figure 2.1) can help you present your raw data in the best way. The inverted pyramid depicts four levels of communication, from the most basic form of conveying data to the highest level of suggesting its meaning for the future by sharing a vision. This framework highlights your challenge: to use your talk not to regurgitate raw data, perhaps even with fancy slides, but to convert data into higher-level communication that will stir your audience and trigger a response. The focus of your presentation should not be on presenting raw data, which though forming the base of the pyramid, should take the least amount of your presentation's time, but rather on engaging your audience in interpreting the data, expanding on the ideas, often using

Gaining Commitment: When you stir viewers' emotions and entertain them in the process, their retention of information will be higher and your presentation's impact much greater. Your audience will be more willing to commit to action and support you and your recommendations when they understand the total picture.

Figure 2.1
The Communication Pyramid

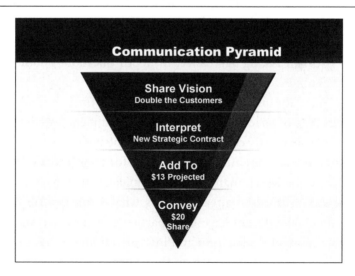

questions and answers, and working together to create and share a vision. When you, as a presenter, can find ways to engage your audience by truly sharing a vision, you are essentially spending time connecting with that audience. Do more of sharing a vision than conveying information. This is especially essential when speaking to executives.

Here is how you would talk using the words you see in the Communication Pyramid.

Convey: At the moment our shares are $20.

Add to: We are very satisfied since our best-case projections were for $13.

Interpret: This increase is due to the efforts of our sales force, who have signed a long-term contract with a new customer who is using our product in ways we had not envisioned. Let me share a story of how our new customer is using the product.

Share vision: Now that we really see it is possible to set up these types of contracts, we have our salespeople prospecting for more customers in this category. We are also thinking about analyzing similar industries to see whether or not we should modify or expand on our product line.

You might just show a slide with the $20 and then talk through the rest of the pyramid. This is up to you and your audience's interests. Keep asking yourself, "Am I doing more than conveying data?" Note that, when you share your vision, you invite your audience to participate in a creative and brainstorming process. This is an important part of creating a connection.

There are many presentation types, such as marketing updates and engineering proposals, which lend themselves to the presenter speaking up the communication pyramid. However, many presenters fail to seize the opportunity that this type of presentation offers. What most presenters do is read the data—and maybe if the audience is fortunate, present it in some logical manner. But what the presenter is supposed to do is interpret the data for the audience, explain the analysis, and satisfy their curiosity. Your audience wants to be able to use their brains and digest what you are saying. Some audiences really want to be intellectually challenged. Don't disappoint them by just reading your information. Most presenters are not being paid just to collect data, but to analyze it and provide the audience information about what to do.

One of my consulting engagements consisted of working with a product manager in a Fortune 500 company. Every month she presented information about key products to upper management. Her presentation was full of graphs and charts, but at the end everyone was trying to make sense of her charts. She asked to work with me because her manager said that the executives were not happy with her presentation, but he could not tell her why, which frustrated her. Together we figured out the problems.

She was making several common mistakes. First, her audience could not understand the data in the way it was presented and, second, they were being asked to listen to something they did not know how to interpret. What my client came to realize is that she was being paid not to present a flood of information but rather, based on her experience, to choose which was the essential data to show and then interpret it for her audience in order to assist them in making the decisions that they needed to make.

Know Your Audience and Speak to Their Interests

You may be asked to give a project overview update to different groups in your company. Let's say you will give an overview to the executives in your company, then a bit more detail to people at your boss's level, and then also a presentation to your peers. The executives are not interested in hearing all the details that your peers will want to know about. And the reason is fairly obvious. They have not been working on your project and aren't familiar with everything that has gone on. They don't want to know about it. They have other issues to think about. So, since you will be doing three presentations, you need to think about chunking. You will chunk your presentation in levels. Your focus as well as the level of detail you provide should change from one presentation to another. For example, in a presentation where you, as a product developer, could be discussing a negative sales trend, the management committee will want to hear what is being done to reverse this trend (new product development, technology enhancements), whereas the technical people will want to hear the nitty-gritty details concerning the product itself and its manufacturing. When you cater to the knowledge needs of each audience, you will connect with them.

Ask Questions

One of the most important characteristics of an effective salesperson, consultant, or technical specialist is the ability to ask questions, listen for the answer, and change plans based on that answer. If you want to establish rapport with your audience, you

POWERPOINT TIP

PowerPoint has a wonderful feature you can use to vary the number of slides in your presentation. It is called Custom Show. You can take one presentation file, choose slides from that file, and give a presentation with only those slides. Here's all you do.

- Go to *Slide Show > Custom Shows.*

- Create a presentation from the file you have open. That's it.

- 2007: *Slide Show > Custom Slide Show > Custom Shows.*

This is also useful when you present one set of slides to one functional area and another set of slides to another area. You can make many custom shows from one file. This is much better than creating a new file every time. Why? Because there will come a time when you need to change a slide and if you have many separate presentation files, you'll have to remember to change the slide in all the files.

will ask many questions about your audience. The worst mistake presenters make is to assume they know the needs and interests of their audience and to give a talk based on these perceptions. To succeed in the future, you will want to ask questions of members of your audience before the talk as well as during the talk. If you are a "performance presenter" who just likes to give the talk and take questions at the end, your tendency will be not to ask questions. If you are an "interactive presenter," then you will love the idea of asking questions and customizing the presentation around the responses. Not only is it acceptable to ask questions during the talk, but I strongly encourage you to do so. People like to talk. They don't like to listen too long.

Here are some "before" questions to ask:

1. What do you want to do that you are not able to do now with the system?

2. What goals do you have that you are not able to reach due to . . . ?

3. How do you see our product helping you achieve certain goals?

4. What is frustrating you right now in your business?

5. What one "major fix" in your business would make the most difference to you?

6. Tell me about how the system would work in your ideal world.

7. What interests you about donating to our foundation?

Asking questions before the presentation gives you content and a way to tailor your presentation to your audience. Let's suppose that you are giving your presentation and you sense that your audience is bored or not going along with your ideas. You wonder how to create interaction. No one is talking. Of course, in some cultures no one will talk, but let's assume that in the culture in which you are presenting, people will interact during a talk. How do you get that going?

Here's what not to do. Don't ask, "Do you understand?" Most people will say yes, even if they do not. What can you ask? You can ask closed questions to find out whether you are on the right track. Closed questions usually require a yes or no answer: "Do you want more details about this now?" "Am I giving you too many details?" "Would you like to talk about x or y next?"

You can also ask more interactive, open questions. They usually leave the answer open and let the responder frame a response. Here are some examples:

1. How do you see this solution fitting into your business?

2. You mentioned a problem with x during our discussion on the phone last week. Here's some information about that problem. How does this information fit with your view of the situation?

3. What additions or changes do you have for this recommendation?

4. Given what I have covered so far, what other information would you like?

To be an effective presenter in the future, you will need to sharpen your question-asking abilities. If you are unsure about what to ask, sometimes silence and a pause will get people talking. Which reminds me, if you ask a question and keep talking, it is likely no one will respond. You need some silence so people feel there is space to answer. Also, if you talk too fast, your audience will probably be quiet. They will not feel there is space for them to engage with you.

Have Some Fun

Finally, you can connect to your audience by having some fun. When that is possible, try it. Some presentations have lots of information, so it is hard to get people to pay attention throughout the whole talk. Heather Stefl with the consulting firm Computer Science Corporation does work for a federal agency in

Washington, D.C. She helped them create ways to get people to listen. For the last three years she has created games at the end of the agency's presentations that cover information technology and data-sharing topics. There are other ways to have fun, depending on the audience. You can ask them to brainstorm with you when you are doing problem-solving presentations. You can seek their support by having them suggest ideas. People like to be creative, particularly in situations that are non-threatening. How does one go about this? One option is to use interactive slides.

The example shown in Figure 2.2 is from a game based on the popular ABC game show "Who Wants to Be a Millionaire?" The game begins with the theme playing in the background. The presenter then clicks one of these images on the slide: 50/50, picture of three people (ask the audience), or phone (phone a friend). The questions and answers were all in the original presentation's content, so the audience really had to listen. The questions get tricky as the game progresses. When a person selects a wrong answer, the slide gives them a buzzer sound. When someone chooses the right answer, the slide has a crowd clapping with joy. If the person makes it to the "lightning" round, he or she receives a prize that has something to do with the subject matter or something from a local vendor. This type of presentation was actually done by an agency. These talks are

Figure 2.2
Sample Quiz Game Slide

POWERPOINT TIP

Create a separate PowerPoint Show for use during intermissions. Here are what some of the intermission shows can be about: brain teasers or trivia about TV, movies, sports, and famous quotations. Ask a question on one slide and give the answer on the following slide. Have the slides advance every ten to fifteen seconds. This is a great way to take a break from the subject of the talk but keep the minds of the audience active and entertained. It's also a good icebreaker, as people start to talk to each other about the questions and answers.

2003: *Slide Show>Custom Animation>Fade or Box Out>Medium Speed>Advance Slides Automatically After (10 seconds)>Apply to All Slides*

2007: *Animations>Custom Animation>* (looks the same as 2003)

now requested all around the world. Most people really listen to the presentations, and the subject matter always sticks in their heads.

CONNECTING BASED ON SPECIFIC PRESENTATIONS

You now have some general guidelines about how to connect and keep engaged with your audience. Based on the specific type of presentation, you will adjust your presentation organization and focus that you worked on in Chapter 1. Following are some different types of presentations and how to make them the best for your listeners.

The Selling Presentation

There are many selling situations. You may be "selling" your ideas to colleagues or upper management. You may actually be selling a product or a service. This section covers both of these situations.

Open Focused on the Customer   *Don't stick to your standard, off-the-shelf presentation.* Frequently, your content will have to be modified. An audience can tell whether a salesperson is just giving the same talk he or she gave yesterday to another potential customer. That no longer works, if it ever did. The whole point of giving a laptop presentation is that it is easy to customize, even at the last moment. Yet many presenters simply don't bother.

I imagine that if we looked at twenty sales presentations, almost all would start with many slides about the company that is selling the product. Some would even have twenty slides before they even acknowledge the customer's products, interests, or needs. This is not customization. What might an opening slide look like?

Gaining Trust: The first slide for a potential prospect is the slide about their company and its needs, not about your company.

Figure 2.3 shows an example of an opening used by a consultant who is being interviewed by a company that is seeking assistance in addressing a negative sales trend. The most convincing sales pitch, in this case, is to demonstrate that the consultant knows something about the company and its priorities. The best of all possible credentials is for the consultant to "WOW" the potential client by addressing the client's needs first.

Figure 2.3
Your Priorities: Additions and Comments

> ### Your Priorities: Additions and Comments ?
>
> ➢ Put products on your shelves that sell fast
> ➢ Offer new state-of-the art products
> ➢ Use coupons to drive people to your store
> ➢ Set up marketing campaigns that bring new customers to the store

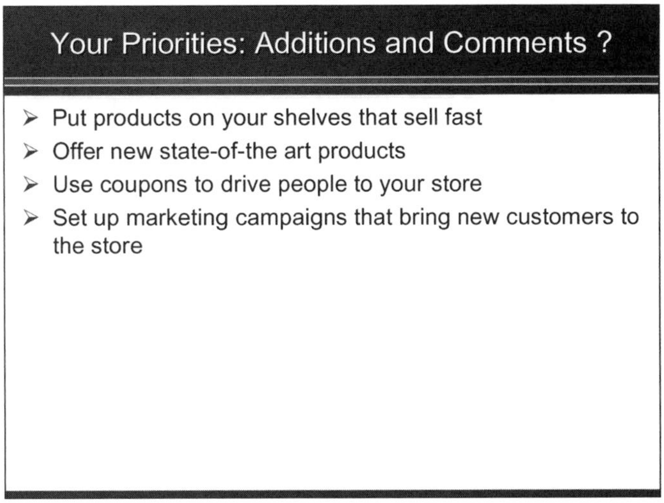

Audiences love to feel they are part of the presentation. They become more involved and retain more of what you say. They also realize that you spent some time thinking about them when creating your presentation.

If you are presenting and your customers want you to start immediately, go along. Then, after speaking only several minutes, ask them a few questions to start them talking. Be persistent in getting them to discuss their issues and concerns before you launch into your slides. You may not be able to formally go around the room and ask everyone, but you can write down people's responses for all to see. Involve everyone by discussing their key concerns first. You know what you plan to say; learn their views so you can truly talk to their comments.

Customize While You Are Talking   Companies spend hours and lots of money trying to keep up with the latest slide technology, but sophisticated slides are not enough. In fact, sometimes they are a distraction. An effective presentation will not just be judged by comparing its bells and whistles with those of a competitor. The difference will be in how well the presentation was focused on the audience and whether the audience was allowed input into the content or structure of the talk.

Greg Rocco, a technical systems engineer at Mercury Computer Systems, has an elaborate, effective way of talking only about his audience's interests. Here's what he says he does:

> "First, the businessperson from Mercury puts up the agenda. This has been discussed in advance. It may now change due to whomever is in our audience, which may be different than what was planned for. We never just start with the first point on the agenda. The businessperson asks, 'Are these the topics you want to discuss? In what particular order do you want to discuss them?' I start showing a PowerPoint slide listing all my favorite customer presentations with hypertext links. But I do have another slide with less frequently used presentations just in case someone mentions something during the opening agenda discussion. Based on what I hear, I make suggestions about what we cover first.
>
> "Now I start with the first presentation. On that opening slide is a detailed outline of the presentation. My outline slide has links to various parts of the presentation so I can quickly get to particular

details. Based on what they say at this point, I choose which show version of that topic to present. For every presentation, I create one or more custom shows of those slides. I explain that there are multiple versions of the subject and assess what level of detail they want to know about these subjects. At this point I look for nonverbal cues from the customer as well as from Mercury people from the local office, as they usually know the customer better than I. When talking about Mercury people in this context, I think it is worth pointing out that I am a person from corporate and generally do not have as close a relationship with the customer as the local account manager and application engineer. I also let them know that I can send them a copy of the slides so we don't have to cover every single detail about a product."

On his agenda slide, Figure 2.4, hyperlinks (underlined words) are set up so that Greg can go to any section of the talk. At the bottom he has created three custom show versions of the talk. Depending on the level of interest in the room, he can go from providing an overview to a little detail to a lot of detail.

Figure 2.4
Agenda Slide

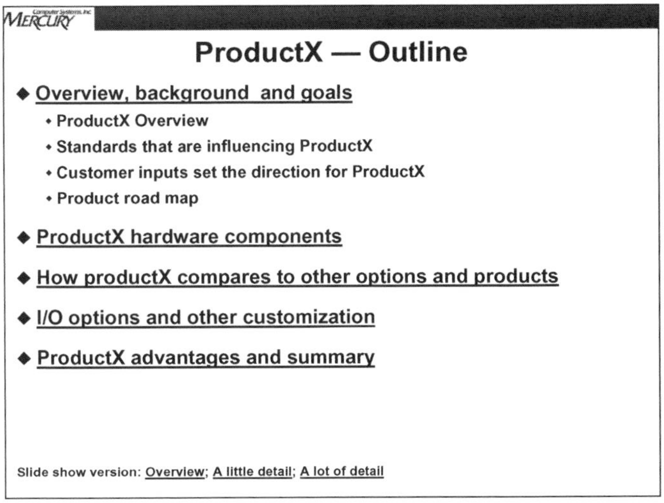

MERCURY

ProductX — Outline

◆ <u>Overview, background and goals</u>
  • ProductX Overview
  • Standards that are influencing ProductX
  • Customer inputs set the direction for ProductX
  • Product road map

◆ <u>ProductX hardware components</u>

◆ <u>How productX compares to other options and products</u>

◆ <u>I/O options and other customization</u>

◆ <u>ProductX advantages and summary</u>

Slide show version: <u>Overview</u>; <u>A little detail</u>; <u>A lot of detail</u>

Greg states, "For me, I am always assessing how much or how little information my client wants right now. Then I can use my hyperlinks and custom shows to provide that level of information. Another technique I use is to have a link at the bottom of some slides, which points to a more detailed slide in case there is interest. I am constantly choosing what level of detail to discuss based on what the customer is most interested in and where I think we should spend the valuable time we have remaining."

The above example focuses on giving the customer a unique "sales experience." As much as possible, the customer is directing how much or how little information is presented. This is as it should be. Imagine how happy audiences will be when they can choose to listen to the "overview," not the "lot of detail" presentation.

Here are some examples of how people customize their talks and find better ways to sell their ideas.

1. **Use Drawings to Illustrate a Situation.** A sales manager for a large company recounts the following: "One of our product designs—a hi-def plasma TV—had a frustrating problem. I needed to get our Japanese engineers to understand the problem and fix it, because it would drive customers nuts. Rather than type out a problem description, which would never be translated properly anyway, I instead illustrated the problem with simple drawings and clip-art customers, the latter happily changing channels on our competitor's sets and frustrated with our set. Our local product planners forwarded my PowerPoint to Japan, and lo and behold, the problem rose to the top of the fix list. The Japanese engineers used the PowerPoint as leverage with their subcontractor for TV tuners and fixed the problem."

2. **Quote Sources.** I like to put short quotes of respected third-party news sources or famous writers, politicians, or sports legends. These make presentations seem up-to-the-minute and are very handy to drive questions to the group and get them to voice opinions that will support my own story. I try to use quotes familiar to my audience.

3. **Let the Customer Be in Charge.** If you are presenting to more than one or two people, you will be standing in front of them. If you are seated, you have a choice. You can hold the remote or you can give it to the customer to hold and click when he or she wants. This might be threatening

to some presenters, but this is certainly a way to let the customer/prospect/manager/trainee be in charge.

4. **Consistently Confirm Interest and Agreement.** As you talk, refer back to their requirements and needs and discuss your ability to fulfill those needs. Before you go on to another product or service description, ask whether they want to hear more about any of the specifics.

5. **Briefly Respond to Questions.** Sometimes you truly know what the questioner was asking and you just answer it and stop. If you aren't clear about the question, don't ramble on and on. Some of your colleagues in the audience can ask follow-up questions to discover exactly what the person is asking before you or someone else responds. After answering, ask, "Do you want more details now?" Let people know that any and all questions are worth your time. If you do not want people to ask questions, then respond to the first question with a five-minute answer. No one will want to ask a question after that.

6. **Ask Questions About the Meeting's Direction.** Part-way through a day-long or multiple-day meeting, check out what people are thinking or feeling about the meeting so far. Ask questions like "Based on what we've covered so far and how we've discussed the issues, what shall we continue, start, or stop doing when we resume after lunch?" "What's been effective for you about our session, and what changes do you suggest we make after the break?" Even though everyone seems engaged and interested, it never hurts to check out what they are really thinking. Then you can make modifications right then and there.

The Technical Presentation

Certain technical presentations set up many challenges to staying engaged with an audience. You may find yourself, as the technical person, having to present information that half of your audience will not understand.

For example, you are supposed to show the engineers in the group that your company really does know the business, while at the same time keep the upper-level managers engaged. This can be almost impossible to do.

First, remember that your non-technical people do not like to feel stupid. To avoid this situation, you are better off to first give a general overview talk. This could be your executive summary. Then tell the non-technical people that for the next fifteen minutes you are going to get into the nitty-gritty technical "stuff" that may not interest them. Give them a choice of whether to stay or leave for fifteen minutes.

If you cannot separate the group, then say only what is needed to convince the technical people in the audience that you know what you are talking about. Say it slowly. Take your cues from your listeners about the speed and level of detail they want to hear at the moment. The real issue with most technical presentations that I see is that they are so full of details, sentences, and models that even a sophisticated audience can be overwhelmed with the amount of information the person is attempting to cover in such a short amount of time. It's as if the person presenting thinks he or she has to prove competency in the subject by covering everything. Moreover, the person has forty slides for a twenty-minute talk. This is a recipe for an almost guaranteed way to discourage your listeners from paying attention. So, when you are the technical expert, only tell your listeners what they want and need to know at a speed at which they can actually process the information.

The Financial Presentation

Financial presentations have their own challenges. First, the audience needs to be able to read the numbers when projected on a screen. Second, after seeing five almost identical pie charts, the audience's eyes need a break. Show the information another way. Someone once asked me, "But what if you have a graph with many numbers and no one can read it? Should you summarize with phrases on the next slide?" Well, the answer is that you should not include such a graph on the slide. Maybe simplify the graph or change the scale of the graph to make it readable. Or perhaps hand out the slide and let people look at it on a piece of paper if you have an audience that really wants to involve itself in the detail. Or maybe just have a slide that summarizes the data and what it means. In my experience I have yet to have a client make a successful case for showing something on the screen that no one can read!

What is just as important as having the information readable is having the person presenting the numbers interpret them for the audience. So what is the best way to present numbers? First, don't read off all your numbers. Many times I see someone reading all the numbers that are on the slide and then going to the next slide. This is utterly boring to your audience. Remember, they can read faster than you can talk.

Second, you must explain the numbers rather than read them. A number is meaningless until it is presented in some form of context. Remember our communication pyramid.

Tell your audience how they should feel about the numbers (excited, depressed, irritated, shocked, intrigued, happy). For example, you might say, "Last year this number was below our projections. This year we met our projected number. This is great news for our company!"

Here's an idea that a colleague of mine got from a client. He said he got tired of just presenting numbers to the board. So one time he made his charts and next to certain numbers he put a smiley face or a frowning face. At first the board members looked a bit surprised, but then they got into it. What he really loved was when a board member said, "I don't agree that that should be a smiley face, seems like we have a problem with. . . ." Now some people I have told think this is a good idea and some have said, "Great, we have now reduced our board meetings to smiley faces." And others have said that finally at least the board saw an interpretation of the numbers. You have to judge what will work in your environment.

The Cross-Cultural Presentation

As so many companies are global, many presenters will find themselves presenting to members of another culture. This is not a time to learn by trial and error. You really do need to prepare or else you and your company's credibility will suffer.

Ask for Advice. Ask for advice from at least two people from that culture. Ask what colors, images, pictures, gestures, acronyms, phrases, words, or competitive references are offensive or not understandable. Find out what type of presenter will be acceptable—what gender, age, and level in the organization. Ask what the audience is used to seeing in the way of visual content and presentation style. Ask about how people express their agreement or disagreement, both verbally and nonverbally. One survey respondent said, "I present three or four times a year outside North America. I've learned that, in some areas of the world (for example, Dubai, the Middle East), when people shake their heads side to side (what Americans know as 'no'), that means 'yes' to them. And when they nod up and down (what Americans know as 'yes'), that means 'no.' If I didn't know this before going there, I would have been surprised and confused by their head nods."

Acknowledge Them and Their Country. Be sure to open with something that shows you know where you are and your appreciation for the person or audience you are speaking to. Personalize slides to that country in some manner.

Put a flag on the slides. Use the country's colors. Find local or regional examples to enliven a concept. Go online and look at how that company's presentations "look" and "feel." Downplay the "Americanization" of a presentation. "Slick" may work in New York City, but perhaps not in cities like Tokyo or London. Learn to say hello, thanks, and good-bye in their language. Make sure you really know the market dynamics and regulations of your business in that country before you offer advice. Read the local paper. A survey respondent said, "I read three papers every day (*The Wall Street Journal, USA Today*, and the local paper) wherever I am. This allows me to reference local events in the presentation and remove things that might be offensive."

Choose Your Slide Language. When deciding which language to make your slides in, consider which language most of the audience can first read and then speak. Another person responded, "I often have to make presentations in Spanish-speaking countries in Spanish, but I use my English slides, as a small minority in the audience does not speak Spanish. Almost everyone in the audience understands English, so they can read my slides. Then only a minority has to listen to interpreters through their earphones." Also, one respondent recommended, "When I travel to the UK, I change to the British spelling of common words like 'colour' and 'theatre.' This shows I took a little extra time to prepare."

Rehearse with a Native. Practice giving the presentation to someone in that country who isn't that familiar with your language. Ask him or her to raise a hand every time you use slang, jargon, offensive words, or colloquialisms. Certain words can have different, very embarrassing meanings in other countries. At the same time, ask to be told whether any of your voice tones, gestures, or slides are offensive and whether you are speaking at the right speed and clearly enough. If you used humor, ask whether it is appropriate in that country. Ask whether you spoke about a topic that is taboo in that country. Usually, you will want to speak more slowly and clearly than you do in your own country. If you can't find a native, run an ad in a local college newspaper and hire a student from the country where your presentation will be given. Have the student sit through your speech and also review your slides. Certain gestures may also be offensive. Avoid using the "thumbs up" or "OK" signs unless you are certain they are acceptable.

Ask About an Interpreter. Before you leave home, find out the language proficiency of your audience and arrange for an interpreter. Here are some more comments from the survey:

"We had a wholesaler fly to Japan to give a presentation to a number of different investment firms. He forgot an interpreter. It didn't take much to summon an interpreter in this case, but imagine the potential chaos attached to such a scenario."

"We have had some funny translations occur when the words were translated but not the concept. For example, blended cup yogurt became 'yogurt mashed in a teacup.' Somehow you need to find a way to trust the interpreter and find out whether your humor works, and test it ahead of time. Practice with an interpreter before you give the presentation. Tell the interpreter to please tell you what you should or should not say to the audience in order to establish rapport."

"One presenter told a joke that did not translate well into Russian. The interpreter knew this and said something like, 'Okay, he's telling a joke now that isn't very funny in Russian. When I tell you, everybody laugh with me.' On cue, the Russians laughed and the presenter laughed too. The presenter went to a different city with a different interpreter. The new interpreter simply translated the joke as it was told. Nobody laughed. The presenter concluded that the residents in the first city had a better sense of humor."

Know How People Answer Questions. In the United States, people are used to saying yes or no when you ask them to do something. In some countries, they do not say no; they will usually say "yes" if asked. But this doesn't mean they will do it. Avoid yes-or-no questions. And don't take head nodding as understanding or agreement. You need to know your culture. Ask the interpreter to help you if you are unsure about what type of questions to ask your audience.

Bring Paper Copies. Here are some comments on this topic from our survey: "I have found that international companies are not reliable when they promise you that they will have equipment ready for you. I use 35 mm slides." "I always carry hard copies of my slides and format them for A4 paper." "I carry paper copies, as there is frequently a loss of electricity." "If the presentation is technical, I hand out a definition of terms to the audience before the presentation." This is good advice for any audience.

Use Text to Increase Understanding. People can frequently read better than they can understand the spoken word. Make the text on the slides useful if the audience speaks your language as a second language. This doesn't mean sentences. It means parallel phrases that all start with verbs or nouns. It means organized content.

This is not the time to have only two words for each bullet point. Use about six bullet points with about six words per point on a slide. Also, many audiences respond better to diagrams and numbers rather than just text on a slide.

Check the Translation. Ensure that anything that is translated means what it should. How to do that? Some people who have lots of time have it translated back. If you don't have the time, have a native speaker go through the slides. Explain technical terms to translators ahead of time.

Plan for a Multiple-Country Presentation Tour. One respondent advised, "When preparing to give the same presentation in multiple countries, create slides in which you can easily drop in images, illustrations, and photos representative of the country in which you are speaking." In many countries people don't ask questions and interact during the presentation. Plan accordingly. A three-hour presentation could take only one hour if there is no interaction.

The Audio or Web Conference

Recently I listened to a web conference on how to give web conferences. At the same time on the screen I could see the presenter's head as well as the slides. I was shocked. The presenter talked so fast that after fifteen minutes I just turned it off. The slides had so many words on them that my eyes revolted at looking at them. Don't do this to your audience.

Let's assume for now that the people listening to you can only hear your voice and/or see your visuals. What do you need to do to keep people's interest? Below is a good checklist. However, first you need to check how your PowerPoint presentation will look on the remote site. Many people who do web conferences have told me that what looks perfectly clear at the home site turns into gibberish at the remote site. If feasible, do a dry run in advance. Take the time to do your real rehearsal in advance.

1. **Noise:** Be sure there is no extra noise around you when talking. Take off bracelets that make noise when touched to the table. Put a big "Do Not Disturb" sign on the door. You don't want to be interrupted when doing your webinar or your on-demand presentation.

2. **Voice:** Your voice may be the only connection to your audience. First, speak in short sentences. You are less likely to be monotone if you speak in short sentences. Second, slow down and then speed up your voice. Don't talk all in the same pace. Third, find ways to emphasize certain key words. If all you do

is talk about numbers then find a way to vary the way the numbers are presented. For example, "In looking at this quarter's numbers, there are three key events to remember. *First.* . . . Then *second.* . . . And *finally.* . . . Emphasize those words. Be sure to pause between each thought and give people time to think. Speak slower than usual. Hint: Remembering to pause is easier than remembering to speak slowly.

3. **Direction:** Tell people where you are in your talk. "Please look at the next slide, 'Planning for the New Product.' The key points you'll want to put into place are. . . ."

4. **Speak to the audience:** In order to connect more to your unseen audience, use words like "you," "you see here," "as you can imagine," "what you will be able to do is. . . ."

5. **Slow down:** Don't talk for more than five minutes without finding some way to engage the audience. First, you will have trouble talking at a pace easy for people to understand and second, people will drift off. Keep bringing people back to your topic.

6. **Put questions on your slides:** If you are using slides, put questions on them for people to answer.

7. **Connect your audience to each other:** Before they talk, ask people to say their names and titles.

8. **Organize the information:** Use one of my formats to organize your data. This makes it so much easier for people to follow your thought process.

Ellen Finkelstein, who has tips for designing presentations for web conferences on her website at www.ellenfinkelstein.com/powerpoint_tip_design_for_web_conferences.html, was gracious enough to provide some additional pointers here. She notes that the design of web presentations needs to be even less busy than for a live presentation, because it's harder for the audience to understand what you're referring to on the slide. They can see your cursor, but often ignore it. There may be markup tools, but they're awkward to use. Also, be sure to include graphics that make your point visually. A presentation full of bulleted text simply looks boring and people just get up and leave. (It's so much easier to leave when the presenter can't see you!) When you present live, you're the most interesting object at the front of the room. Without a person, there's nothing but the slides and your voice.

Don't forget that the audience has no idea when you click your mouse or press a key on the keyboard. If you're giving computer training, for example, you need to verbally explain instructions that involve clicking or pressing a key.

In many cases, the transmission through the web conference software slows down your presentation. Therefore, you need to allow extra time and explain the delay to the audience when nothing happens for two seconds after you click something. Animation may be choppy so it's best to leave it out or minimize it.

If you won't be taking questions during the webinar by phone, initiate some audience participation by asking a question verbally and asking participants to use the Chat feature of the web conferencing software to reply. Then reference their answers as you continue. This helps to involve the audience.

The Academic Presentation

In a business presentation, you are frequently selling something to your audience, be it a product, an idea, or yourself. In an academic presentation, you are arguing for a thesis statement or showing how much you know about a subject.

In academics the presenter is more part of the presentation and its content. The person is being "graded." People don't judge you in business by all the details you know. In an academic context, however, they want to know whether you know all the details. In fact, people are questioning you to see how much you know. In a research facility, your scientific research is questioned to be sure you did all your due diligence work. In some cases, your audience may want to prove you wrong. That's their task—they want to show where you missed something.

Here are some hints about making academic presentations that I have gathered from many sources:

1. Don't apologize by saying you are sorry you don't know more. Some people in the audience may know as much or more than you do, but that doesn't mean you need to apologize. This is a "victim" way to start a presentation and certainly will not endear you to your audience. They will become slightly anxious or irritated by such behavior and lose confidence in you.

2. Don't tell them everything about the field. First, it is impossible and, second, it is boring to them. Use the formats we discussed earlier. Use an executive summary at the end. Also, when you tell them everything, they may feel that you are condescending to them or that you don't believe they are up-to-date in this area.

3. Defend your ideas, but don't start thinking you are defending your person-hood. It's the ideas the audience is asking questions about. Indeed, some-times in academia, especially in research situations, this type of discussion can be extremely productive.

4. Don't be "nervous and forget to think" when asked a question you don't know or have not thought about. Indeed, the audience considers it their job to ask you something you may not have considered. You can acknowl-edge that the question is worth additional consideration and thought.

5. Don't tell yourself that the talk is not important as it is just in a class. Every time you get up in front of people and talk, you want to make it your best. If you don't do that, then when the time comes for you to really impress your audience, you will not have practiced enough in the necessary style.

You will be fortunate in your career if you have someone who pushes you in your academic presentations in the classroom. Here is what Joseph M. Giglio, Ph.D., professor at Northeastern University's College of Business Administration says, "The classroom exercises should be as vigorous and demanding as those in the real world. Business presentations are hard-hitting, cut to the chase, decision-focused, and you need to be well prepared for plenty of questions. It may not always be genteel. We kid ourselves if we believe we are doing students a favor by failing to replicate the true conditions in the business world. Charm is necessary but not suf-ficient. You have to know the subject. We should have high expectations."

When presenting at an academic conference, "It is common to find half a dozen presentations going on at once at these conferences, which means that attendees have to pick and choose which ones they will be able to observe. Some conferees attempt to cover as many as they can by popping in to catch five min-utes of a presentation, grabbing a copy of the handouts, and slipping out to do the same thing at the presentation next door. You can make up a short hand-out for these casual observers who don't stay around for the whole presentation and leave a stack of them near the door" (Zwickel & Pfeiffer, 2006, p. 226). Don't be discouraged when people come and go; that's the nature of the conference. Be sure you do have handouts they can get to during your talk.

The On-Demand Presentation

What is an on-demand presentation? This is a recorded online presentation that your audience can view at any time that is convenient for them. Typically, an on-demand presentation is accessed via a web link that is placed on your company intranet site or website, or it may be delivered as a link within an email.

You may never have heard of this method of presentation, but one-third of the Fortune 100 companies use Brainshark, a company that offers on-demand services, to improve their marketing, sales, training, and communications. It is catching on. With this type of presentation, the listener can listen and watch at any time. Also, the service tracks if the person listened to all of it or when he or she stopped listening.

Some of the applications include sales presentations for company sales representatives to send to their customers and prospects, as well as training in all types of industries, from employee training to training of distribution partners.

So what do you need to do differently when creating a presentation for this type? You need to follow the same guidelines as when giving a motivating web or audio conference. What's nice with this method is that you can stop and re-record your voice on any slide if you so desire. This differs from a live webinar, where you can't stop and do it over if you realize your voice has become monotone or you stumble over a word.

There are some important things to know when your audience is listening to you on-demand. Attention spans are shorter so keep your presentation short and keep it moving. The cadence of your talk should be faster than if you were delivering it in person. And the length should be shorter. You probably want to take only three to five minutes for a marketing-oriented presentation or corporate message and no more than ten to fifteen minutes for a training presentation. Scripting your presentation beforehand is always a good idea with an on-demand presentation, and this approach may feel very different from other ways that you prepare for a presentation. You will be surprised at how much you can say in a short amount of time by eliminating extraneous words and phrases that don't add value and impact to your message. If you find that even with tight scripting you have more content than can be delivered in a few minutes, you can break your presentation out into shorter, more digestible "chunks" of information that can be viewed as a series of mini-presentations.

The Poster Presentation

Colin Purrington, author of *Advice on Designing Scientific Posters* (found on the Internet), offers the following description of a poster presentation: "A scientific poster is a large document that can communicate your research at a scientific meeting, and is composed of a short title, an introduction to your burning question, an overview of your trendy experimental approach, your amazing results, some insightful discussion of aforementioned results, a listing of previously published articles that are important to your research, and some brief acknowledgement of the tremendous assistance and financial support from others. If all text is kept to a minimum, a person could fully read your poster in under ten minutes." Purrington also provides a poster template at www .swarthmore.edu/NatSci/cpurrin1/posteradvice.htm. You will see poster examples and can also read more excellent advice.

The best advice I will give you is to be brief. Go back and look over the executive summaries in Chapter 1. You have to give that type of summary over and over again at a poster event. Once you get into the details, many people will walk away. Give them the high-level talk first. I believe two minutes is long enough. See what they tell you for your poster session, but err on the side of speaking less rather than more. Be careful that, when you are asked a question, you answer it briefly. Don't use the question as a way to then provide all the details you know. Use the poster and its visuals when you are talking. Point out the charts and what they mean. Discuss the photos and how they corroborate your conclusions. In other words, don't just stand there and talk without showing how the poster illustrates your messages.

Decide ahead of time on the number of words and keep cutting them until you get that number. Depending on your style, you will also know as you write the words the images that will go with them. Storyboard, in a high-level manner, your words and images before you start on the final product. Use one of the poster design ideas so you don't start from scratch trying to decide on how to organize the content and images.

CONCLUSION

In your next three presentations, I encourage you to use four new ideas from this chapter on how to connect to your audience. Your audience wants you to have a dialogue with them. You will read how very important this is in Chapter 8: Demonstrate Executive Presence. Let me conclude this chapter by talking about a subject dear to my heart—dancing the Argentine Tango. The saying that it "takes two to tango" is absolutely true. In tango, the leader leads every step. I mean, every step—right foot, left foot, right foot, left foot, etc. Sometimes the follower will add or embellish a step by doing fancy foot- or legwork. At this point, the leader has to wait for the follower. But there is a paradox to this situation.

For the leader, the most important thing in the dance is to be aware of and focused on the follower. In other words, a good leader knows exactly which foot the follower is on at every step. The leader connects to the follower by waiting for the follower to finish her embellishments. The leader connects by first giving an indication about which direction the step is going to take, then steps with the follower. So you could say that, in tango, the dance is about the leader taking cues from the follower, even though the leader is leading. And that is why it is so seductive. There is an incredible connection between two people who are both leading and following, in some manner, at the same time.

That too is what makes up an excellent presentation. Even though you, the presenter, speak most of the time, your presentation should be all about the audience. Through your messaging, stories, engaging questions, and verbal and non-verbal dialogue as well as keeping them engaged by telling them something they do not know, you will stay connected to the audience. You, as a presenter, can "seduce" your audience into listening to you, liking you, believing what you say, and finally agreeing with what you are asking them to do. As our motto stated in the beginning: "First and always I establish and keep rapport with the audience by following their cues." You set the lead, but if you are smart, you will follow their direction. In the end you and the audience will have taken turns leading and following throughout your talk.

This chapter gave you ideas about how you, by what you do and do not do, can connect and "Tango" with your audience. The next chapter offers recommendations on how to set up your slide background look and consistent slide design images so you can connect with your audience through your slides.

Use the Connect Checklist in Exhibit 2.2 to prepare yourself for truly engaging with your audience.

Exhibit 2.2
Connect Checklist

	Yes	Not Necessary or Appropriate
1. I have at least three things I'm telling them they don't know (facts, figures, examples, latest development).		
2. I have created two ways of setting up a dialogue.		
3. I have logically organized the information and stories and am only speaking about key "chunks" of information.		
4. I add value to what is on the screen and tell the audience information not on the slide.		
5. Having gone over my talk, I cut out all the irrelevant information the audience does not care to hear about.		
6. I have questions to ask them and other ways to get the audience talking with each other or me.		
7. I have added humor and fun into my talk.		

Use Specific PowerPoint Features

Situation today: You believe that since you know Word or another computer program that you can use PowerPoint. You treat it like a word-processing program. You make each slide a separate design project. You find features you like that you may have learned in a class and you use them indiscriminately.

Key problems: You're wasting hours trying myriad menu choices—fonts, alignments, drawing options, graphic adjustments, and so on. While you play the "graphic designer" role, you rob time from tasks with a higher goal payoff.

    Key opportunities: Make your time work for you. Learn the key features that speed you toward professional-looking slides.

    Solution: Spend some time learning these key features. Practice them, mesh them into your skill repertoire.

    Story: Jessica, a product marketing manager, created all the presentations for her product. She then sent them out to the people in the field. She loved creating the slides. Unfortunately, it took hours when someone else tried to modify them. She did not set them up so they were easy to change. After attending one of my "Creating PowerPoint Presentations That Get Your Point Across" sessions, she changed her way of creating the presentations. She also sent out guidelines advising people on how to modify the slides. She received comments such as, "This is great. I customized your opening to my client in no time."

Chapter Motto: *Use only the important "business" features in PowerPoint.*

HOW POWERPOINT CAN HELP YOU

- PowerPoint Features That Will Save Time and Make Your Slides Look More Professional

  ○ Use the Slide Master: Make more than one slide master look

  ○ Keep letters the size you want

  ○ Settle on a harmonizing color scheme and stick with it

  ○ Rely on Format Painter

  ○ Re-position the guides and align your objects to them

  ○ Compress your pictures

- Engage Your Audience Using Certain PowerPoint Features

  ○ Custom Shows: Create various custom presentations targeted for specific audiences

  ○ Hyperlinks: Set up clickable links to instantly jump to the exact slide that answers your audience's question

  ○ Slide Key: Jump directly to any slide by typing its number

  ○ Blank screen: Turn the screen all black or white in order to connect more to your audience

  ○ Pen for screen: Draw on the screen with the pen to highlight images or numbers

  ○ Animations: Use easy-on-the-eyes builds to tell a story

This chapter is for those of you who do have to or choose to use PowerPoint. It is only an overview of certain features that I have seen my clients really appreciate knowing about. I suggest that in your process to create an effective, winning presentation, you learn how to effectively and correctly use these certain features in PowerPoint. Also, find a way (read a book, take a class, get individual tutoring, look online) to learn more about PowerPoint to save even more time creating your presentations. Be sure you take a class where they teach you how to create an effective presentation, not where they teach you all the features in PowerPoint. In this chapter, I'll cover the following:

- *First*, you will learn some hints on using PowerPoint to create your slides.

- *Second*, you will learn some hints on using PowerPoint features when you actually are presenting. These tips will make it easier for you to engage your audience in a dialogue. Remember, one of your goals as a presenter is to establish a connection with your audience and to do that you need to get them talking. This sounds simple, but takes some planning to make it happen.

- *Third*, Geetesh Bajaj of Indezine, Microsoft PowerPoint MVP, and author of four PowerPoint books, has graciously written some of the key differences between the 2003 and 2007 versions of PowerPoint.

- *Fourth*, you will begin to think of giving a non-linear presentation. What is that? Most presenters start at Slide 1 and go straight through to Slide 12, without asking whether the audience would prefer to hear the information in another order. Frequently, this may work just fine. But sometimes you want to ask your audience in what order they prefer to hear the information. This chapter explains how to use hyperlinks to customize your presentation.

POWERPOINT FEATURES THAT WILL SAVE TIME AND MAKE YOUR SLIDES LOOK MORE PROFESSIONAL

Use the Slide Master: Make More Than One Slide Master Look

The Slide Master is the look that you create that sets the design for all your slides. On the Slide Master you put such items as the background look, the text sizes you want, the bullet look, the "confidential statement." Then, when creating slides, you can just insert a slide and you have the look that is connected to a particular Slide Master. In many versions of PowerPoint you can have more than one Slide Master look.

To create a slide master in PowerPoint 2002 and 2003, go to *View>Master>Slide Master*. On the left you will see the slide masters that are now in your presentation. To create another slide master go to *Insert>Duplicate Slide Master*. You can now make a new slide master with a new look. For example, you may have one for using with text, another one for photos, and a completely white one for large or complex flow charts, research images, or tables.

Your Slide Master and its theme set the look and feel for all your slides. When you insert a new slide, the color of your titles, the size of your fonts, and the size and shape of your bullets come from the Slide Master. You will save hours of time when you don't design each slide from scratch.

PowerPoint 2007: PowerPoint 2007 users can have more than one Slide Master look in a presentation as well. In addition, each Slide Master can include several slide layouts—each of these layouts can include a little variation to create a set of coordinated layouts.

Once your Slide Master and slide layouts are set up, go to *Home>Down Arrow Next to New Slide Button*. You will see all the layouts. Click any of the layouts to insert a new slide based on that layout. Avoid using the Text Box in the Shapes gallery to put text on your slide. When you insert a certain slide layout, there will be a placeholder for text. Type your text in there. Then your text and look will match the Slide Master.

Keep Letters the Size You Want

This hint is for those of your who, when typing text in PowerPoint, notice that it keeps changing size. It can be annoying to keep seeing your text change sizes as you type. Here's the fix. Go to *Tools>AutoCorrect Options>AutoFormat as You Type*. Uncheck "AutoFit title text to placeholder," "AutoFit body text to placeholder," and "Automatic layout for inserted objects." Now, as you type, your text won't keep changing size in the placeholder.

PowerPoint 2007: Go to *Office Button>PowerPoint Options>Proofing> AutoCorrect Options>AutoFormat as You Type*. Uncheck "AutoFit title text to placeholder" and "AutoFit body text to placeholder."

Settle on a Harmonizing Color Scheme and Stick with It

There is a place in PowerPoint to designate a color scheme for your slides. Go to *Design>Color Schemes>Edit Color Schemes>Custom*. You can change these colors so that they all harmonize. The bottom four colors are the default colors for your charts. The fills color is the default color for your autoshapes. This means that every time you draw an arrow, call-out, or any shape, it turns the fills color. The accent and hyperlink color is the color that your hyperlinked text turns to when you set up a hyperlink. After you use the hyperlink during a presentation, it turns into the accent and followed hyperlink color.

When you use these colors, your slides will all look like they go together. Most of us really don't know a lot about how to put colors together. I suggest you find a professional designer to give you a really effective color combination. Color mismatch is one way to make your audience unhappy with your slides. You hurt your audience's eyes when you deliver slide after slide of bright yellow text over a bright blue background.

PowerPoint 2007: Go to *Slide Master>Colors>Create New Theme Colors.* Accent 5, Accent 6, Hyperlink, and Followed Hyperlink are the color scheme from your earlier version of PowerPoint. To see the same standard and custom colors menu that the other versions of PowerPoint had, click on the arrow by a theme color, then go to more colors.

Rely on Format Painter

How do you change the colors on a flow chart or change the text size on many slides or on a diagram very easily and quickly?

It is easy. Use the Format Painter. It's the paintbrush icon on your toolbar, in both Microsoft Word and PowerPoint. If you can't find it, go to the help menu. For boxes in a flow chart, select a color for one box, double-click the format painter icon, and click on all the other boxes to automatically select the same color. If you click Format Painter only once, then it changes only the next object you click on. If you double-click Format Painter, you may change as many objects as you want. This is a very quick way to make changes on one or multiple slides. Once you discover the Format Painter, you will save hours.

PowerPoint 2007: Go to the Home tab on the Ribbon.

Re-Position the Guides and Align Your Objects to Them

You may have become frustrated trying to line up images or text on a slide. Use the guides instead. Let's say you want to put photos on many slides. You also want them to be all in the same location. Set up guides on your slide exactly where you want to place your pictures. Now you can put the pictures at a certain place on every slide. This means that as you click from slide to slide the images will all be on the same place on the screen.

To turn on and set up your guides, go to *View>Grid and Guides* and then check "Display drawing guides on screen" and "Snap objects to grid." Duplicate a guide by clicking on it, holding down the CTRL key, and dragging the guide.

PowerPoint 2007: In the Home tab on the Ribbon, choose *Arrange> Align>Grid Settings* and then check "Display drawing guides on screen."

The following guides appear on all the slides in the same position:

- Vertical: below the title, on the placeholder line, center, bottom
- Horizontal: left side on placeholder, center, right side on placeholder

Using the guides makes it easier to place your objects in a consistent location on the slide. For example, when you have four charts, you can place them on the same spot on every slide.

Compress Your Pictures

You have many pictures in your file—it's just getting bigger and bigger. You can't send it to anyone. Maybe you don't have any room left on the company's shared space. What are you going to do with this gigantic file? In PowerPoint 2003 and 2007, you can compress all your pictures by selecting just one of them. Some of my clients' files have been reduced by more than half. Here's how:

PowerPoint 2003: Select a picture and your picture toolbar should open. If not, then go to *View>Toolbars>Picture.* Select the Compress Pictures icon (a square with four arrows pointing inward at each corner). In the compress pictures dialogue box, *Apply to>All pictures in the document* and *Change resolution>Web/Screen* and *Options>Compress pictures and Delete cropped areas of pictures.*

PowerPoint 2007: Select a picture, then go to *Picture Tools Format tab>Compress Pictures icon* (a square with four arrows pointing inwards at each corner)*>Options>Compression options: check both and Target output>Email (96 ppi).* Click OK to get back to the previous dialogue box. Click OK again to apply the compression.

Now save your file under a new name and see the difference in your file size.

NxPowerLite—Compression Program for PowerPoint: With a click of the button you can reduce your files. I've taken a file from 15 mg to 5mg. You can download a trial version at their site. www.nxpowerlite.com

ENGAGE YOUR AUDIENCE USING CERTAIN POWERPOINT FEATURES

PowerPoint itself provides several good hints that can be accessed when you are in Slide Show by simply pressing F1. Many of the following hints can be very useful in giving a non-linear talk or one that is more focused on your audience's interests.

Custom Shows: Create Various Custom Presentations Targeted for Specific Audiences

How many times do you go somewhere to give a talk and are told you only have fifteen minutes instead of thirty minutes? If you are like some people, you just talk faster and usually run out of time. This type of behavior certainly does not engage your audience. How can you be prepared in advance for both the thirty-minute and the fifteen-minute version? Easy. Prepare ahead by making a custom show. Go to *Slide Show>Custom Shows*. To create a new show, select New, and add slides from the presentation to the custom show. You will name each show, which means you can have as many custom shows as you desire.

PowerPoint 2007: Click the Slide Show tab on the Ribbon, then click Custom Slide Shows.

Here is a personal example: I was giving a talk at an Investor Relations conference in Mexico. Although I planned for about one hour and twenty minutes, I also made an hour-long custom show. Sure enough, a previous speaker exceeded his time, leaving me with an hour. I wasn't unnerved; all I had to do was open my hour-long custom version and use it to talk. Now that's a useful feature! More importantly, I could engage my audience, since I wasn't nervous about my talk and its length. I had several versions of my presentation ready to go.

How many of you have made a copy of a presentation, renaming it for another group? Then you used that same presentation, but perhaps cut out slides for another group. Still later, you made a shorter version of that talk for another situation. Pretty soon, you have six different files of the same presentation with minor changes in each version. At one point, you changed the numbers on one of the slides in one of the files. Now you have to fix the numbers in all the versions, but you can't remember which file has the correct numbers. This is the second scenario in which a custom show can be useful. You only have one file.

A third way to use a custom show is when you create a presentation to give to many different levels in your organization. You can have a custom show with just a few slides for the executives and a different custom show with more of your slides for your peers from different departments. Then you can show all of your slides to your colleagues in your department who will understand the technical words and flow charts. This is certainly easier than creating three presentations.

Hyperlinks: Set Up Clickable Links to Instantly Jump to the Exact Slide That Answers Your Audience's Question

Here's how to create hyperlinks:

- Click on your object or select text.

- Then go to *Slide Show>Action Settings>Hyperlink* to (pick what you want to link to).

- Click OK and then run the slide show.

To use the hyperlink, click on your object or the text. When you move the cursor over whatever you have used to create the hyperlink (picture or text), the cursor will be a hand instead of the arrow. If you've used words for your hyperlink, the words will be underlined. The change of color in the hyperlinked words comes from the Slide Color Scheme. The "Accent and hyperlink" box in the color scheme shows the color of your hyperlink in PowerPoint. After you use the hyperlink, the words turn a different color. The "Accent and followed hyperlink" box shows that color. After linking, when you want to go back to the original slide, right click the mouse and go to "last viewed."

PowerPoint 2007: Select an object, then *Insert>Hyperlink*. You will see all the link-to places on the left. If you've used words for your hyperlink, the words will be underlined and of a different color. The color is shown on the "Accent and hyperlink" in the slide color scheme. Now run the slide show. To use the hyperlink when in Slide Show, run your arrow over the link and your arrow will turn into a hand. Click, and the slide you want will appear.

People's level of interest and retention is heightened when they are actively involved in a presentation, rather than just watching it. Interactivity can be an effective approach to creating such involvement.

A presentation can be designed in a number of ways to encourage audience interaction. The most common way is to set up a main menu with "hot buttons"

POWERPOINT TIP

An action button can be very helpful. You can put an action button on any slide and use that button to hyperlink the slide being shown to any other slide of your choice. To set up an action button:

- Go to your Slide Master. On your Slide Master, draw an action button using *AutoShape>Action Buttons.*

- The Action Settings dialog box will automatically pop up. If it does not pop up, select the Action Button, then go to *Slide Show>Action Settings.* Hyperlink this button to go back to your slide with all your links.

- Now no matter what slide you are on, you can click the action button on the slide and go right back to the slides with all your links.

PowerPoint 2007:

- Go to your Slide Master. Draw an action button by going to *Insert>Shapes>Action Buttons.* The Action Settings dialog box will automatically pop up. If it does not pop up, select the Action Button, then go to *Insert>Action.* Set this button to go back to your slide with all your links.

next to each subject or with hyperlinks for the different subject areas. The presenter uses the main menu to trigger interaction with the audience, asking them to choose the subjects of interest. Figure 3.1 is an example of this type of menu.

The slide in Figure 3.1 contains a list of all the steps in this particular presentation, similar to a table of contents. Every step has a hyperlink to that part of the talk. I can start by asking the audience what they want to hear about first, click on that link, and go to those slides. Then on every slide in my talk I have an action button in the bottom left corner. I usually make this button a color the audience cannot see. This button takes me back to the first slide with all the hyperlinks. I can then navigate through my presentation in any order of the steps. Or I can only talk about the steps the audience wants to discuss. (Hint: I put this action button on my different Slide Masters. I did not copy and paste it on every slide.)

Figure 3.1
Ten Steps to Your Success

10 Steps to Your Success

1. Channel Your Nervousness
2. Define Your Objective
3. Organize Everything
4. Create and Use Visuals
5. Energize Yourself
6. Motivate Your Listeners
7. Conclude with Conviction
8. Manage Questions
9. Recommend Next Steps
10. Take the Leap!

www.wilderpresentations.com

One of the benefits of an electronic presentation is that, during the presentation, you can change the slide sequence. If you set up your slides in advance, you can easily go to another presentation file or to another slide in that file. So you can feel comfortable using your hyperlinks, practice ahead of time.

Linking to previous slide: When I design presentations for our officers, they are not always comfortable with the technology. They told me they just want the ability to go back to the previous slide very easily. Therefore, I have a particular spot on the slide (lower left corner) where I put an "unfilled rectangle" that links to the previous slide. I put this hyperlink on the master slide, so it will be in exactly the same place on each slide. The presenter just has to point to the lower left corner. When he sees the hand, he clicks and instantly returns to the previous slide.

Slide Key: Jump Directly to Any Slide by Typing Its Number

Sometimes you want to go to another slide in the presentation, but you don't know how. One way is to key in the number of a selected slide and press enter. To make use of this feature, print out a hard copy of your slides (six to nine on a page) and number them. This way, at any moment you can have access to all your slides.

This is especially useful when responding to questions. In preparation for questions, create several, not too many, "back pocket" slides (ones at the end of your file) to bring up on the screen when answering specific questions. As you bring them up on the screen, you will leave an impression with the audience of being a well-prepared presenter.

There is another way to get to your different slides. When in Slide Show, right click and you will see Go to Slide and then a list of your slide titles. This works very well when you have created informative slide titles. You will also see on this list Previous Viewed. Here's an example of how to use this feature. After you have typed in the number of a slide and shown that slide, you want to go back to where you were in the presentation, so right click and go to Previous Viewed.

Blank Screen: Turn the Screen All Black or White in Order to Connect More to Your Audience

There are many reasons to blank out the screen. You can start your talk without having a slide on the screen. This tells your audience that you don't need your slides to start your talk. You can give your audience a rest from the screen and allow them to focus on you while you tell a story, give examples, offer your opinion about the topic or get them to talk among themselves. You can also blank it out while people in a meeting are in a heated discussion. Then you won't just be standing there by the screen feeling a bit uncomfortable. You can also end your talk without a slide being shown.

To black out the screen, while in Slide Show, touch the B key. Or touch the W key and your screen will go white. When you want the screen to appear, again touch the B key or click your remote.

Pen for Screen: Draw on the Screen with the Pen to Highlight Images or Numbers

There are times when you will want to highlight different numbers, images on a screen, or parts in a flow chart. You may need to answer a question by pointing out something. You can make your cursor into a pen and then draw on the screen. To do this, while in Slide Show press CTRL then P. Your cursor is now a pen. You can draw on the screen. When you want to go back to the arrow, press CTRL then A. That's all there is to it.

Animations: Use Easy-on-the-Eyes Builds to Tell a Story

Many presentations include too many animations. In Chapter 5 you can read more about animations. How to animate:

> First, select the text or image you want to animate. Then go to *Slide Show>Custom Animation.*

> **PowerPoint 2007:** Go to *Animations>Custom Animation.*

Unless you are doing a big presentation for someone's birthday, don't have your text and your images swirl around and shrink and grow. No dissolves, spins, flys. A dissolve in a financial presentation does not send the right visual message. Here are some of my favorite animations. Again, consider your audience and the topic of your talk. Don't get carried away.

- Text: wipe from left, fade.
- Images: circle, diamond, appear.

CONCLUSION

As you begin to use these key features in PowerPoint, you will discover that you are not spending so much time creating your slides. You will also discover that by using such features as Custom Show, you can have many varied presentations in one PowerPoint file. The motto you want to follow is once again: Use only the important "business" features in PowerPoint. Now that you know how to use certain key features in PowerPoint, Chapter 4 provides you with ideas of how to save even more time by setting up the background looks and slide design ideas in a separate file that you use again and again.

The checklist in Exhibit 3.1 will help ensure that your PowerPoint presentations are as polished and audience-friendly as they can be.

Exhibit 3.1
Using PowerPoint Checklist

	Yes	Not Necessary or Appropriate
1. I have several Slide Master looks for my presentation background.		
2. The font sizes are large—at least 20-point and mostly 28-point.		
3. I have a color scheme that is appropriate for the objective of my presentation.		
4. I have set up my guides so the information and pictures on my slides are in the same place.		
5. I have made my file size small by compressing the pictures as well as using a compression program, if necessary.		
6. I have not used one fly animation. My animations are easy on the eyes.		
7. I have made custom shows of my presentation—in case I have less time, I am prepared with a shorter version.		
8. I put in some hyperlinks so that the audience can choose in what order to discuss the topics.		
9. I have not put everything I know on all the slides. I have only put what is essential.		

Design Professional Slide Looks

Situation today: Everyone is creating his or her own PowerPoint slides. They may use the company background, but frequently it was made by the ad agency by someone who has no idea how to create a background that works in PowerPoint. Most slides do not look professional, and many are unreadable by the audience. Presenters stand up and read their slides, which is an embarrassment for the presenter and the organization.

Key problems: People spend way too much time creating slides rather than focusing on their real work, such as prospecting for new contacts to grow the business or researching to find the specific compound they need. Most of the slides are text slides. Also, there is no corporate look presented to the public. Maybe there is the same background look, but all the actual images put on the slides have no color coordination or similar slide look.

   Key opportunities: Save hours of time. Provide a corporate image for everyone to use. Make sure the important messages are put on the slides.

   Solution: *First,* there should be a series of effective slides people can use to explain the company.

   Second, there should be a series of empty slides that people can use to display their own content.

   Story: An ad agency created one background look in PowerPoint for the product marketing group in a large Fortune 500 company. The product marketing person used it to create seventy slides for the sales force to use when talking about the latest new product. Most of the slides were filled with text; there were only a few with product pictures. The product marketing group sent out the seventy-slide deck to the sales staff of one hundred people. They now had to make their own slides from the ones they received. Many of the salespeople were dissatisfied and had to make significant changes in order to tailor the slides to their particular clients' interests. On average, they each spent a minimum of four hours. That amounted to a total of four hundred hours. And what was there to show at the end? One hundred new and different presentations, many with text—and probably some creative ideas thrown in that none of the other salespeople would ever see. The Western Region of this company hired me to take the seventy slides from marketing and redo them to be appropriate for the sales staff. I reduced the seventy slides to fifteen, made sure the slides focused on the key product messages, and made several background looks so the slides were more interesting to look at. The sales staff could now use the slides to engage their audience and focus more on selling, rather than boring their audience with endless text slides. They could now take that four hours saved on redoing the slides to focus on key accounts and finding new customers.

Chapter Motto: *Upgrade your talk with a set of professionally designed slide looks.*

In this chapter we will focus on the following topics:

- Create Specific Content Slides
- Create Professionally Designed "Empty" Content Slides

This chapter will provide a cheaper, quicker, and easier strategy for the thousands of people who are trying to create effective, audience-focused and audience-motivating slides. The benefits accrued from a company creating its own set of design slides are described below.

Time Savings. When people don't have to start every slide from scratch, they will save hours. For example, in many companies, if a technical person needs a comparison slide without a blue background, he has to create such a slide. He will save time if that type of slide is already in existence.

Consistent Corporate Image and Message. The company will have one corporate image in the marketplace. With a pre-defined color scheme and many different slide designs, the slides will be easy to mix and match between presentations. People will look forward to using all the different designs and not go off on their own, either creating horrid color combinations or just giving up and creating text slide after text slide. With a consistent corporate image for the slides, not just a background, the presentations will—just by the structure and design—subtly tell audiences a great deal about the mission and goals of the company.

Higher Standards of Professionalism. Companies will have professional-looking slides for their presentations, showing their audiences that they took the time and energy to create well-conceived slide designs.

Ability to Focus on Other Business Concerns. People will be able to spend more time on the real work of creating the company's future. The businessperson can think about the larger issues of business expansion and customer satisfaction.

Ease of Delivery. Presenters will be more interested in speaking if they don't have to look at the same slide design hour after hour. Variety in the slide look enables the presenter to have more variety in voice tone, gestures, and audience interaction.

If you want your company presenters to be smarter about creating and delivering presentations, then provide a library of formats and slide designs that employees can use to create professional and consistent slides for their presentations. One background and slide look is not enough.

CREATE SPECIFIC CONTENT SLIDES

What do I mean by specific content slides? These are slides for such presentations as a corporate overview, product presentations, project updates, and client proposals. For these general presentations done over and over, the general content slides are the ones that the company hopes the presenters will use. Someone spent a lot of time thinking about the messages that are on the slides. Someone decided on the order of data. Someone chunked the information so it is logically organized and easy to present. And hopefully, someone made the presentation so it is easy to present a high level of information or drill down into more detail.

When I am asked to help managers prepare for their annual meeting with the executive team, I wish someone had provided a common template with many slide designs to help people organize their information Why? I frequently coach presenters on their delivery; however, I find that I have to spend a lot of time on the slides before even addressing issues of delivery. The problems include: slides do not look professional, colors do not go together, too many slides for the time allotted, and the information is not presented in a logical, systematic manner. If someone gave managers each four professionally designed slides and asked them to fill in the information in a particular manner, that would save everyone hours of time. Of course, people could add to or change the structure and look, but they would all have a starting point. This starting point would make everyone's time better utilized.

Figures 4.1 through 4.11 provide a sample of the general content slides for Harvard Medical International's Corporate Overview. My thanks to Julie Terberg of Terberg Designs, who designed these slides. These slides are used to explain the organization's mission and purpose. Their look and feel presents a unique, branded image to their partners around the world. The organization of this presentation can be seen in Figure 4.1. Here you see how a presenter can choose which slides to present in each area. With this organization, it is easy to create a custom show for a particular audience. I suggest that if you are presenting variations on a standard presentation to many different audiences, organize your slides in this manner. You will save a lot of time once you have the structure and the "chunks" of information grouped together.

Figure 4.1
Harvard Medical International Custom Show Organization

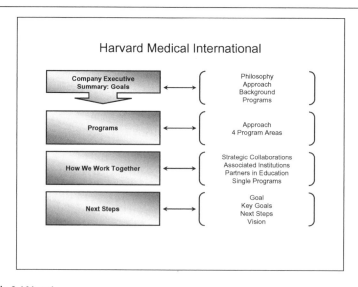

Figure 4.2
Executive Summary Slide
This brief summary of Harvard Medical International makes it easy for the speaker to elaborate on the areas of interest to the audience.

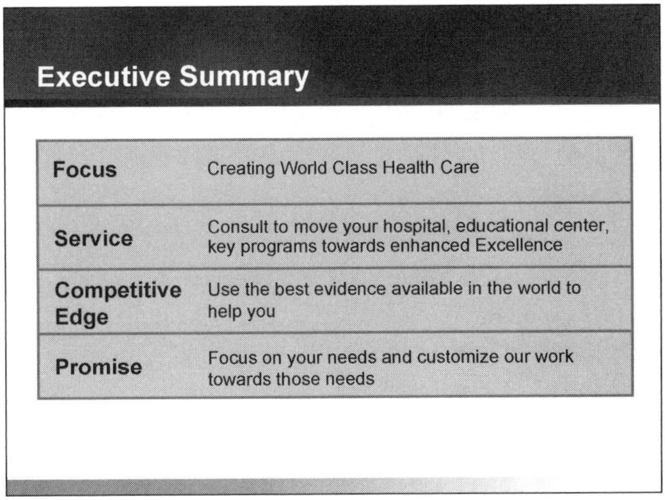

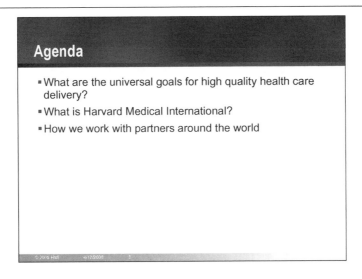

Figure 4.3
Agenda
This is an example of a question agenda. It is not a list of everything that is to be covered. I suggest you try this idea for an agenda.

Figure 4.4
Guiding Philosophy
This is a brief but wonderful statement combined with a very powerful photograph. This elicits the emotional connection that is so desirable. And coupled with a story of how they are going about this task, it makes the philosophy come alive.

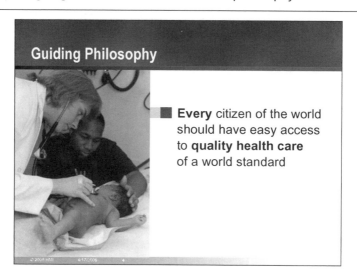

Figure 4.5
Summary of HMI's Approach
This type of slide look can also be used for specific projects.

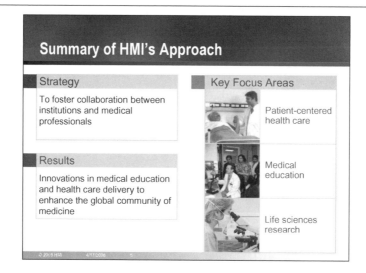

Figure 4.6
Background
The information is so easy to see that it does not have to be all read out loud. The presenter can pick one piece of information to talk about.

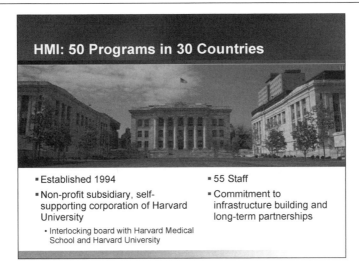

Figure 4.7
Harvard-Affiliated Medical Institutions
A very simple and straightforward way of demonstrating the size and reach of this organization. There is very little text but very impressive numbers. Notice that all the numbers are listed first.

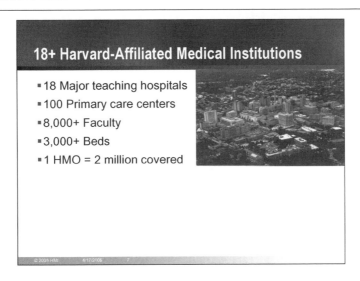

Figure 4.8
Global Partnership Sites

Now very visually, the audience grasps the global reach of their work. With this slide the presenter can add many interesting examples regarding how the partnerships operate, particular country issues, and interesting personal experiences.

Figure 4.9
Programs Around the World

This is an overview. Depending on the audience, they will pick which area to discuss.

Figure 4.10
How We Work Together

A photograph showing people from different ethnic backgrounds enhances the actual points set forth on the slide and brings out the cultural diversity of the organization.

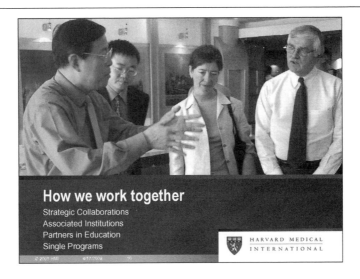

Figure 4.11
Building the Excellent Team

A visual of all the types of people who are working together. This is a much more interesting and involving conclusion than a slide with lots of text on it.

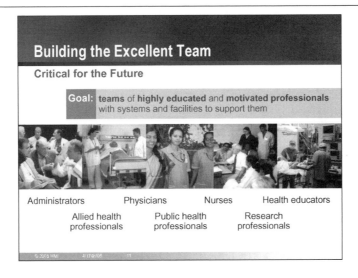

CREATE PROFESSIONALLY DESIGNED "EMPTY" CONTENT SLIDES

You've seen how you can create specific content slides focused on a corporate overview. You can do the same for many product overviews, project descriptions, and investor presentations. Notice that this is not a sixty-slide presentation. It is an overview. But you also need another type of slide look. This is the specially designed "empty" content slide that is waiting for content to be put on it. When you look at these next presentation slides, you will notice that there are designs for showing chunks of data. There are timelines and process slides. Everyone benefits by having slides already made so that they can just enter the text, images, or pictures.

Let's continue to consider Harvard Medical International. They have strategic partners around the world. Their partner work is divided into four areas: Strategic Collaborations, Associated Institutions, Partners in Education, and Single Programs. They explain this work in a summary fashion without elaborating more than is necessary.

Figure 4.12
Harvard Medical International Strategic Collaboration Slide
So here we see one slide design that provides the audience with an overview of one particular strategic collaboration.

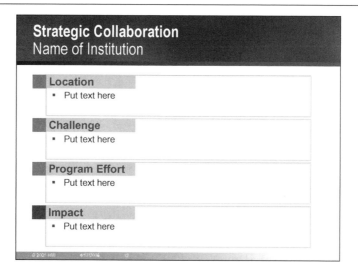

The type of design in Figure 4.12 forces the creator of the slide to not put too much information on it. But at the same time the design is set up to give an executive summary of one collaboration.

Now the presenter can have some fun. The presenter can have five of these slides about different projects and, based on the audience's interest, the presenter, through hyperlinks, can only show the projects of interest to the audience. Also, the presenter can have several slides of just pictures about any program.

So what type of slides do you need for your presentations? Figures 4.13 through 4.29 below are some examples that will get you thinking about how to present information and explain it. Some people are very creative and can come up with their own slide design looks. Others look at the designs here and then say, "Oh, I can put my information into this look. It will be organized more clearly for the audience to understand." Once you have a series of professionally designed slides in one file, your presentation creation time will be cut in half, your slides will have fewer words on them, and, consequently, your delivery will be much better.

The slide in Figure 4.13 makes it easier to present the information and much easier for the audience to comprehend the company's mission. Notice how this slide blends a focus on the company with benefits to the potential client.

Figure 4.13
Mission Statement

Rather than put your mission statement in one or two sentences, cut it down and do something more interesting with it.

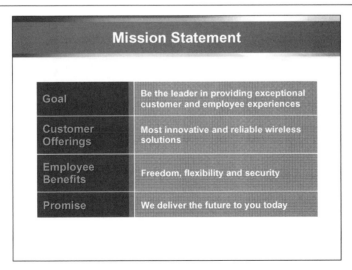

Figure 4.14
Question and Answer Opening
Engaging your audience with questions is another way to open.

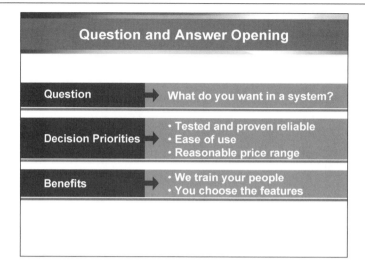

You may want to encourage your salespeople to open the way shown in Figure 4.14, because it forces them to focus on what the client wants and enables them to tailor the rest of the presentation to what is important for the client.

Again, the slide in Figure 4.15 is a customer-oriented slide that ties in well with the product. It can be very useful to respond to questions like, "What are the benefits of this product and what can it do for us?" and "Why should we replace what is currently working well?"

Figure 4.15
Product Summary

Product Summary: Wireless Headset	
Focus	Hear your clients better Save your neck Make notes while you listen
Products	Completely wireless headsets
Competitive Edge	Range of 300 feet Noise-canceling, crystal clear 8 hours of talk time
Promise	You'll wonder how you worked without it!

Figure 4.16
Grouping Information for Variety

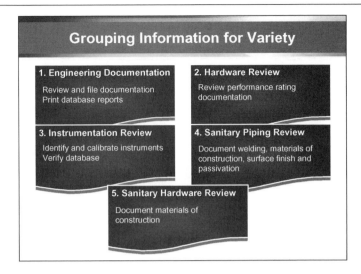

In Figure 4.16, you see a way to put text in images rather than just make a list on the slide. The data, in categories, is much easier to look at on the screen.

Now you see the information from Figure 4.16 shown in another way. The slide in Figure 4.17 shows a simple way to keep the same text on a slide but to highlight the key points. Your audience can read only the top-level information and/or concentrate on the more detailed descriptions.

Figure 4.17
For a Slide with Key Points and Subpoints

Figure 4.18
Timeline Slide

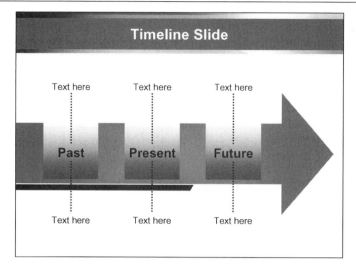

Figure 4.18 shows one way to give an overview of what has happened, what is happening, and what will happen in the future. This is not just a straight arrow but has some variety to it. I have seen many clients take this idea and then use it to explain changes in a department. This timeline has many uses.

Figure 4.19 shows another type of timeline, commonly used to show project milestones. It is much easier to follow dates across a page than be presented with a list of dates with text next to them. But you will notice we have only the key dates shown on this slide. That detailed timeline of twenty dates works better as a handout.

Figure 4.19
Implementation Timeline

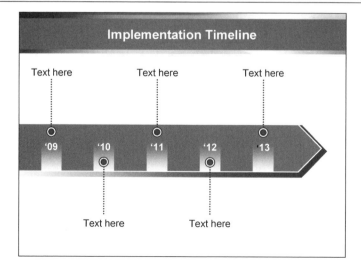

Figure 4.20
Change from Present to Future

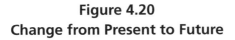

Change from Present to Future		
	Present	**Future**
HR Data	Centralized control	Integrated access
HR Functions	Independent	Integrated
Employee Focus	Mutual loyalty Sacrifice	Personal focus Immediate benefits
Jobs	Static	Dynamic
Orientation	Long-term	Short-term

You can illustrate how you are making a change by showing the present state and then the future, as seen in Figure 4.20. You can show the chart, let people read it, and then pick several of the points to talk about. You don't have to explain every detail in the chart unless the information is not self-explanatory.

Figure 4.21 uses an executive summary format to illustrate what resources you need. The resources can be financial, equipment, or people. You choose what is most relevant.

Figure 4.21
Strategies and Resources Needed

Moving from Paper to On-Line	
Strategy	**Resource**
1. Roll out system	$350,000
2. Train key employees	1 trainer for 6 months
3. Train key customers	1 trainer for 1 year

Figure 4.22 shows a very simple way for your audience to guess some numbers. When you see this slide on the CD, you can see how the question comes up first and then the statistic. This style of presenting statistics can create a dialogue with you and your audience. It is certainly more interesting than having someone read you all the numbers.

Figure 4.22
What Are Your Answers?
Let your audience guess some numbers.

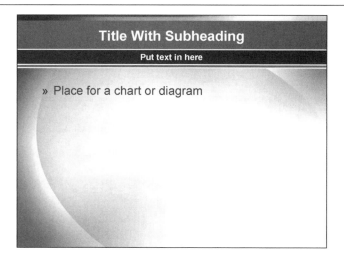

From *Speak Like a CEO* by Suzanne Bates

Figure 4.23
Title with Subheading
You might put a chart in this space and have two headings, the name of the chart at the top and the key point of the chart in the subheading.

SURVEY

Lack of Subject-Relevant Images and Graphs: Only 15 percent of the professionals say their companies provide specific graphic designs such as arrow images, good-looking tables, and comparison charts to use. The other 85 percent resort to designing their own charts and images. Among those professionals for whom company-designed PowerPoint templates or backgrounds are available, more than 40 percent think they are ineffective or not worth using.

Figures 4.24 through 4.29 all go together. These slides show the presenter how to logically present information.

Figure 4.24
The Opening Slide of This Series

This slide might be used for discussing phases or a process, key products, research experiments, or key parts of a proposal. In the arrows you can put your own text. You might make a slide like this with only three arrows.

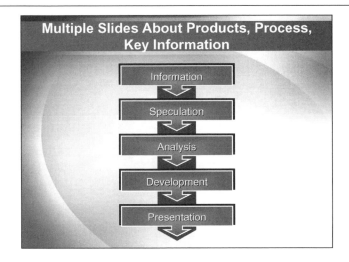

Figure 4.25
The First Slide in the Series
The first arrow or section is highlighted and there is text or a chart beside it. You could make the arrows smaller if you needed more room to show a chart. Each subsequent slide in this series would then have the next arrow/section highlighted, as shown in Figures 4.26 through 4.29.

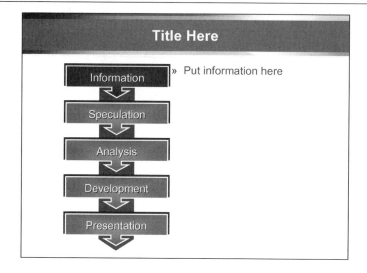

Figure 4.26
The Second Slide in the Series

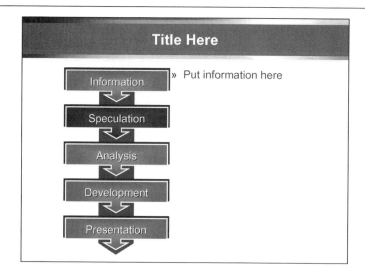

Figure 4.27
The Third Slide in the Series

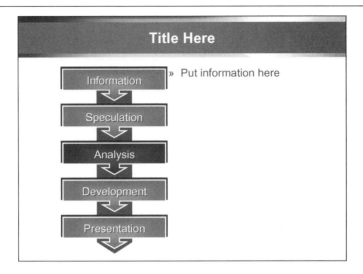

Figure 4.28
The Fourth Slide in the Series

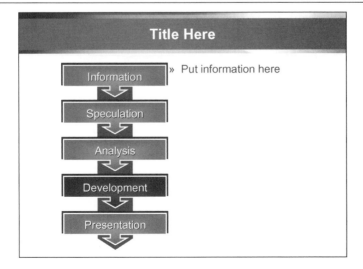

Figure 4.29
The Fifth Slide in the Series

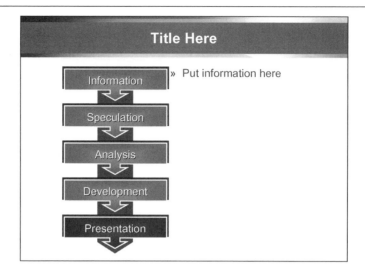

CONCLUSION

When you have both a set of specific content slides for key presentations and professionally designed "empty" content slides, you will experience how much more quickly you can organize your key messages. You and others in your organization can be more productive and creative by using the designed "empty" slides for content. I love watching clients in my classes look at slides like this. You can see their eyes light up. They say, "Oh, I can group my data and put it in these arrow slides" or "I can cut down my information then use a timeline." Some people just need the beginnings of an idea and then they can go from there. Do yourself and your audience a favor by following our chapter motto: Upgrade your talk with a set of professionally designed slide looks. Once you pay a designer to create the slides to fit your presentations, you will be set for several years. The investment will save you days of time, give you a professional image in front of your audience, and teach you how to put fewer words and more images on your slides.

The next chapter is on taking slides you have already created and making them more effective so as to connect and engage your audience.

The checklist in Exhibit 4.1 can help you think about what professional slide looks you want to create for your organization. I'm sure you will create your own list of looks.

Exhibit 4.1
Slide Looks for Your Library Checklist

	Yes	Not Necessary or Appropriate
1. Mission/Project Statement		
2. Question and Answer Opening Slide or Question Slide During the Talk		
3. Product Summary Slide		
4. Hyperlink Slide		
5. Get Rid of the Text Slide		
6. Timeline Slide		
7. Comparison Slide: Past to Future or Old to New Process		
8. Strategies and Resources Slide		
9. Title with Subheading Slide		
10. Organizing Chunks of Data Slide		
11. Statistics Slide		
12. Photo with Text Slide		

Increase Your Credibility with Effective Slides

Situation today: People are creating Word documents on PowerPoint slides. The information is impossible to read. Even when using photos, the photos are many times too small to make an impression. And people make excuses by saying, "Well, I want people to be able to read the information later and understand it" or "I don't want to forget anything" or "Well, they ought to see all the pictures of these properties we have."

Key problems: People literally cannot read the slides or see the images that are shown on the screen and become frustrated. More importantly, they cannot possibly process all the information that is being conveyed. Their brains just quit trying at a certain point.

   Key opportunities: Create fewer slides, but make every slide count. Make the slides readable and focused on your messages. Don't fill the presentation with too many images and diagrams.

   Solution: A set of criteria must be established so that the slides are created according to specific guidelines. Audiences must be asked, anonymously, about the effectiveness of the presentation's slides.

   Story: A company was interested in obtaining more venture capital money and decided to put together a presentation regarding its ideas for future products. The company was fairly new and was comprised of many individuals who were research and technologically oriented. These individuals met, and each person was assigned the task of creating slides that reflected his or her particular work in the business. The result was a nightmare set of slides. Each person created a slightly different slide background and covered the slides with long passages of text. In total, there were forty slides. There was no focus to the presentation, and the slides appeared formidable in terms of the quantity of information being presented. The head of the company became concerned, and I was brought in to advise them. The first thing that we did was to prepare the presentation following the guidelines in Chapter 1. We then started looking at the slides and shortening and eliminating what did not support the presentation. This was not the easiest or fastest process, as many people were very attached to their lists of ten points on a slide. By the end of our work together, they had only fifteen slides. Over half of these slides had images, diagrams, or tables. The titles were informative and helped tell their story in an organized and convincing way. The managers spoke clearly and concisely because they were not overwhelmed by the information on the slides, but were guided by the short phrases and diagrams. Moreover, they could elaborate with more flexibility and had an opportunity to truly showcase their knowledge. The presenters went into the conference with confidence and received the funding they desired. They were very happy.

Chapter Motto: *Make your slides increase your credibility—not reduce it.*

In this chapter we will focus on the following topics:

- Choose How Many Slides Are Necessary
- Limit the Text to What Is Essential
- Follow the Criteria for Effective Slides

  ◦ Criterion 1: Harmonize Background and Colors to Meet Your Objective

  ◦ Criterion 2: Organize the Text into Groups of Information

  ◦ Criterion 3: Don't Cover the Whole Slide

  ◦ Criterion 4: Write Informative or Action-Oriented Titles

  ◦ Criterion 5: Use Tables and Images Whenever Possible

  ◦ Criterion 6: Make Your Pictures and Video Clips Count

- Criterion 7: Simplify Your Charts and Diagrams
- Criterion 8: Use Callout Boxes
- Criterion 9: Use Animations to Tell Your Story
- Criterion 10: Include Emotional Connection Slides
- Criterion 11: Lay Out All of the Slides and Look at Them

You are sitting at your desk looking at text on your PowerPoint slide and thinking, "There must be a better way. What can I do to make this a better slide? How can I make this interesting?" This chapter answers these questions. You are going to see examples of how to create better slides, with explanations of why the slides are better. All of these examples are on the CD that accompanies this book so you can see them in color. To really motivate you to make effective slides, here are several comments audiences make about PowerPoint presentations.

> "I would rather read a white paper than try to read information from a slide. I can't stand overly complicated slides no one can read, with every possible animation used."

> "PowerPoint should be taken away from anyone who allows the presentation to be driven by the slides, or who reads the content of the slides to the audience. PowerPoint is a flip chart on steroids. It obviously has some great capabilities, but the presenters need to remember that *they* are the presentation, and not a talking meat puppet who narrates a slide show."

If you like humor, go see the three-minute video called *Life After Death by PowerPoint* at http://vids.myspace.com/index.cfm?fuseaction=vids.individual& videoID=1529637984. The author calls too many animations "pointless motion."

So how do you start with the process of putting together effective slides? First you will read about deciding on the number of slides. Then you will think about ideas on how to reduce the text. Finally you will be able to check your slides against eleven criteria for effective slides.

CHOOSE HOW MANY SLIDES ARE NECESSARY

Recently, I consulted with a person giving a twenty-five-minute talk at a conference. She had sixty-two slides. She had to cut out more than half her slides. She did so much more work than was necessary, as her slides were filled with charts, images, and graphics. They took many hours to create. Next time, she will first list her talk's overall objective and then decide how many slides she needs in order to reach it. Plus, she will consider her time constraints and plan her slides accordingly.

Ask yourself, "What is the purpose of my slides?"

Share information: You are sharing some information and that's it. In this case, it may be that people will not look at your slides after the talk, so you can design your slides with only the actual talk in mind.

Talk and also send slides to people who were not there: Now you need to make your slides easy to understand by someone who can't hear you explain them. Perhaps it would be better to send them a summary in a Word document. Or include speaker notes so they can read about the slides as they look through them. This is a time when you may be inclined to put whole sentences on your slides as you convince yourself that people will really read your slides at some future time. But do not. My question to you is, "Have you ever asked these people if they really do look at the slide decks sent to them?"

Make a decision: If people are going to make a decision based on your information, then you may show only several slides and then hand out more detailed charts and tables that people can really read. Make your audience productive. Organize the information in a systematic manner so your audience will feel comfortable making a decision. They can analyze whether you are correct in your logic, but they should not have to spend time trying to figure out how to organize the data. You don't need more slides to help people make a decision; you need the right slides with the right amount of information.

Second, decide how many slides will be necessary to focus on the key messages (Chapter 1). Don't make too many slides and cover the same points two to three times. Neither you nor your audience has that kind of time to waste. Also, less really is better most of the time. Determining the number of slides can be tricky. You may read advice that tells you to speak one slide per minute or one slide per three minutes. This timing totally depends on your content. For example, a management update probably means you won't spend more than several minutes speaking about each slide—except the one with the discussion points on how to handle certain unexpected situations. A technical presentation can sometimes mean the presenter spends four to five minutes on one slide. Think about your slides and their purpose, then consider and write down how many slides you will probably need to make your point and fill the time. Practicing out loud is the only way to know how long it will take. (Speaking it in your mind won't give you a sense of how long it will take.) But for those of you who want some guidelines, here they are. And you can decide whether you will count the opening slide, the agenda slide, and the closing slide. Those usually don't take up much time.

- Ten-minute speech: five to ten slides

- Twenty-minute speech: ten to twenty slides

- Forty-minute speech: twenty to thirty slides

Also, if you will take questions during your speech, create fewer slides. You may spend much of your time answering questions. Of course, you can show slides that clarify your responses.

Third, know your audience. Some audiences expect so many slides and if you do not give them that, you are not considered effective. Upper-level managers want fewer slides. They have no time to sit through the details. When presenting in English to an audience where English is not their first language, you may want to have more slides so people can read the words. People can usually better understand another language by reading it rather than just listening.

LIMIT THE TEXT TO WHAT IS ESSENTIAL

Are you the kind of person who can't just give the recipe and be quiet? When someone asks you for the recipe for a cake, do you tell him about the history of the flour you use and the origin of the first cake? Or are you someone who says, for example, mix flour, milk, butter, sugar, and chocolate and then bake. In creating slides, you need to find a happy medium between telling all and not providing enough details. Think about yourself and your presence as being the necessary filler when creating slides. Remember the Communication Pyramid in Chapter 2. You are going to add value to the information that your audience sees.

Limiting the text deserves a whole section because of what I see on so many slides. The amount of text one sees on slides these days is ridiculous and totally out of control. Your real goal is to make slides that reinforce what you say in your presentation and don't just repeat what you say. Some research has been done that suggests that people do not learn as well when they see the same words on the screen that they hear being read to them (Kalyuga, Chandler, & Sweller, 2004). While many people assume that presenting the same material in written and spoken form benefits learning and understanding, this assumption may be incorrect. This type of presentation does not permit the audience to be as involved with the presenter as in one where the speaker is elaborating from a short summary or actually interpreting a chart.

"A woman who was working at a marketing company was giving a pitch to a new client. The gentleman complained that he couldn't read the words on the screen. Although the woman was frustrated at hearing this, she had little choice at the time but to continue giving her presentation. When it was over, he commented to her superior and said, 'If they couldn't put together an adequate presentation for me to look at, how will they be able to put together a competitive marketing scheme?' The woman was given the choice to accept an assistant position or find another job."

Think about the situation in which you show a slide with lots of text. Your audience is trying to read it and you are talking them through it. They read faster. So consequently, they are neither reading well for comprehension as you are talking nor listening to you as they are reading. This process really does not help your audience comprehend, let alone think about what you are saying. By the very fact that there is lots of text on a slide, the text has to be made smaller and smaller. This means your audience probably will not be able to read the slides. Not being about to read the slides is a frustrating experience for your listeners.

Everyone has his or her own rules about how many words should go on a slide. For example, I can arbitrarily say, "Have no more than six lines and six words per line." But what does that mean? Maybe, if it is a presentation for a board of directors, the advice would be fine, but if it is a technical presentation and more words are necessary, then one must include them. For me, what's more important than counting words is to ask oneself, "What critical information does the audience need to see on a slide in order for us to reach the presentation's objective as a group?"

In practice, what I have found increasingly true is that the more words on the slide, the less understandable it is . . . literally. The sentences don't make sense and the ideas don't flow. Frequently, the slide will read like someone's free-floating brainstorm that never was distilled into concrete ideas and organized into a logical structure. So be careful. If you have to have many words, make sure your phrases are in order and the thought process is clear.

Setting a limit for the number of words: "By limiting my students to no more than fifty words on all their visuals—not per visual, but for all the visuals in the presentation—the amount of text read to the audience drops dramatically. This exercise forces them to choose each word carefully, weighing its value before using it in their presentation."

—Steve Zwickel, professor, College of Engineering, UW Madison

Here is what to do when you look at a slide with too much text.

- **Same word one time on slide.** Try to have the same word on the slide only one time. Don't repeat the same word five times on a slide. Find ways to make tables or reorganize the text.

- **No filler words.** Leave out filler words and phrases such as "in the meantime," "we are hoping to," "in the future we plan to," "approximately," or "as of December 26."

- **Group data.** Chunk the information so it is not just listed in sentences on the slide.

- **No sentences.** Cut the sentences down to phrases. Don't put a sentence on a slide unless it is a quote. And make your quotes brief.

- **Start all phrases with verbs or nouns.** This phrase structure makes it easier to talk and easier for the audience to follow.

- **Refuse to give up white space.** Some people believe in filling every single corner of a slide. Don't do that. Make it a rule to leave white space (empty space) around the border of your slide.

Reflect for a day: After you have finished a slide, sleep on it. Come back the next day and simplify it, no matter how simple it was yesterday. Pay attention to small details by enlarging then refining the details—even if only you can notice them. The psychological impact of these actions will boost your confidence when delivering.

FOLLOW THE CRITERIA FOR EFFECTIVE SLIDES

Now let's go through a set of criteria that you can follow to truly have slides that enhance your message and credibility. As a presenter, it is extremely important to know what an audience thinks and feels about your presentation slides. They may not volunteer any opinion to you, but it is probable that they will talk to others. You will likely never find out what they think unless you ask. That is why it pays to hand out questionnaires. Use the questionnaires as guides; don't be demoralized if you receive negative comments. Evaluate them, talk to your colleagues, and, if appropriate, apply the feedback to your slides. Some of those very comments will be responsible in the future for your success. To keep you on track, check to be sure your slides meet the following criteria.

Criterion 1: Harmonize Background and Colors to Meet Your Objective

I always laugh to myself when someone asks me what it costs to make a background. They seem to think that they can order a background like you go to the fast-food restaurant and order French fries. A background is not a fast-food item! A background serves many purposes—especially today when, in PowerPoint, you can have more than one background look in the same talk.

Make a Template Appropriate to Your Corporate Image   What type of image do you want to project? Conservative, aggressive, or futuristic? For example, a plain blue background is a conservative image. Remember that you sometimes cannot match your print and corporate packaging with your PowerPoint. All major presentation programs come with a variety of ready-made templates. The reality is that most of these should never be used in business. I suggest you never (well almost never) use a PowerPoint-provided background. Everyone has seen them. They will know you used a canned background and that you didn't take much care in putting together your talk. Consequently, presenters have to purchase a pre-made background, pay a designer to create a background, or create it themselves. Some of the pre-made backgrounds are beautiful and very professional. You can see some on the CD. If you decide to create one yourself, don't be tempted by the broad array of features and possibilities in PowerPoint to presume that you can design something without experience.

Here is a hypothetical situation of what happens when a manager decides to become a graphic designer. Suppose you are bored with the templates you have been using and decide to create your own. You also know that management is bored with canned templates and, after all, this will be an important presentation and you need to make an impression. You like the color lavender and believe that others should also like it because it is soothing. So you pick a lavender background with circular shapes on it for your presentation, the object of which is to convince the management committee to give you $50,000 more for your project.

The management committee members look at the slides and can't figure out how your subject fits with the lavender color and round shapes that they see on the screen. Probably unconsciously, they don't like looking at the busy background, and the color is not that appealing. Indeed, they conclude that it is strange and for some reason it makes them uncomfortable. The result is that your very objective may be frustrated by the design you used. Suddenly, what seemed to be obvious to you is being resisted by the management committee. Maybe they won't admit that their resistance results from your choice of background, but they are nevertheless becoming concerned about giving you the money. And they may never really realize that your gaudy-looking slides made them question your credibility.

Here are some key considerations in selecting a template design with a color scheme for business use.

Background choices: You only have two choices: a light background or a dark background. Perhaps around the edges of the slide you can vary it, but in the center, where the text and images fit, you need either dark or light.

With a dark background you must use light yellow or white letters so the audience can read them. With a light background you can use black, dark blue, or green text. Don't use a background that starts light at the top and ends up dark at the bottom. Why? You then have to use dark letters at the top on the light background and then light letters on the bottom for the dark background. Now the slide looks inconsistent, which does not send the best message to your audience. Always ask yourself which colors have the best contrast, and then use them, as long as the colors are easy on the audience's eyes. In designing the slide don't lose track of the fact that the message is important.

Note that about 10 percent of the male population and 5 percent of the female population is red/green color-blind, so they won't be able to see the difference between red and green on the screen.

Color choices: You have fewer color choices than you think. Look at the color chart in your software program. Most of you will not be using the pinks, the light greens, the reds, or the browns as a background. You might use a certain type of red for the title area, but not for the whole slide. When you take out those colors, you don't have that many choices. You can use shades of blue, green, and maybe gold. In the end, the color has to match the presentation's objective. Some people like black as a background color. It is very solemn. It is also not very interesting to look at for hour after hour. You want to keep your audience awake. On the other hand, a white background isn't that interesting either. When you use white so that you can show your charts and technical data, at least make the title area a color.

Slide color scheme: The slide color scheme needs to be determined when the background is designed. They go together. Make a slide color scheme and use it. I am consistently surprised that companies will send out a "background" to their employees, but no color scheme that goes with it. Make your own and use it.

Unless you are a color expert, find a designer to at least give you a color scheme. The money will be well worth it. Better yet, do some research and include your company colors in your color scheme.

Exhibit 5.1 lists a number of available colors, their emotional associations, and how each may best be used.

Know the Audience's Preferences   What type of audience will you have? Serious investors, participants in a training class, board members, company employees, customers? For example, if you are doing a two-day training class, you may wish to have several backgrounds that look light and energizing. If you are speaking to board members, you may wish to cut the graphics down and just show the information they need to know. If you are talking to company employees, then you want to present the company image so that everyone can identify with it.

Identify the Presentation's Objective   What is your objective? Do you want to motivate, to update, to present good or bad news, to sell? A motivational speech will have a different background than a speech to cancer patients about their disease. A caring physician is not going to have a background with smiling faces and dancing figures when telling patients about their disease. A simple light-colored background is appropriate.

So let's review from simple to more complex backgrounds.

All the same color: I personally do not like backgrounds that are all the same color. For me, the title needs to be set apart with a different color or a different value of the same color. This encourages the eye to first focus on the title.

Figure 5.2
Background with Enough Space for Two Lines

The title text may have to be 36 point or smaller as well as Arial Narrow so all the words fit.

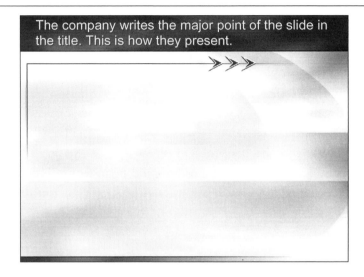

The company writes the major point of the slide in the title. This is how they present.

Figure 5.3
Background with Subheading Under Title

This can be especially useful when you have a chart on the slide. The subheading can state the key point of the chart. You will notice this is a white slide. That is because this slide will be used for charts and the background of Figure 5.2 would be too busy to use for charts. Also, the title space is smaller.

Background with Subheading Under Title

Sub-heading goes here: sentence case

Think about all these options before you ask someone to create backgrounds so that you can guide the designer in creating several looks you know will help convey your information. As a result, your data will fit on your slides and your messages will be easier to convey. Once you have these background looks, then you can consider how you will convey groups of information on each slide.

Criterion 2: Organize the Text into Groups of Information

I believe that many people just sit down and start typing on a slide. The slide shown in Figure 5.4 looks like that. Long lists of information portray the presenter as not organized, a bit lazy, and certainly not the person who will be asked to present to upper management. When I watch a presenter who has trouble talking through the content, the problem is usually that the text and images are set up incorrectly for the speaker. No one should be in front of a group looking at a slide wondering what to say about it. No one should be forced by the slide

Figure 5.4
Before: Ways You Can Practice Calming Your Nervousness Before and During a Talk

Too many of these lists during a presentation will make your listeners look down at their BlackBerries. Ask yourself this question when you see a list like this: How can I put this information into some categories that would make it easier to explain and discuss?

Ways You Can Practice Calming Your Nervousness Before and During a Talk

- You have to breathe when you are talking in front of people.
- Too many customer care Issues.
- You have to rehearse out loud at least one time. Try to rehearse at least two to three times.
- While you are waiting to present, take some deep breaths.
- Get some people to listen to you as you rehearse. They can give you useful feedback.
- Be nice to yourself and encourage yourself as you speak.
  - Yes, you sound confident.
  - Yes, you recuperated very well after that last question.
- When you tell stories, you relax and can use some emotion.
- Stories engage the audience and they like to then go tell others the story you may have told.
- *Don't say these comments to yourself.*
  - *I don't know what I am talking about.*
  - *I know I sound nervous and my voice cracks.*

Figure 5.5
After: Calm Yourself When Presenting

The information is put into chunks for easier readability and understanding. This is much easier on the eyes and can set up a dialogue with your audience. You can say, "As you look at these ideas, which ones appeal to you?" Notice the difference in how your eyes feel about this one as compared to Figure 5.4.

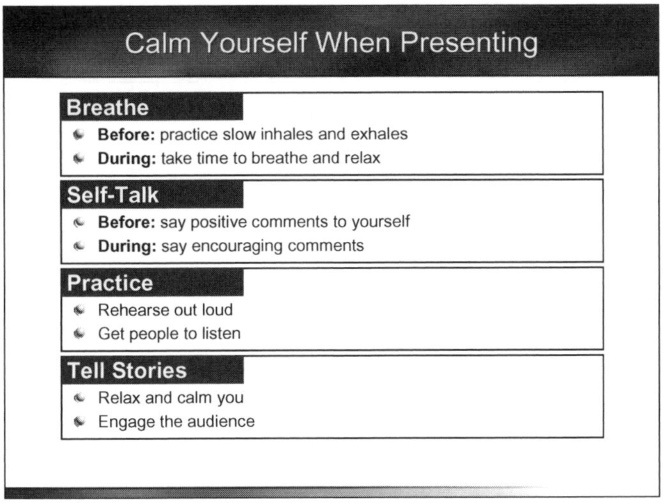

Calm Yourself When Presenting

Breathe
- **Before:** practice slow inhales and exhales
- **During:** take time to breathe and relax

Self-Talk
- **Before:** say positive comments to yourself
- **During:** say encouraging comments

Practice
- Rehearse out loud
- Get people to listen

Tell Stories
- Relax and calm you
- Engage the audience

Getting someone to let you change a slide: I find it is easier to not ask someone whether I can change the slide. I just redo it with fewer words and then say something like, "I know this is different, but what do you think?" Then I ask, "Try presenting both of them and see what works better." Rarely does someone prefer the slide with all the words.

design to have to read all the words to the group. Instead, the content of the slide should assist the presenter to easily and naturally begin talking about the subject. Another big "hint" that the slide is not making sense is if I have trouble looking at the content and understanding it. Surprising as it may sound, I frequently see slides that are incomprehensible.

Figure 5.6
Before: Product Strategy

This company's business overview had eight slides like this, filled with very technical words. Some companies like to use many slides when telling the audience what they do. Sentence after sentence pops up on the screen. Each slide has a lot of text with words that only a select few understand. People tell me that it is very hard to look interested when they have to listen to someone speaking in industry jargon for half an hour. They say, "The worst is that, even when the talk is done, I still don't know what the company does, or, more importantly, how its products and services can help my company attain its business objectives."

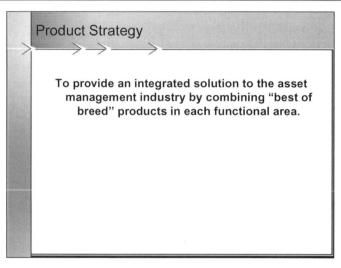

Figure 5.7
After: Serving Your Customer Needs

Rather than eight slides, make one that summarizes the business. This is the executive summary of your business. Then selectively present only certain information that will drill down into these areas. Now, at least, the audience has an overview of your company and won't by mystified by jargon.

Serving Your Customer Needs

- ◪ Product
  - Portfolio accounting software
  - Performance measurement software
- ◪ Users
  - Institutional asset managers
- ◪ Focus
  - Make it easy to use
- ◪ Strategy
  - Combine best products in each functional area

Figure 5.8
Before: Commercial Banks Held Steady with Jumbo CDs Compensating for Deposits Lost Elsewhere

Here we have a chart that is readable but could be made easier and quicker to understand.

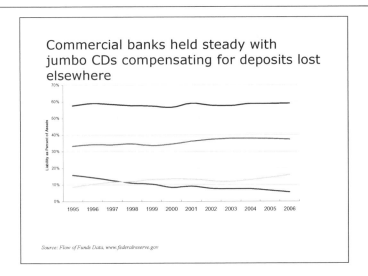

Figure 5.9
After: Commercial Banks Held Steady

First, the title has two parts. The top title is the point of the chart. The title underneath explains the reason for the top title. The names of the lines are put next to them so it is quicker to read. The source has a place in the bottom left. When you see this on the CD, click on the image around the chart. You will see it was put on top to frame the chart.

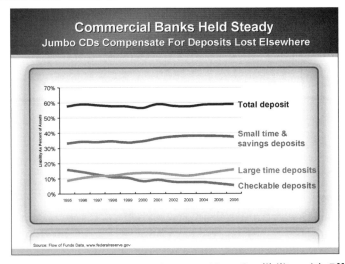

Criterion 3: Don't Cover the Whole Slide

People seem to think that a slide totally saturated with images and/or text makes a point. What it really does is cause one's eyes to keep looking all over the slide for a place to start. Leave some white space.

Figure 5.10
Before: What Really Matters Is Moving to Drivers

There is a lot going on in this slide. There's the left side bar with the company, the model in the middle of the slide, the big arrow on the right, and lots of text on the bottom. Also, the title is long. "What really matters" is what the presenter can say. This is a transition phrase that does not belong on the slide. When you put your transition phrases on the slide, you have nothing to say.

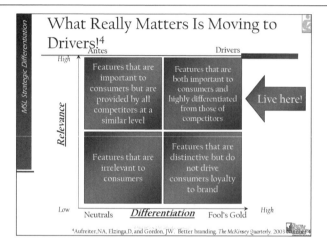

Figure 5.11
After: Make Your Features the Drivers!

The title now says the point of the slide. The word "features," which was on the slide four times, has been taken out of the model, as it is now in the title. The slide is less cluttered with images. The arrow is gone because the box it was pointing to is now bigger. On the CD you will see the box is animated. The footnote in the corner has been reduced to size 8 font. Also, the slide colors harmonize to make it easier on the eyes.

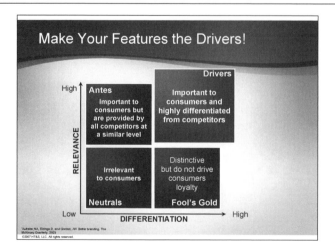

Figure 5.12
Before: Corporate Barriers That Hamper Agility

This slide is impossible to really read. Imagine trying to talk through this slide. Frequently I see pie charts that just do not need to be pie charts. Recently, someone had created six pie charts, each chart only having two or three numbers. We took all those numbers and made a wonderful animated list. This more compact information was all his audience wanted to know.

Figure 5.13
After: Reduce Barriers That Hamper Agility

Look at how much easier it is to understand with just the text. We reduced the number of barriers from ten to five. In reality, they only have time to talk about the key barriers. Why not just show the key barriers? Make it less complicated so there can be a focused discussion. Also, the title is changed to be action-oriented.

Reduce Barriers That Hamper Agility

Overly centralized, complex decision-making processes	26%
Poor coordination and control of multiple initiatives	13%
Inconsistent communication of objectives, targets	13%
Boundaries, real or imagined, that impede free flow of information and ideas	13%
Unclear accountability	12%

Criterion 4: Write Informative or Action-Oriented Titles

You just saw in Figure 5.13 that the title was made more action-oriented in relation to the material on the slide. Also, the transition phrase the presenter might say was taken out of the title. Slide titles are all too often boring and dull. Plus, they lack information. It is frustrating for the audience when the title says nothing about the slide.

Here is what one person says about slide titles: "I make sure every slide has a title—even when the whole slide is covered by a picture or something else. That creates an outline that quickly identifies each slide."

Give yourself a challenge. Create a presentation that you could potentially give with only slide titles. How easy would it be for you to talk? This is very important when you are giving a round-table presentation where everyone is looking at the booklet you are using to present. Consider, for example, a presentation where there are pie or bar charts on almost every slide. If you had titles that summarized the key message in these charts, your audience could follow better. In addition, they could actually look at the handouts later and understand the meaning of a page of information. Now consider a presentation with many charts. Make these charts understandable by showing three levels of information: an informative slide title, a subheading explaining the chart's key points, then the chart itself.

Exhibit 5.2 shows some ideas on how to change your slide titles into something that is informative. If you still want the "before" word on the slide, put it in 12-point font in the upper left corner.

Exhibit 5.2
Title Changes

Before	After
Summary	13 Percent Ahead in Projected Sales
Our Team	The Team That Beat Last Year's Record
2007 Financials	10 Percent Growth in Product Sales
Implementation Plan	Plan to Achieve On-Time Installations—Every Time

Criterion 5: Use Tables and Images Whenever Possible

Throughout this book you have seen how to take information and do something with it besides just leaving it as text. You have also seen how information can be shown in many different ways.

Figures 5.14 through 5.20 bring us to another point about showing models. Technical presenters like to show models. This can really be useful for a particular audience. But don't show your audience six different models in a presentation of thirty minutes—unless that is the point of your talk. Too many different frameworks with technical or non-familiar words just confuse and irritate people. This is especially true when they cannot follow all of it.

Figure 5.14
Before: In Better Locations

Here we have a pie chart. It is readable, which is good, but I am not a fan of 3D charts. You will see on the CD that the colors are quite bright.

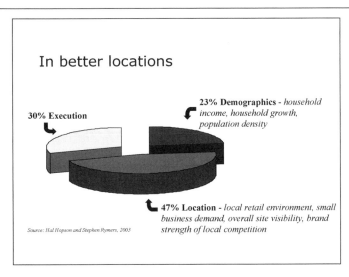

Figure 5.15
After: What Is the Best Predictor of Branch Profitability?

Now we see a cleaner and more professional-looking slide. The colors all harmonize together. The slide title asks a question and the pie chart answers it. Figure 5.16 shows another way to portray this same information.

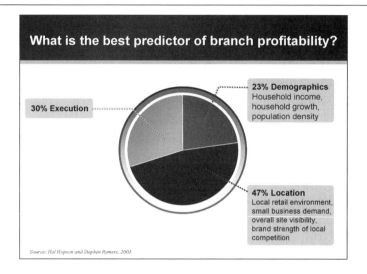

Figure 5.16
After: Predicting Branch Behavior

The title is the subject of the slide. You can see how to use images to categorize information for clear viewing of the data. The percents are organized from less to more.

Figure 5.17
Before: Working Upward Toward Action

Yes, do use images and models, but preferably not two on one slide. There is just too much going on in this slide, plus the background images as well. And there are too many points being made on this slide.

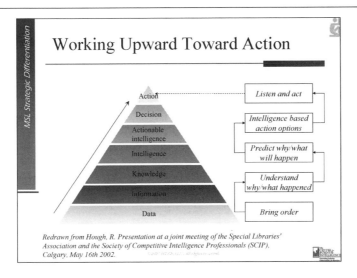

Figure 5.18
After: Moving from Data to Action

The title is clearer and easier to understand. It has an action included. Now see how easy it is to look at one model on a slide. Your eyes follow the boxes and the presenter can talk. Also, this background look fits the presenter's talk about flowing into the future.

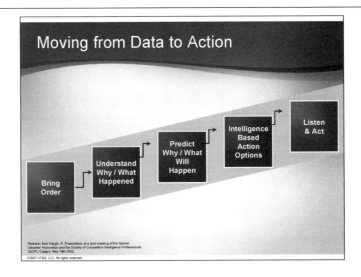

Figure 5.19
Before: GPA Distribution for Graduating Seniors

This is clear and easy to follow. You see all the numbers and these specific colors are used to depict the different racial backgrounds throughout the presentation. These slides are from the Center for Urban Education at the University of Southern California.

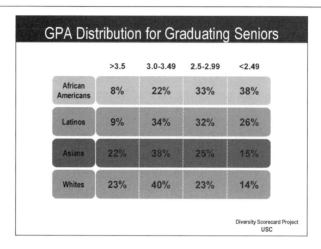

GPA Distribution for Graduating Seniors

	>3.5	3.0-3.49	2.5-2.99	<2.49
African Americans	8%	22%	33%	38%
Latinos	9%	34%	32%	26%
Asians	22%	38%	25%	15%
Whites	23%	40%	23%	14%

Diversity Scorecard Project
USC

The slide in Figure 5.19 follows many of our guidelines. The numbers are 24-font size so they are readable on the screen. There is white space around the table. The same colors are used throughout the presentation to depict the different racial backgrounds. Let's take it one step further. Look at Figure 5.20.

Figure 5.20
After: Who Needs the Most Tutoring?

By adding up some of the numbers on the chart, the audience is able to see the real differences between the racial populations. This chart shows you that by having fewer numbers the differences can be more clearly seen and compared.

GPA Distribution for Graduating Seniors

	>3.5	3.0-3.49	2.5-2.99	<2.49	
African Americans	8%	22%			=71%
Latinos	9%	34%			=58%
Asians	22%	38%			=40%
Whites	23%	40%			=37%

Diversity Scorecard Project
USC

Criterion 6: Make Your Pictures and Video Clips Count

Pictures and video clips add variety to a presentation and can make it easier to understand. Keep in mind that most people are visually oriented. They grasp information better through pictorial images. Also be aware, however, that extraneous or inappropriate pictures can get in the way of your message. Show pictures relevant to your topic and to your audience. See Figures 5.21 and 5.22 for examples.

Another issue with pictures and images is whether you can send the file to others, if this is important. There are many programs that reduce the size of your file.

The following are some other questions to ask yourself when you are using photos:

- **Why add:** Am I adding this picture or video clip simply because I have access to it, or does it further my point?

- **Appropriate:** Is there anything in the picture that may offend or exclude part of my audience? Are there only men or only women in the pictures? Are the pictures only of a certain ethnicity? You must show variety in today's diverse workforce.

Figure 5.21
Ultimately, MSLs Can Create More Value by Seeing Broader Landscapes

So here we have a picture, but with it too much other information. The title is too long. The background images on the slide get in the way of you just focusing on the picture. And the words at the bottom are something that should be left for the presenter to say rather than shown on the slide.

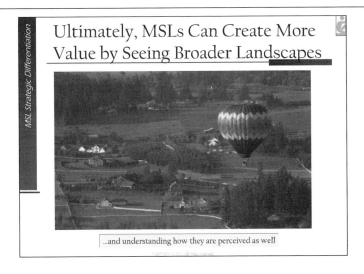

Figure 5.22
MSLs Create More Value

Now the picture takes up the whole slide. The presenter can speak about it. The picture is much more inviting. You can feel a big burst of emotion when you look at it, especially if you have, at one time, gone up in a hot air balloon.

- **Color:** Will the colors of the pictures look the same at the presentation location as they do on my laptop in my office?

- **Picture explanation:** Am I prepared to explain and comment on the picture? Have you ever suffered through a presentation in which the presenter showed many pictures, one after the other, but never explained the point of each one? A picture may be worth a thousand words, but unless it is given context and meaning, it can mean something different to everyone in the audience. Most pictures need to be accompanied by a title or phrase that makes the point and by an explanation from you.

Here are some considerations for video clips.

Video clips can now be created using a digital camera. Just be sure that the video is of good quality. I have seen many video clips of the president of a company or a customer talking that looked terrible. Be sure you don't end up in one of those "homemade" video clip scenes. Also, don't make your video clips too long. Here are ways video (and possibly sound) clips can be of genuine value:

- Video clips of company employees introduce them to customers or to other employees.

- Displays of products and manufacturing processes bring the products to life.

- Video clips of plant locations take the audience to places they may not have an opportunity to visit. They also show the audience that it is a real business.

- Customer or employee testimonials support your sales points.

Criterion 7: Simplify Your Charts and Diagrams

Just because your software program will make a graph twelve lines across doesn't mean you should make one. Only show the numbers you truly believe your audience wants to see. Sometimes a trend line is enough. After showing the trend line, you may want to bring up on the screen the key number that interests your audience. Here are some other considerations for your charts and graphs:

- Make thick lines if you are showing trends. I have seen many narrow lines that are almost invisible on the screen.

- Make the lines in bright colors, but not yellow. Yellow can only be seen on a dark background.

- Don't put more than five lines or sets of bars on one chart. It is frustrating since they may be too small to see.

- Guide the eye to the main point of the chart with an arrow, a different color, a box, or by the heading title.

- Shorten all the numbers as much as possible. For example, put '01 instead of 2001.

- Use rounded numbers that are as short as possible. Instead of $10,400.34, show $10K (or $10.4 if the .4 is significant to your audience).

- Use a sans serif font such as Arial. The numbers are much easier to read when on the screen.

  Figures 5.23 through 5.27 show examples of these points.

Figure 5.23
Before: Agenda (cont.)

This is the right idea of using an image, but is there a way to simplify it so the arrows are less obvious and don't interfere with reading the text?

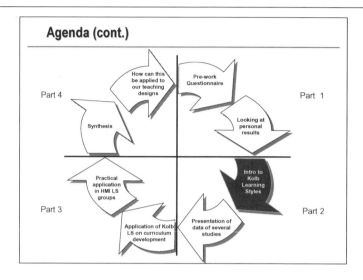

Figure 5.24
After: Agenda

The arrows as they were, even when made simpler, kept the text too small. So we made a circle instead. The font size went from size 13 to 20 bold. Now it is possible to read on the screen.

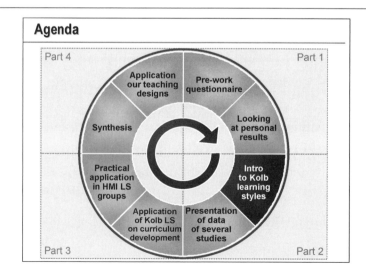

Figure 5.25
Growth in Services

Here we see a typical 3D bar chart. People show them all the time. But there is a problem. How do you read the 3D bar and figure out exactly what value it represents? If you read the front of the 3D bar, you get one number. If you read the back, you get another. And since the numbers are not on the chart, this can cause confusion as people are discussing a situation as it relates to the numbers. They may each be thinking of a different number during the discussion! I suggest you do not use 3D bars. They confuse the data.

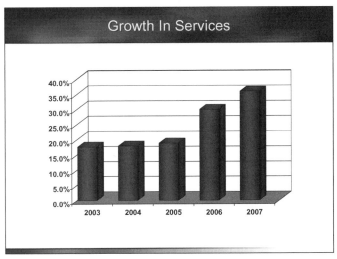

Figure 5.26
Growth in Services

Now here we see just a simple bar chart. You can read the numbers on the chart, but the gridlines get in the way. There's a lot of extra clutter on the chart that is not needed.

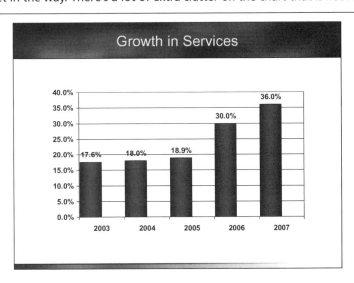

Figure 5.27
Service Growth Due to New Customer
Now the numbers are easy to read. The chart is interesting from a style point of view. The title gives us more information about why the numbers are going up in 2007.

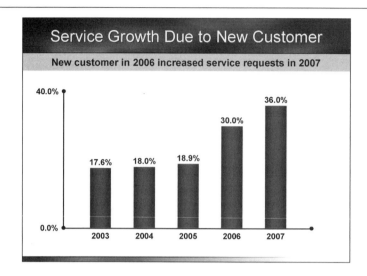

Criterion 8: Use Callout Boxes

Callout boxes are underutilized on presentation slides. There are many ways to use callout boxes, such as highlighting a certain part on a piece of equipment. You can use callout boxes on screen shots as well. You show the screen shot and then use a callout box to point out the exact place you want your audience to look and remember. You can also use them to add important detail or to point out certain numbers on charts that might otherwise be difficult to read. Ideally, you want to find another way to present lots of numbers, but if you have a chart that you've been told you must use, callouts can really help highlight certain numbers.

Callout boxes that are simple and that look like the ones shown in Figure 5.28 work best. These callouts are used to point to a certain piece on this valve gate. When you see it on the CD, you will notice that the last callout box is animated. This is a way to change the pace. I would not animate all these callout boxes.

Figure 5.28
Valve Gates

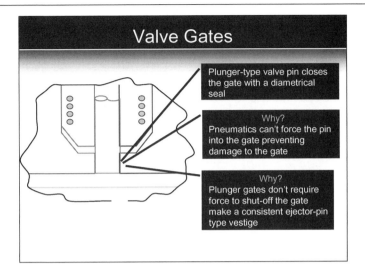

Criterion 9: Use Animations to Tell Your Story

Many presenters like to have text shooting in from all directions. There are many reasons not to do this. First, your colleagues at work are probably wondering how you can afford to spend all that time doing animations. Don't you have something better to do? Second, too many animations are really not fun to look at. They hurt the eyes. Third, animations get in the way of the message.

But animations can also help you tell the story and reveal certain images at the right moment. They help you keep connected to your audience as you explain a situation. Use animations for text if you want to explain a process and it makes sense to reveal one point at a time. Don't set up every slide with the text that comes in one phrase at a time. This will not please your audience. Just because you can animate almost anything on your screen doesn't mean you should. Don't overdo it! Animate less than one-eighth of your slides, and then only to tell a story to make it easier for your audience to understand your information. In electronic presentations, animations can lead your audience from one point to the next. They control the viewers' attention between messages. How can you use the transitions and builds to enhance the effectiveness of your presentation without overloading it with too many effects that distract your audience?

Here are hints for using animations. Use only a few in a presentation. Maybe animate three to five slides out of ten. Use only certain animations. Don't use more than a couple of different animations in one presentation. Audiences don't want phrases and images flying in from all directions of the screen, and you don't want to compete with your presentation for attention.

- Only animate certain pictures and diagrams, not every one. When deciding which ones to animate, ask yourself, "Will the animation of this picture or diagram contribute to the clarity and effectiveness of the presentation?"

- Only use three different transition effects on the slides throughout the presentation. Having too many different transition effects distracts the audience.

- Don't use slide transition effects between slides. It is just too much stress on the eyes.

- Change the pace. Don't do a build on every screen. Audiences really dislike this waiting around, and their eyes start to bother them.

- Don't use "fly" animations. They are very distracting and disturbing to the eyes.

- Use a remote mouse even when presenting to only one person as you both look at your laptop. If you don't use a remote mouse, you will have more trouble animating your slides because you will have to stand by your computer and push the arrow keys.

Transitions and builds are really movie-making techniques. Use them to enhance your story. All this being said, you must really be judicious about their use because so many people really dislike seeing transition and build effects. One person said, "I'll go to a movie when I want to see lots of movie effects. Presentations are for sharing information. Just give me a few effects."

The selection of slide transitions and build effects provides a unique feel to a presentation—just as the color scheme does. For instance, imagine two presentations, one to a conservative group of bankers and another to a gathering of employees during their lunch hour (most of whom would rather be spending their lunch hour somewhere else). Does the presentation to the group of conservative investors call for a different tone, color scheme, and set of transitions and build effects than the training session on workplace safety during the lunch hour? Yes!

For the employee meeting, a lively box-out transition when changing agenda points, combined with certain text wiping and picture zooming techniques may help keep everyone's attention. These same effects may jar the conservative sensibilities of a financial audience and be unnecessary distractions.

In Chapter 5 on the CD, there is a PowerPoint file called "animation examples." I have taken the slides in this chapter and shown you some effective and ineffective animations. Read the comment boxes on the slides to learn more.

Criterion 10: Include Emotional Connection Slides

So what is an emotional connection slide? A slide with a lot of text is probably not going to get your audience to feel anything positive or help you connect with the audience. When such a slide appears on the screen, most people will not feel a sense of awe, happiness, excitement, or anger. Well, maybe anger because this is the tenth text slide. And maybe excitement if you are presenting them their financial portfolio results for the year and the numbers are fabulous. But most of the time, text just does not incite emotion. You have a better chance with a good graph to at least arouse some curiosity. Speaking of graphs and numbers, one way to unintentionally demotivate your audience is to show financials and use a red accent color. Red in finances means not good, even if it is only the color of your title area. I would change the title area for a financial presentation. On the CD you will see one slide in red and the other in green. Which works better for you for a financial presentation? See Figures 5.29 and 5.30 to compare the effects.

Figure 5.29
Financials with Red

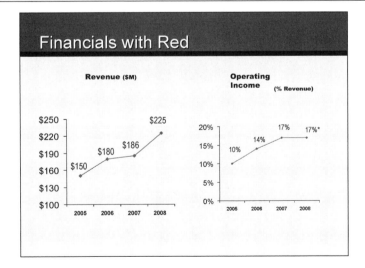

Figure 5.30
Finances with a Neutral Color

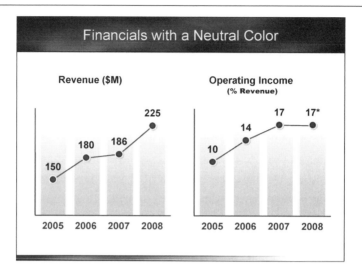

So how does one go about arousing emotion besides presenting a good or poor number, some startling facts, or a fascinating diagram that piques someone's interest? Photos, which are really underutilized by many presenters, have the best chance. Presenters need to take the opportunity to use their photos to the best of their capability. Make them big. Let them pop up on the screen and leave them there. Use a photo to tell a story. This will truly engage your audience. Emphasize a point by using an image that has impact. This is done in advertising on a daily basis. You can purchase a photo, but you can also use one of your own. Figure 5.31 is a photo from my trip to Glacier National Park in Montana. If I were pitching a new program I could show this photo and say, "I'm showing you this photo for you to really get a sense of my vision for this product. We can go a long way with it. There is a path we can follow that will take us further than we can imagine." Once you have a photo idea, ask several people for their opinions about using it for a particular presentation.

Criterion 11: Lay Out All of the Slides and Look at Them

Once you have created and analyzed all your slides, print them out, one slide per page, lay them out on a table, and look at them. They don't have to be in color. Yes, you can see them on the computer screen in slide sorter, but you can't

Figure 5.31
Picture

SURVEY

Excessive Length: When asked what they would change about their presentations if given the chance, 88 percent of respondents said they would provide less information, shorten their presentation, and/or make their slides more readable by eliminating sentences. Nearly half believe their presentations are at least 20 percent too long, and most of these people attribute the excessive length to the number of slides. In fact, about half of those surveyed admit to running through twenty to thirty slides, on average, during a thirty-minute talk. That's one slide every sixty to ninety seconds. That is way too much information. Presenters mistakenly assume that if the number of slides is modest, the audience will not believe the presentation adds much value. Consequently, people tend to present too much information too quickly. Ironically, the result for the recipient is to absorb *less* information and lose the most salient points in the minutiae.

see them all at once. Also, you don't get the same sense as when you lay them out and see how they all look together. Make sure the presentation slides follow the guidelines set forth in this chapter. When you lay them out, you can also see what information or slides you can delete.

Now that you believe your slides are ready, have someone else look at them on the table and edit them. That extra pair of eyes will save you embarrassment in front of your audience. Spell check does not catch all the errors.

As you have seen in this chapter, a high-impact slide can enable you to present with more confidence and energy. Each slide has the potential of connecting you with your audience on an emotional level. Design them with great care so that they support you—the Wow! —in the presentation. Use photos in slides to create emotional connection as well as to give you an opportunity to be a storyteller. For in truth, that is what a presentation is all about—connecting with your audience and imparting your knowledge, emotional commitment, and enthusiasm so that they also believe in what you are offering, be it a product, a service, or an idea.

So now let's look at how to improve on your slides by examining how a professional designer goes about making a slide presentation work. Kelly Ellis, who is a fabulous slide designer, received a set of slides that the company Senture wanted to improve on. She laid them out and looked at them. Senture told her they wanted slides that the salespeople could use while feeling proud of the company as they talked. Senture service offerings include 24/7/365 contact center support, including help desk, fulfillment, order processing, and warehousing to a host of clients in the federal, state, and commercial sectors. In addition, the company offers security solutions, secure credentialing and information technology services.

They wanted to impress their customers by showing that they took the time to really dazzle their audience with the visuals as well as the delivery. Then Kelly did her magic. You can see the difference in the slides. (See Figures 5.32 through 5.41.) She is a graphic designer by trade, so you are seeing some very high-level, gorgeous slides. You would use these when you are prospecting for a potentially big client.

Figure 5.32
Before: Senture: Who We Are

Senture – Who We Are

- Senture is a faith-based company that values every employee, customer and community in which it serves

- Senture is an American company

- Senture is a team and results-oriented company

- Senture is a futuristic technology-based solutions provider

Figure 5.33
After: Senture: A Solutions Provider

The slide is interesting, uncluttered, and has a lot of movement, which fits with Senture's message of being a futuristic company. The photographs are integrated into the slide design.

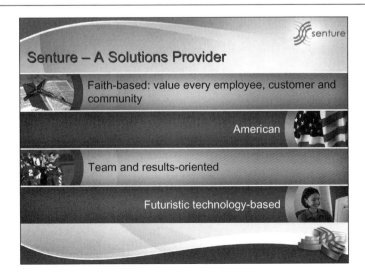

Senture – A Solutions Provider

Faith-based: value every employee, customer and community

American

Team and results-oriented

Futuristic technology-based

Figure 5.34
Before: Highlights of Organization

Highlights of Organization

- Management staff has an average of 15 years experience working together in similar functions
- CSRs have an average of 4.5 years experience
- Total seat capacity
  - Current = 810
  - At 9/30/07 = 1,235
  - At full utilization = 3,050

Figure 5.35
After: Experienced, Competent Staff

Again, this slide has movement in it and it appeals to emotion by showing a smiling and receptive person communicating.

Figure 5.36
Before: Our Core Values

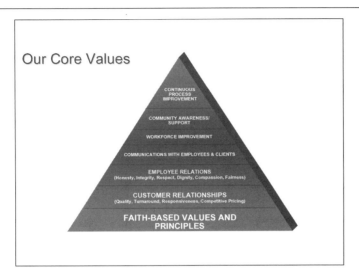

Figure 5.37
After: Our Core Values

This circle is a more effective way to illustrate how the core values go together to make a whole. And again we have movement in the slide.

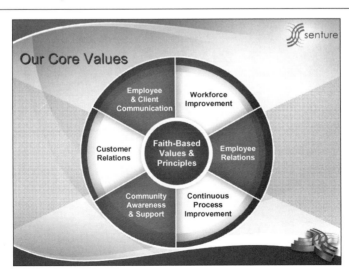

Figure 5.38
Before: Senture Business Units

Figure 5.39
After: Business Units Set Up to Serve You

The circle idea is carried through again in this slide. The puzzle piece now has meaning—fitting the units together. The title is action-oriented.

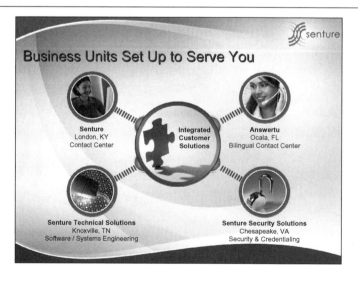

Figure 5.40
Before: Better Customer Service—A Definition

Better Customer Service – A Definition

- Target clients' needs and wants
- Respond more quickly to our client's problems
- Let our clients know we care
- Show our clients we stand behind what we sell
- Obtain invaluable feedback of the client's impressions
  - Correct "problems" with own products / services
- Ensure future product offerings are on target

Figure 5.41
After: We Target Client Needs and Wants

This slide connects the definition with the importance of customer service to Senture and uses a photo of a smiling person to do so. The emotional appeal of the slide is greater and the slide is very pleasant to look at. The focus of the slide is on the person and what she is holding.

CONCLUSION

As you look back through the slides in this chapter, you will notice there is text on many of them. There are images and diagrams. Perhaps, in an ideal world, you could just stand up and show a picture, but I focused this chapter and this book to all those people who are expected to show diagrams, images, and text on the slides. Your competence in the eyes of your audience will increase when your diagrams are clearer, you use fewer words, and you show more images and photos. The motto of this chapter is: Make your slides increase your credibility—not reduce it. That's my desire for you—and I believe your desire for yourself as well.

The next chapter, Prepare for Technology Success, will make sure you can show the fabulous slides you made.

Following are two checklists. As you lay out your slides on the table and then look at them, use Exhibit 5.3, the Total Visual Checklist. Then, analyze each slide using Exhibit 5.4, the Single Visual Checklist. These are your guidelines for creating and/or modifying your slides in order to keep your slides on message and your audience paying attention.

Exhibit 5.3
Total Visual Checklist

Attribute	Description	✓
1. Organization		
Agenda	The agenda and/or executive summary are shown in the first three slides.	
Logical Flow/ Data Chunked	The content flow follows the format and agenda. All information related to one topic is together.	
2. Content/Flow		
Variety	The slides don't all look the same. There are not six pie charts or six text slides in a row. Flow charts, tables, and/or diagrams convey a complex message colorfully and accurately.	

Necessity of Slide	All the slides are necessary. They help illustrate and support the key messages and presentation objective.	
3. Look		
Appropriate Template	Background(s) matches presentation objective and audience expectations. The colors reinforce the message and the words are all readable. Logos are not used on every slide unless essential for the message.	
Informative Headings	There is a different heading on every slide. It states one of the key points of the slide.	
Graphics	Graphics accurately and appropriately represent the topic and message. Graphics are appropriate for the audience.	
Animations	There are almost no slide transition animations, except to highlight something that is going to be on a slide. Text and image animations are subtle and used only on a limited number of slides.	
4. Other Ideas		
Client Customization	Include slides of client information.	
Table of Contents	Include a table of contents as an aid to the audience for easy reference.	
Appropriate Chart	Ensure the type of chart chosen is the best way to display the data.	
Handouts	If printed in black and white, charts are understandable. For example, bar charts in different colors, without textures, may look all the same in black and white.	
Sound	There are no sound effects in the talk, unless appropriate.	

Exhibit 5.4
Single Visual Checklist

Attribute	Description	☑
1. Organization		
Major Focal Point	There is one major point being made on the slide.	
Chunked Images and Text	The eye can easily follow the images and text on the slide.	
Lists	Numbers are used with a list when there is an order of importance to delineate.	
2. Understanding		
Titles	Titles are informative and tell your audience the importance of the slide within three seconds. Titles are not "Summary," but "Up 18–20 Percent in Production 2007."	
Phrases with Limited Words	Short phrases, not sentences, are on the slide. The same word is only on the slide one time. Words are in sentence case, not all capital letters.	
Parallel Structure	All phrases on the same slide start the same way: verbs or nouns.	
Fonts	Use 24-point font for text; no less than 18-point if absolutely necessary. Use sans serif typeface such as Arial.	
Charts and Graphs	The charts and graphs are clear and the data points are well placed and readable. Arrows or symbols draw attention to the important part of the chart, photo, or diagram.	
Abbreviations/ Jargon	Limited and spelled out, if appropriate.	

3. Look		
Clip Art	Clip art not used unless there is a rationale and audience used to seeing it.	
Sizing Photos/ Clip Art	Images are sized to the appropriate scale, and when shown on many slides, they are in the same place on every slide.	

Prepare for Technology Success

Situation today: People take the technology marvels available to them for granted. They work on computers as if they will not break. They assume that the PowerPoint version they have on their laptops will work with anyone's laptop. Many people don't even know what version of PowerPoint they are using. They sometimes don't take a backup in case the computer crashes.

Key problems: When your computer crashes just before a presentation, you are not prepared. You don't have it on a USB drive and you don't have hard copy. Even if you do have a file of your talk, it may not work on someone else's computer.

Key opportunities: Save yourself the embarrassment of having to talk without notes. Save yourself the frustration of having to redo your work because you did not back it up.

Solution: You must plan and act as if your computer will break down. You need to be familiar with PowerPoint in order to be prepared to use your backup on other computers.

First, know what could go wrong and prepare in advance.

Second, have a contingency plan in case the computer fails just before you make your presentation.

Story: I recently was asked to do a presentation in Las Vegas. The presentation was complicated by the fact that I would do the beginning totally in Spanish. On the way to Las Vegas, indeed, as I was writing this book, my laptop crashed. Fortunately, I had just backed up my chapters on a USB drive, so I didn't care all that much. For some reason or other, the computer seemed to work well after the crash, so I became confident that it would perform for my presentation in Las Vegas. Just before the presentation itself, although the computer was turned on, we could not get the image up on the screen for all to see. I gave someone my USB drive in order to put my presentation on his computer. Meanwhile, the vice president of sales introduced me to the predominantly Spanish-speaking audience and I had to begin without my slides on the screen. I shudder to think of what could have happened if I had not prepared a hard copy of the notes and slides. Fortunately, I had printed out a hard copy. So I put them in front of me and talked for about ten minutes. While it wasn't the way that I had rehearsed doing this introduction, I felt confident even though this was the first seminar I had ever given in Spanish. After about ten minutes, we managed to get the slides on the screen so that the participants could see my presentation.

Chapter Motto: *Do preventative and contingent planning—then you'll always be able to present with confidence.*

Here are the topics we'll cover in this chapter:

- Prepare Days Ahead
- Recheck Just Before Your Talk
- Keep Track of Your Laptop and Its Contents
- Present Internationally with Ease
- Learn from Other People's Stories
- The Future of Technology

When this book was first published in 1996 we were all experiencing technology glitches. Now some are fixed, and some are still happening. And many of us are more prepared for the glitches as I was in Las Vegas. The most important glitch these days is not being able to access your presentation. So make a backup plan. "Plan for bad luck!"

This chapter is meant to give you ideas on how to prepare for unexpected problems and to convince you that you really need to do that preparation.

PREPARE DAYS AHEAD

Buy a Wireless Microphone. Some people spend their lives presenting in big conference centers and hotels. Since audio is a very large part of a presentation, it may be worth the money and your reputation to carry your own system.

Use the Partner System. For high-level key presentations, always go in twos. If something happens with the technology, one of you can speak to the audience while the other troubleshoots the equipment. A good pairing consists of the speaker and the expert on the technology. It is not a good idea to pair two speakers who are novices concerning the equipment or software program, or two technical experts who are inexperienced speakers.

Have Several Backups. First, why do you need backups? Here are some things that could go wrong: You forget the power cord and your battery is about out. The electricity goes out. There is no electrical outlet or the outlet is not good. Your computer or the LCD projector breaks. Your hard drive crashes. You corrupt the presentation while trying to "tweak" it on a low battery. You drop your laptop on the way to catching a plane. You spill something on it. Someone steals it. I am not making these up. There are real stories behind these scenarios.

You need a reliable, quick backup plan that lets you have no more than a five-minute delay between something not working and your continuing on with the speech. And during that transition, someone else should implement your backup plan so you can keep speaking. You need a partner or designated helper who can do that for you. Here are some backup plans. Pick several that will work for you.

- Copy the presentation to a USB. At this point USB drives seem to be the best choice. Pretty soon, many of us will be carrying our presentations on our phones.

- Make sure the video and other files that you are using in the presentation are in the same folder in which you create your presentation file. PowerPoint serves as a stage and just points to the location of the video file. If the file isn't there, then you won't get a video. Just remember to always put sound and video files in the same folder as your presentation when it is created, and you should be able to avoid hyperlink problems. Then, if you have to copy and move the folder, you will be moving everything at once.

- Do a rehearsal with the USB backup, just in case you have to use it. Many presenters have opened a backup only to see the dreaded red X's through many of their slides.

- If you have special fonts, including bullets, put them on your laptop as well—and on the laptops of any of those people who are keeping your file in case you need it. When using special fonts, keep copies of the font files used. You may need to give them to someone else. You can also embed your fonts in your presentation. Here's how. Go to *File>Save As>Tools>Save Options>Embed True Type Fonts>Embed all characters.*

- Check your backup files. Every video driver is a bit different, and you may have some unexpected problems, mostly with the transition effects. Check your effects to be sure they look presentable.

- Store the file on a network that you can access. Some people suggest that you have someone back in the office keep a copy of the presentation. The idea is that you can call at a moment's notice and have it sent via email. There are two major problems. No one answers the phone anymore. You can call, but that doesn't mean anyone will be there. You can email, but again you may not receive an instant answer. Second, the file size may be too big to download through the available network.

- Always have paper copies of the slides. This is a must! You need to have some notes to speak from if all else fails. I have heard and read about too many people who ended up giving a speech without any notes at all. Don't set yourself up for this kind of experience. A colleague said to me, "Sometimes I design my handouts so I can do my presentation directly from them if all electronic media options fail."

- If you are presenting with a group from your office, bring more than one laptop. When you are presenting with other colleagues, odds are one of your laptops will work.

- Send the presentation to someone at the company who will be in the audience. That way you can use the company's system if yours doesn't work.

- Bring two sets of equipment if this is a very important presentation, but also bring some type of non-electric backup. Here is one story I received about electrical issues: "We brought two of everything—two laptops and two projectors. What we didn't plan on is that the electric sockets in the room would be unusable." And here is another: "I happened to have the only electrical socket in the whole San Francisco Moscone Conference Center that didn't work."

- Find the name of the local audiovisual vendor in case you have to buy a cable or connector. When you are using the equipment in a hotel, be sure to ask whether the AV person will be there to make sure everything is working. Some hotels just have equipment dropped off in the room and it's up to you to put it all together.

Practice for the Worst Scenario. For those crucial presentations, do a real practice run. During your rehearsal, start presenting and then pretend that you can no longer use the laptop. Give the speech using your backup plan. If your backup plan is another set of equipment, that's fine, but practice continuing to speak without the slides while the second system is being set up. Better yet, pretend both systems crashed. Then decide what you will do.

The following section describes equipment checks you should make prior to your presentation.

Check Your Batteries. Use your batteries once in a while, even if you have an AC power cord. Replace your batteries if you notice the battery that used to last three hours now lasts only forty minutes. Remember that batteries have a shelf life. They do not keep the charge forever. Regularly drain your laptop battery (at least once a month) until it totally runs out and then recharge.

Make Sure You Have a Fast Enough Computer. Your fades in and out may look great on your laptop, but be sure that the actual equipment you'll use for your presentation can also handle the speed. Otherwise, transitions will be unbearably slow and will put you in an awkward position as you struggle to figure out what to say during the slow transitions. Also, check if you use a different version of PowerPoint that your animations look OK. Reverting to an older version of PowerPoint may change many of your animations.

Check Your Projector and Screen. Try the presentation on the same size screen you will be using. Colors look different on different size screens. Images look different and can change clarity on different size screens. The most common mistake people make is to believe that what is readable on the laptop computer screen will be readable on a seven-foot screen by an audience member in the last row. Fonts have to be 24-point or larger just to be sure the text will be readable by everyone in the audience.

Don't Let Someone "Fix" Your Computer. Recently, I was at a company and someone set up my laptop to work with the projector. I didn't pay any attention. Two days later I was in another company and I couldn't get the screen to work with the projector, even with the assistance of the IT person and some other people who wanted to help. Several hours later, after I had been using another computer with my USB drive (backup files), someone figured out the problem. I vowed not to let anyone change anything on my computer unless I am watching and can then change it back myself.

Practice Using a Remote Mouse. This is essential. No one should stand by a laptop and push the page-down keys when presenting. And don't have someone else push the keys for you. In my opinion, all presenters need remotes. Why? Because (1) you are not confined to the area by your laptop; (2) you are not distracted by having to press the forward key to move to the next slide; (3) you are not distracting others who watch you continually walking back to your computer to manually advance the next slide; and (4) you are not interrupting your talk by saying, "next slide please," which is totally distracting and breaks the flow of the speech.

Buy your own remote and practice with it. This way you can seamlessly and unobtrusively advance to the next slide without stopping your presentation, breaking eye contact with the audience, walking up to the computer, and looking for the right button to press. There are a wide variety of remotes on the market. Try them out and see what is comfortable. You will look so much more professional when using one. See my favorite remote at www.powerremote.com.

Here are some tips when considering what type of remote to buy. When you go shopping, check out these features. Better yet, find someone who has a remote, try it, and if you like it, buy that one.

- *Must fit in your hand.* Some are big and will not easily fit in your hand. This sounds like a small point but it's not when you are holding it for one to six hours at a time. Some people like to put the remote in a pocket, so if that's true for you, your guideline is that it must fit in your pocket.

- *Must be easy to use.* Some remotes are very difficult to use. If you don't do a lot of presentations, then you want a remote that is easy to use from the first time you use it. You can't afford to stumble and look inept for several presentations until you get used to it. And by easy to use I mean it must not advance slides just because you very gently put your finger on a button. That can be embarrassing.

- *The laser pointer dot must be big enough to see on a big screen.* Some have such a small red dot that you can't readily find it on the screen. Unless you need to point to specific parts on the screen such as complicated diagrams or charts, you won't need a laser pointer. You can use animations to highlight your key images on your slide. That's one of the advantages of laptop presentations. (But be careful about using too many animations these days. They can and will actually detract from your presentation!)

RECHECK JUST BEFORE YOUR TALK

Be sure you confirm with your company contact the time you will meet. Find out what to do should your contact arrive late. There is nothing worse than sitting in a company lobby and having only one contact. People do get sick, get stuck in traffic, or have emergencies and fail to come to work on time. Also, many times the equipment is not there and you will have to find the person who is supposed to bring it to the room. That can take time. Once in the room, be sure the equipment is set up properly. Run through your slides one time to make sure everything is working and the colors on the slides look like the colors they are supposed to be. For example, golds can turn bright yellow and watermarks can disappear.

Communicate with the Technical Crew

Set aside time prior to the beginning of the presentation to discuss the format of your presentation with any technical crew. This will also allow them time to instruct you in the proper use of the wireless microphone and to make sure any PowerPoint is loaded and ready to go. Good communication with the crew usually results in a smoother presentation and less chance of a technical mistake.

The Room

Before you give a presentation, it is a good idea to be familiar with the room in which you will present.

Check the Room Layout. Change the room layout if it is not conducive to your presentation style. Lately, I have been having to move big plants around. It is not too conducive to be presenting when a plant's leaves are poking out behind your head. Move the chairs around. Set up the room so that you have the best chance to succeed and so that most people have a good view of you and the screen. Most people arrange the room in a rectangle.

Here are some specific room guidelines. Let's say a screen is eight feet wide by six feet tall. The front row needs to be at least twice the screen height away from the screen. Thus, the front row should never be closer than twelve feet from the screen. The back row should never be more than six times the screen height away from the screen. Consequently, the back row should not be more than thirty-six feet back from the screen. Clearly, this rule is designed around letting the audience see what is on the screen. Too close, and your audience will be overpowered by the screen. If the screen is too far away, the audience will be unable to see the content. There is also a rule of thumb for width that is intended to maximize the screen's visibility to the audience and allow for a comfortable viewing experience. The front row should never be more than four times the screen width; in this example, thirty-two feet wide. The back row should never be more than eight times the screen width; in this case, sixty-four feet wide. If these numbers are exceeded, then the participants at the edges will feel uncomfortable having to crane their necks during the presentation or to settle for seeing only half the screen.

If the screen is not large enough, put it on a table or chair. That way the people in the back of the room can see the bottom of the screen. No sense presenting when half the audience can only see half the screen.

Fix the Lighting, If Possible. Lighting features in some rooms can be fantastic. There are buttons that turn off different portions of the room's lights. Or the lighting can be horrendous, with bulbs that shine on your screen and blur your messages. Be brave. Ask the hotel to undo the lights that are shining on the screen. In a company conference room, unscrew the bulbs yourself.

The Laptop

Here's some specific advice about the laptop when you're using it to present.

Plug in the Laptop. Don't do your presentation using only battery power. Use your plug and have the battery charged just in case you need it for a little while. Plug it in somewhere to rehearse. And then plug it in again when it is your turn to present. There are too many stories about batteries going dead while someone was waiting to speak. Also, boot the laptop ahead of time. It can be very uncomfortable being in front of an audience waiting for your laptop to start.

Turn Off Certain Functions. Turn off the screen-saver function. Also, turn off little pop-up boxes that say things like, "Your battery is now fully charged." Be sure the projector's screen saver is off as well. Turn off the sound. Most people dislike the sounds of phrases flying in. If that is the only sound you plan to have, then turn it off, unless you are speaking to your neighborhood seven-year-olds. Turn off your automatic updates that go on every day at a certain time.

Move or Tape Down Cords. Position and tape down the cords so that you won't trip over them. We heard from one presenter who had people come up to her after the speech to tell her that they were worried she was going to trip over a cord. At least tape them down for your audience's peace of mind. When possible, hide the wires and cords so the audience doesn't see them. A participant in one of my seminars shared this story: "The presenter was not conversant in the medium he chose to present with. He had been sloppy in setting up his equipment. His laptop was plugged into an extension cord that snaked around him and was plugged in behind a curtain. During the presentation, he tripped over the power cord and the plug came out of the wall. The computer shut down and the screen went blank. We couldn't understand why his battery did not work; maybe it was dead. He then had to reconnect his equipment, which was difficult because he had to search behind the curtain to find the plug. The audience felt terrible for him, but his antics were causing some participants to snicker. He then restarted the computer and we all waited while he searched through his programs for the right presentation. He didn't have it on his desktop. He became more and more flustered. He then opened the wrong file. Finally, he managed to start the right presentation, but by then he almost forgot where he was in his presentation. In fact, he presented two slides over again."

Test Your Power Source. Make sure both ends of the power supply cord are plugged in. Then make sure the power source is really on by seeing if your battery is on. If you plug your cord into a podium, be sure the power is on. I heard about one CEO who was presenting, when midway through his talk, the low battery signal went on with a loud beeping sound. Everyone had thought the laptop was plugged in. So the CEO continued while someone else got down on hands and knees and moved the plug to the wall outlet. Fortunately, there was an outlet nearby.

Don't Undo Once Connected. After you have set up the equipment and tested it, don't disconnect. That can sometimes cause things not to work. Also, if the colors look funny on the screen, one of the cords may not be totally plugged in.

Have the Presentation on the Screen. After connecting the laptop to the projector, know what keys to press so the presentation is shown on the screen. This is usually Fn plus the display function key. Now, most projectors automatically pick up the computer signal.

Find Your File. Frequently, within a company, employees present using a file stored on the network drive. This can be embarrassing if you can't find the file. Try to go to the conference room early and be sure you can access and open your file. If you don't have to be on the network, place a shortcut icon to the presentation on the desktop. This makes it easier and more professional when you start. This is especially important when you are doing one-on-one presentations. You boot up the laptop and then just click the shortcut icon. You appear in charge and ready to go.

Don't Share Your Laptop. If you let another presenter use your laptop, there is a possibility that someone may inadvertently delete your presentation files or move them around so that you can't find them. If you must share, make sure that you control the keyboard. Don't let anyone else touch it.

This is a fairly comprehensive list. I hope most of you do all these things already. But what happens if things still go wrong? First, don't bad mouth the technology. Just keep going graciously. You picked the technology, and if the equipment belongs to the client, do not complain about their system. Tell yourself that in a few weeks your experience will make a funny or instructive story for someone.

KEEP TRACK OF YOUR LAPTOP AND ITS CONTENTS

Safeware Insurance Agency is a company that offers insurance protection for your laptop. The company says that accidental damage is the number one cause of computer damage. Theft is number two.

Damage

Let's start with accidental damage. Here are some tips they offer in order to take better care of your computer. Realize that these tips come from listening to their clients have problems in these areas.

- Only use approved laptop carrying cases. Don't stuff it in your carry-on case without something around it. I used to do this with my computer until it broke. Now I treat it like a good pearl necklace.

- Don't put your laptop in a bag with heavy items such as books.

- Keep liquids away from your system! Don't put a glass of water by your laptop. Move your laptop before the flight attendant passes a glass of liquid over it. One bump and your laptop could be full of sticky Coke, red wine, or orange juice. None of these sound good for it.

- Extreme temperatures, whether hot or cold, can damage your computer's components. Don't leave your laptop in direct sunlight for a long period of time. The heat will boil its brains!

- A quality surge protector can help prevent damage from a power surge.

Theft

Now that you know how to protect your computer from damage, you need to guard against theft. Did you know that a laptop is stolen every fifty-three seconds? According to the FBI, 97 percent are never recovered. Keep in mind that many of these laptops contain confidential or sensitive information and that 57 percent of corporate crimes are linked to stolen laptops. Interestingly, 40 percent of laptop thefts happen at work. I know, you think that your computer will never be stolen since you watch it all the time. But in reality, such care is a practical impossibility and thieves are also watchful and crafty, always looking for opportunity. Here are some ideas: First, if you have sensitive information on your laptop, make sure that it is not stolen when you lose your laptop. There are many companies whose job it is to help their clients guard confidential information. For example, a program called SafeGuard Easy encrypts your laptop's hard disk drive so data thieves cannot read your files. Find the latest program that offers some way for the thieves not to be able to retrieve your information. Then, if your computer is stolen, at least you will have the peace of mind to know that your data cannot be stolen as well.

To prevent a theft, watch your computer, have someone else watch it, or lock it down. No one is immune. Qualcomm's CEO had his laptop stolen from him during a news conference while he was standing no more than thirty feet away from it. He was surrounded by reporters and then it was gone (Security Focus Website: www.securityfocus.com/infocus/1186). Who would think someone would have the nerve to steal a laptop next to the CEO?

Don't leave your laptop in a conference room unless you have specifically asked someone to stay there and watch it. Don't assume because the door is locked someone will not get in. It is very difficult to truly secure a conference room in a hotel. I know it will be tempting to leave your laptop in a locked room when going out to lunch because it is already hooked up and ready to go.

Resist the temptation and plan for the extra time it takes to reconnect. All thirteen of us at a seminar I taught in Las Vegas took our laptops to lunch. No one was willing to trust the locked door. I just make it a rule never to leave my laptop anywhere unwatched. I take it with me. For those days when I am working at a client site, I go to lunch with my laptop in my briefcase.

Here is something to remember when you are traveling: When something unusual happens, someone spills something on you or someone drops something unexpectedly in front of you, a laptop thief may be behind you just ready to pick it up! Obviously, never leave your laptop in plain view in your car, since that will cost you a broken window as well. And never advertise your new laptop with a fancy traveling case. Some security-minded people never carry a laptop in a bag that looks like a laptop carrying case. Once on the plane, put your laptop near you; don't store it in an overhead compartment far from where you are sitting. Some people always carry it inside the taxi and don't put it in the trunk. This also protects it from being bounced around.

Do not put your PC on the security conveyor belt at an airport until the person in front of you has cleared through the metal detector. If that person doesn't clear and you have to wait, your PC may not be on the other side when you finally get there. Also, calm yourself down as you go through security so you won't forget your computer on the belt. This happens more than anyone will admit.

To prepare for the worst, there are all kinds of sophisticated systems coming out on the market every day to protect against theft. For example, there is a new tracking and retrieval laptop system now available from Computrace. If your computer is stolen, you contact Computrace and their recovery service monitors that computer for its next incoming call. The software agent stealthily calls in with its location as soon as its plugged into a phone line. To find out more, go to www.absolute.com. On their website, Computrace says they recover three out of four computers. There's another company called Steath Signal that claims to have about a 63 percent recovery rate. Sophisticated thieves are also up-to-date on security and may try to bypass these measures by reformatting the hard drive so that there is no signal.

Stop a minute and think about how secure you keep your laptop. What are the times when you take it for granted that no one is going to take it? Should you be locking it up in the hotel room? Do you leave it in a conference room at a big conference? Are you careful to keep your laptop in view, as much as possible, when you go through security?

Company-Provided Services

If you work in a company, then there are policies and procedures to follow if your computer crashes. Check out what they are so that you know the right numbers to phone. If you work on your own, then you need to know those laptop service numbers to call from wherever you are. Try to call and see whether you can get through. Now! Before it breaks, find out what type of service you have. If you plan to travel, then call in advance and see what services exist at your destination. Can you get the laptop back in twenty-four or thirty-six hours? Does the particular service have parts for your computer? What are their service charges?

Backing Up

This brings up the issue of backing up the laptop. Do you back it up? Imagine now that your laptop is gone forever. How long would it take you to get going again?

Back up your computer every day. When traveling, back up the files you create on your laptop onto a USB drive. Ask yourself: If my hard drive was destroyed or stolen, how long would it take me to re-create the files I had on my hard drive? If you, like many others, simply cringe at the thought, start backing up your files.

Words of Wisdom

One of my colleagues recounted the following story about a laptop crash: "I live in Venezuela. I had just arrived in Miami on Friday to teach a seminar on Monday. I was checking my email and my laptop froze and didn't come back to life. I called the laptop maker's hotline and tried to reboot. The hard drive was fried. I had to run around and buy a new laptop. Luckily and thank goodness, I had made backup files of everything, but the backup files were in Caracas! I called the Caracas office and had them email me the files and key documents I would need for the Monday presentation. By 8:30 on Friday night, I had my new laptop up and running. I learned some valuable lessons. First, during an emergency like this I had to relax. My brain was running at a thousand miles per hour and didn't let me find good solutions. Anger would not resolve the situation. Second, I turned the negative into a positive. I went shopping for a brand new machine and I found this excellent deal at a distributor. And third, I continue to back up my files frequently."

But even with all the planning you do, you may experience a problem. Below are some funny ideas of what you can say. Be creative when unexpected problems occur. People love to laugh.

- When you have a technology failure say, "There is a lesson to be learned here. If something does not work right, it does not necessarily mean that it won't make a lot of money!"
- If your screen goes blank you could say, "I guess someone did not pay the electric bill" or "Looks like you are really going to be in the dark now."
- When you have a problem with PowerPoint, you could say, "Well, regardless, I still wish that I had bought Microsoft stock years ago."
- You drop the remote and say, "Wow, that's one mouse that's difficult to catch."

PRESENT INTERNATIONALLY WITH EASE

You may find yourself traveling around the world with your laptop. Here are a few technology considerations.

Carry Certain Equipment. Bring an international power adapter kit (power conversion plugs) so you can charge your laptop using various types of electrical outlets. Says one presenter: "I always carry a copy of the PowerPoint software on CD. I also save my PowerPoint file to HTML, just in case I have to borrow a machine that finds my files hard to read. These all fit nicely on the USB."

Use Your Own Laptop. As it is much easier to present with your laptop, take it when you can. If it's too heavy, think of getting a lighter one for travel.

Personally Confirm AV Requirements. Call ahead to confirm your AV equipment needs. Discuss compatibility and connectivity issues. Find out whether the images will be projected on a big screen or on small monitors. Once your needs are confirmed, then call ahead to be sure the equipment is reserved. Once there, get help to be sure you are connecting everything correctly. Travel can take its toll on remembering that things are different and you may plug in the wrong connections. One presenter said: "I had a power strip explode in Holland because I forgot the voltage was 220VAC."

Keep a Native PowerPoint Expert Nearby. Many people have discovered that they need to have a translator available to look at the slides. Some presenters advised: "Make sure that you have somebody familiar with PowerPoint, since the menus are in the local language. At an international meeting, I had difficulty with

PowerPoint versions that have non-Roman alphabet characters, like Chinese or Arabic. At least with French or German, I can fudge my way around the menus."

"In Eastern Europe I had to merge someone else's slides with Russian fonts into my slides. I did not have the correct fonts loaded, and couldn't tell because I couldn't read any of it anyway."

LEARN FROM OTHER PEOPLE'S STORIES

Here are some short anecdotes I have gathered to motivate you to take the time to prepare appropriately. Many times taking an additional hour to prepare will prevent problems or at least enable you to overcome them quickly.

Dead Laptop. A presenter recounted the following: "My laptop died and I had no backup so couldn't use someone else's computer. I ended up drawing on a whiteboard and the meeting went very well. It pays to know what you are going to present and be familiar with the material. Now I plan for computer crashes. And actually, I sometimes use the whiteboard now instead of my PowerPoint. My decision depends on the audience. Some audiences seem to like the whiteboard interaction more than the PowerPoint talk. "

Dead Batteries. While it is always advisable to plug in your laptop instead of using batteries, sometimes dead batteries can be a problem. A colleague who was assisting a friend recounted the following: "My friend's batteries died in his remote just before the talk was to begin and there was no time to get a new battery. I was sitting by the laptop and I advanced the slides using the space bar while he pointed the remote, as though he were clicking. No one in the audience noticed."

The Auto Save Feature. Sometimes a situation seems to be an emergency. People tend to overreact and not consider the consequences of what they are doing. This can be disastrous on the computer. A colleague who had prepared a comprehensive presentation tells the following story: "Twenty minutes before a speech I was asked to produce a handout. Quickly I deleted all the unwanted slides, making the presentation ten instead of forty slides. The auto save feature was on and had overwritten the file. I did not have a backup file. However, one of my associates had made a disk of the speech. When asked why he had it, he said, 'I always expect the unexpected.'"

First in the Morning or Right After Lunch. And this story comes from an experienced speaker: "I try very hard to be the first presenter on in the morning or the first after lunch so I can run through the presentation at least once before 'show time,' since no one else will be around before that time. I have uncovered a multitude of errors this way. Sometimes I have to adjust the background of the slide because of the projection equipment. It is easy to do when I can run through it in advance. Sometimes sound is a problem and can be worked out in advance. When I plan to use the Internet, I have my sites 'cached' so there are no snags. If I don't have an opportunity to run through the presentation on-site in advance, I consider refusing the engagement."

Changes at the Last Minute. Of course, even the best-made plans must sometimes give way to rank: "One time with the military, I went there a week before to set everything up and try it all out. The day of the speech, five minutes before start time, I was informed the general wanted the room. We were delegated to a room with only an overhead projector. When I advised my audience of the situation, they all understood and accepted the limitations without question."

It pays to keep a cool head and not complain when something goes wrong. A presenter recounts the following: "I arrived very early for a training session. I found the room I had been assigned and set it all up. It looked great. I was sitting and speaking to a participant about fifteen minutes before the training was to start. Someone came in and told me I was in the wrong room. The 'right' room, according to someone else, turned out to be one-third the size of the room I had. Good for five people, not the ten I had. I swallowed hard, smiled, and taught all day. Although I did later receive an apology for the mix-up, it didn't help the cramped day my class experienced. Several months later I saw one of the participants from that day's training and he said, 'I really admired how you kept your spirits up after we ended up in that terrible windowless room.'" In this case the presenter's choice not to complain but to do the seminar with a pleasant demeanor saved the day, notwithstanding the bad room.

Above All, Do No Harm, Literally. Sometimes other people can unintentionally cause problems and make it very difficult to keep one's temper from flaring. A very experienced (and forgiving) speaker tells the following. "I was about to present a sixty-slide PR program overseas to a group of sixty-five European product managers. The hotel's technician started messing around with the electrical plugs as I stood over him repeatedly saying, 'PLEASE, SIR, don't touch that one.' He pulled my three-prong American plug out of the adapter I brought and twisted it into the two-prong Italian socket. My laptop emitted a bright flash and went completely, utterly, and irrevocably dead. All the lights in the room went out as well.

After the lights went back on, the technician then refused to leave the stage until I accepted his apology. At that point I had already started presenting extemporaneously. My client later said, 'Those who don't know you would never have guessed that anything was wrong. Those of us who do know you were very impressed that you managed not to harm the technician.'"

The Laptop and Cold/Hot Car. Watch out for both hot and cold weather. Let the equipment come to room temperature before turning it on. "I kept my LCD projector in my car overnight during freezing weather. I plugged it in when it wasn't warmed up and instantly "POW"—the expensive bulb was gone. Not only was it a costly, but I didn't have a spare bulb." Also, remember that very cold cars can deplete the battery charges on laptops. If you do leave your laptop in the car, let the laptop literally warm up before you try to boot it up.

Shared Projectors. Different people in an office may share the same LCD projector. It is crucial to check whether everything is there before you set off for your presentation. "I expected to use a remote to advance my slide presentation rather than being tied to arm's reach of the computer key pad. The necessary items were not put back in the box by the last user."

The Fireworks Crash. Keep an eye on what is going on. Here is one person who wasn't watching the screen: "I was doing a presentation when the audience, spontaneously, began to mumble elongated ohhhs and ahhhs. I turned around to view the screen, as I knew my presentation was not worthy of the ohhhs and ahhhs one would hear during fireworks. My laptop was in the process of crashing and in a blaze of glory it went out with a dramatic 'light show.'"

The Smoky Laptop. When I was writing this book in a coffee shop, the person next to me noticed the topic and told me this story. He said he was at a prospect's office and plugged his laptop into a projector. Within a few minutes, his laptop started to smoke. He unplugged the laptop from the projector and it stopped. That was the end of his computer. The prospect said, "This happened to the last laptop that was plugged into the projector."

Be Sure It Is Off Before You Put It in a Carrying Case. A laptop that is on while in an enclosed bag will continue to generate heat and, with no air circulation, may melt.

Operate Your Laptop on a Hard Surface So That the Air Can Circulate. Be sure your vents are free and clear so air can move around. I actually forgot about this the other day while driving with someone. I put my laptop on a pillow on my lap and worked on it for a while. Then I felt the bottom of the laptop. It was hot.

Check Where You Are Writing. If you use a screen and whiteboard interchangeably, don't accidentally sketch or write on the screen, especially with a permanent marker. Someone wrote me this note, "I couldn't believe I did it. I wrote with my marker on the screen."

"Once I was using the live Internet connection and the line went down. I didn't have a backup. Never again! I now give my presentation without a live Internet connection. It's just too uncertain. I show the screen shots."

When the Stakes Are High, Pack Your Own Equipment. Don't trust what people say they will have in terms of equipment. If you have to, rent what you need; if you can't, at least find out as soon as you can what equipment is actually available. A person who was actually judging several presenters tells the following: "The setting was a surgery resident research competition. Each resident had a maximum of ten minutes to present, then five minutes for questions. One resident brought a CD, but the computer didn't have a CD-ROM drive, so he spent ten minutes trying to find a laptop with a CD. He was then told he had five minutes left. He spoke without his visuals for five minutes and sat down. The next day I privately saw his presentation about his research. His research was fantastic. I was one of the judges and would have certainly given the resident first prize; not to mention that many chairs of departments would have been interested in recruiting him. This simple mistake was a career-crippling experience."

Plan for Delayed Flights. A company representative who had arranged for a wholesaler of his product to present to a room full of brokers recounts the following story:

> "Problem 1: We had a wholesaler who flew to his destination only to arrive several hours later than planned. Problem 2: He had checked his laptop and discovered at the hotel that he had a huge hole in the middle of the screen. Problem 3: He had fifteen minutes to get to the meeting and he had no USB drive with the presentation on it, no hard copy, nothing. Problem 4: He attempted to persuade fifty brokers to sell our products with zero slides, zero handouts, and no map to guide his presentation. Problem 5: How to go back and convince the brokers that the products really are excellent."

THE FUTURE OF TECHNOLOGY

I asked Dan Drop, sales team lead, ADTECH Systems in Sudbury, Massachusetts, to give me some ideas about how presenters will be presenting in the future. Here's what he said.

"Traditionally, presenters have traveled with suitcases filled with notebook PCs, heavy and bulky projectors, and cabling. They relied on a team of support personnel to ensure that it all worked properly when required. Much of that has changed. In fact, they do not even need to carry a notebook or any cables (save for power) at all. And the projector can be as light as two pounds!

"The biggest burden, literally depending on what size laptop one has, is the need to have a projector and a notebook with them all the time. When a presenter copies a presentation file to a compact, portable storage device (like the USB 'pen drives'), it saves the need to carry the laptop. The industry calls this 'PC-less projection.' It is a potential dream-come-true for many presenters, especially those who travel frequently, travel light, and perform the same presentation time and again.

"This procedure is not without caveats, however. The most commonly used presentation package is PowerPoint. This package, along with other commercially available packages, is 'closed source,' that is, the underlying application code is not publicly available. That means that only Microsoft can make PowerPoint run on any system that it chooses to support. None of the projectors that support PC-less projection are able to run PowerPoint presentations easily. Instead, the presenter (or his or her IT support staff) has to run the presentation through another application to convert it to something the projector will understand. In many cases, it is necessary to change each slide to a flat JPEG file. Some manufacturers allow animations and transitions if their own software converter is used in conjunction with their projector.

"With the prevalence of Internet access at virtually all corners of the globe, wireless network connectivity is now virtually standard in all notebook PCs. While an enormous convenience for the traveling businessperson, not only to stay connected with the office, clients, and family, it also provides a convenient solution for connecting a PC with a projector. Again, this solution comes with many caveats. Wireless Internet access is made possible through cards installed into PCs and access-points connected to the Internet via landline routers. While speed and access for over-the-air connections are reliable and quick enough for routine Internet applications, making full screen video reliable over that same connection will require substantial additional resources not currently available. As such, a WiFi connection between PC and projector will be adequate for static images such as photographs that do not need to be displayed in rapid succession (less than ten seconds apart) or for slides with text and images combined. Additionally, the software required to send the screen data to the projector via the PC's WiFi card is only really compatible with Microsoft Windows-based PCs, and often causes the PC to be less reliable than when not used.

"Many presenters also use online resources during their presentations, accessing web pages, web movies, and online documents to support their presentations. Accessing these online resources while using a WiFi connection between the PC and the projector is not possible, and therefore, all the presenter's resources will need to be stored locally on his or her PC.

"So is there a happy medium, whereby a traveling presenter does not need to carry an entire office each time he or she needs to make a presentation? Indeed there may be. Most businesspeople travel with a cellular phone and a PDA of some sort. These two are often combined into one device, called a Smartphone. Microsoft has created a variation of its Windows brand to run on some Smartphones and PDAs, called Windows Smartphone, Windows Mobile, or Windows CE. Often, these devices ship with a scaled-down version of PowerPoint, right within the device. Depending on the device, it may be fitted with a WiFi card. By simply synchronizing the Windows Mobile device with the desktop or notebook PC, the presenter can connect the Windows Mobile device to a wifi-enabled projector and play back the entire presentation, as he or she had authored it in PowerPoint on a PC. This solution combines all the advantages of having less gear to transport, the simplicity of a common platform

(Microsoft Windows and PowerPoint), and a compact projector. The caveat is that the PDA may play movie content a bit slower than a full-fledged computer will, and that the WiFi connection still limits the presenter to relatively simple, static slides, rather than the media-rich content that many employ in their presentations."

CONCLUSION

In our ideal technological world, the presenter would carry everything and nothing would go wrong. Batteries would last forever and thieves would be gainfully employed. Everything would be standard and what worked in Idaho could also be used in China without a hitch. If it were really ideal, someone else would carry the equipment and the presenter would tag along! OK. We do not live in an ideal world, so I suggest you use lighter, more portable equipment. What are the basics? It is good to have a laptop, a remote, and an LCD projector. That way you are used to the equipment, know it works, and, over time, will gain experience on how to use it. The novice presenter should have two hot-line numbers to call for the just-in-case situations.

One of the main themes that runs through this chapter is *don't use unfamiliar equipment*. Part of your job, regardless of what the topic of your presentation is, is to inspire confidence in your audience. So obviously, if you master your equipment and your presentation, you will clearly inspire confidence. On the other hand, if you are trying to sell people a product and you have problems operating your own equipment, fumble around with cords, and otherwise make errors running your software, they may ask themselves, "How good can she be? How good can this company's customer service be if they send out people who can't run some simple equipment?" That isn't the kind of impression you want to make. If you don't know how to run certain equipment, find someone who can teach you how to do it. Find out about some of the trouble spots that can occur with the equipment and know what to do. Find someone who has been using the equipment for a while and ask what has gone wrong. You owe it to yourself and to your audience to be able to make it work.

The other theme is in our chapter motto: Do preventative and contingent planning—then you'll always be able to present with confidence. And have a contingency plan just in case. I know you are saying, "Yes, that's a good idea." Remember, it may take ten minutes or so to set up your backup plan and you may be rushed. But you may lose more than those ten minutes if you don't have a backup contingency plan.

You've got your equipment under control. Now you want to rehearse. The next chapter gives you the steps for doing a real rehearsal. You really must practice out loud at least once before you give the talk.

The checklist in Exhibit 6.1 contains some general issues to resolve surrounding technology.

Exhibit 6.1
Technology Checklist

	Yes	I better do this
1. I have a comprehensive backup plan for my information. I could be up and running within a day if my computer crashed and have all my data available.		
2. At work, I have ways to make sure my laptop is difficult to steal.		
3. I have encrypted my data, if necessary, so no one could see or use it.		
4. I know what version of the program I'm using, so if I need to put it on another computer, I will know which version I need.		
5. When traveling, I carry a USB drive to use to back up my information, especially if I'm creating a presentation.		
6. I carry my computer in a way that it isn't easy to pick up and carry away. For example, I keep it with all my papers in my carry-on roller bag.		

Rehearse Like It's the Real Thing

Situation today: Very few people rehearse the talk they are going to give. This seems to be true whether the presentation is going to be given to the executives in the company, a potential customer, or colleagues. Everyone has too much to do without the time to do it. Many people say that their rehearsal is thinking about the talk in their heads while on the way to the presentation.

Key problems: People spend too much time creating too much content and, by 1 A.M. the night before the talk, they are too tired to practice. An unrehearsed presenter will be anxious before and during the talk and will tend to read his or her slides rather than find ways to connect with the audience. In addition, the presenter will have no idea how long the talk will actually take and will not know whether the points are really in the right order and make sense. Incredibly, many people are afraid to rehearse with colleagues. Rather than practice ahead of time before a live audience, they prefer to take their chances and "hope" they will do fine speaking it out loud the first time in front of a real audience.

   Key opportunities: Don't throw away a chance to impress your audience by not practicing. Gain credibility with the audience. Look and sound more confident. Find out the defects in the presentation and correct them before you go "live."

   Solution: You must practice out loud before giving the actual presentation. Not only will it prepare you for the talk, but it will also give you confidence.

   Story: A client came to me for advice because she said that some of the customers at the quarterly customer conference complained about her talks, saying that she was unprepared. After discussing the issue, it appeared that she did know the information; however, she finally confessed to not practicing her talk before she actually had to give it. So we discussed the reasons why it was critical to her that she rehearse and she agreed. She then rehearsed her talk with me as well as with someone who knew the customers and their hot buttons. We taped her sessions and then played them back so that she could watch herself. She was surprised when she saw herself swaying from side to side and speaking in a monotone. We found ways to correct these habits and, after her next presentation at the quarterly customer conference, several customers complimented her.

Chapter Motto: *Practice out loud to create your ability to look, sound, and feel confident.*

Here are our topics for this chapter:

- Talk Through Your Slides Out Loud as You Create Them
- Do a Real Rehearsal
- Present with Confidence
- Do a Mini-Rehearsal Just Before Your Talk
- Be Yourself While Engaging the Audience

You have done an enormous amount of work putting together your talk. Do not waste that effort by not practicing. This would be like cooking a fabulous dinner and then serving it cold. Or having a wedding ceremony without a rehearsal. Don't sabotage your own success. This chapter gives you ideas on how to increase your success while presenting. When you follow the processes and use the checklists in the other chapters, you will have time to practice. In Figure 7.1, the Real Rehearsal Flow Chart, you see the rehearsal process that will lead you to your success. This chapter takes you through this rehearsal process.

TALK THROUGH YOUR SLIDES OUT LOUD AS YOU CREATE THEM

Let's assume you have followed the suggestions in Chapter 1 about how to organize your content. After creating your executive summary, practice it out loud. Listen to how the phrases will sound to your audience. As you create your other

Figure 7.1
Real Rehearsal Flow Chart

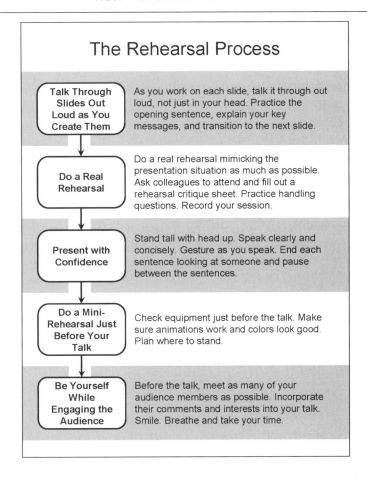

slides, rehearse as you create them. After you finish a slide, speak it softly to yourself, or loudly if you have a closed-in office. Don't think about it in your head. Actually say the words you will say during the talk. Then practice the transition sentence to the next slide you are going to create. Or, if you have created five slides because you are full of creative energy, then speak through those five slides before you go on.

This is a very quick way to practice and discover whether the slide makes sense. Why? When you rehearse as you create the slides, you will know what needs to be changed right then and there. What may look good on paper may not sound as good when you are speaking. Furthermore, you won't be surprised later on when you see that you have the wrong content on the slide, too much content to talk effectively, or content that doesn't make it easy for you to transition from slide to slide.

DO A REAL REHEARSAL

You want to do a real rehearsal so you can get the presentation in you. You put the messages in yourself so you will sound authentic and passionate when in front of your audience. You want to be relaxed during the real talk and have a better possibility of truly being your best. Then do a real rehearsal. Ideally, the full dress rehearsal is you giving the speech with the same equipment in the same size room with the same clothes you plan to wear. You can test everything out. You want to try your hyperlinks again to be sure you link to the slide you planned. You may think you know where you will stand so you can see your laptop or the screen. You may think you can use that remote mouse you bought yesterday. But until you actually practice the speech, you don't really know how you will give it. The only way you can know is to practice in the same type of room with the same equipment you will be using. If you don't, you may be in for some unexpected surprises.

Of course, this may not always be possible. When giving a talk to two thousand people you probably can't go down to the nearest hotel and ask to borrow one of their big conference rooms for an hour. But you can find a big room in your company and at least get a feeling for what it will be like to speak in a large room.

I have heard many reasons why people don't rehearse their speeches. The following are some of the typical excuses. You may recognize some of these yourself!

- "I don't have time."
- "I've been doing this for ages. I don't need to rehearse."
- "This isn't an important presentation. I won't bother to practice."
- "I'm too busy getting the information and proposal done to have time to rehearse."

In reality, the presentation of the material is as important as the material itself. Don't count on the material and excellent slides to make up for your poor delivery skills.

Following is a continuum of the most desirable to the least desirable way to rehearse.

- Ideally, rehearse before some of your colleagues, in the same type of room and wearing the same clothes, as you will on the date of your presentation.

- Tape the talk and watch it. Ideally, watch it with someone who will give you a critique. If that is not possible, watch it by yourself.

- Audiotape the talk and listen to it. Ideally, do this with someone who will give you a critique. Practice this standing up if you will be standing for the talk.

- Practice at home with your spouse, children, or friends listening to you. Give them a critique sheet to use when giving you feedback.

- Sit down in front of your slides and practice out loud. This is only good if you will be sitting for your talk.

- Think about the talk as you drive around. Practice the opening and closing out loud.

SURVEY

Failure to Rehearse: While more than three-quarters of presenters agree that practicing in advance is a good idea, only 38 percent say they actually practice. Among those who do not practice, 83 percent agree that practice could help improve their results.

Hopefully, you will decide to rehearse with others and not by yourself. But before you rehearse with others, I suggest you time how long it takes you to give the whole presentation.

Find out how long you speak about each slide and exactly how long the whole presentation takes to deliver. This is crucial. Many speakers go over their allotted time. Many of them will compensate for this and will start speaking faster and faster as the time comes closer for them to end. I have had managers say, "I worry about Tom. If he can't get the time right on his PowerPoint presentations, I'm not sure how he will manage the big project coming his way." To manage the timing of your talk, use the Rehearse Timings feature in PowerPoint.

POWERPOINT TIP

In PowerPoint 2003, go to *Slide Show>Rehearse Timings.* You will be in Slide Show and will see the timer in the upper left. Practice your presentation out loud. The timer times how long it takes for you to present each slide. When you are done and exit, the following box will come up. "The total time for this slide show was _____. Do you want to keep the new slide timings to use when you view the slide show?" Click yes. Now you will be in Slide Sorter and can see under each slide on the bottom left how long each slide took to present. This is fabulous to use when you are doing any kind of talk that demands you speak for only a certain amount of time.

YOU MUST CHANGE SOMETHING IN POWERPOINT BEFORE ACTUALLY PRESENTING . . .

When you actually present, go to *Slide Show>Set up Show>Advance Slides>Manually.* If you do not do this, your slides will advance according to the timing in which you last presented it.

PowerPoint 2007: Just the same.

Practicing with Others Listening to Your Talk

Now that you have rehearsed by yourself and know approximately how long the talk is going to be, you will feel more comfortable asking someone to listen. You'll know how much time you can ask the person to take away from work to listen to you. It's always a good idea to have at least one person, if not more, watch you rehearse. Preferably, have one colleague who knows your subject and can point out any content inconsistencies or additions. Have another colleague who doesn't know your subject and can point out acronyms and jargon words. Distribute a copy of the feedback form in Exhibit 7.1 (also on the CD) to each person and ask them both to fill out the form as they watch you present. If you must rehearse alone, pretend that you have an audience and that each audience member is being supportive and interested in your subject. Imagine that people are sitting in the chairs and end your sentences by looking at your imaginary audience. This trains you to be prepared to consciously look at someone at the end of a sentence.

Exhibit 7.1
Rehearsal Feedback Form

Presenter's Name:				
Channel Nervousness	**Confident appearance**	High	Medium	Low
	Appears confident (no um's, no shuffling, no fidgeting with mouse)	High	Medium	Low
Logical Flow/ Interesting	**Technical words**	Just right	Too many	Too few
	Transitions clearly said	Yes	Do more	Do less
	Added value and didn't just read words on screen	Yes	Sometimes	Not enough
Non-Verbals	**Eye contact**	Just right	Do more	
	Gestures	Just right	Do more	Do less
	Standing on two feet looking confident	Just right	Do more	
	Silence at end of sentences or key points	Just right	Do more	Do less
	Ends sentences looking at someone, not the screen	Yes	Sometimes	No
	Posture	Just right	Too stiff	Too loose
	Uses face to express meaning	Just right	Overly done	More expression
	Used filler words such as "uhs" or "ums"	No	Some	Too many
	Movement	Just right	Too much	Do less
Voice	**Voice volume**	Just right	Speak louder	Speak softer
	Voice pace: changes the speed. For example, slows down when making a key point.	Just right	Vary speed	Too much variation
	Convincing tone	Yes	More emphasis on key points	

Conclude with Conviction	Strong last sentence	Yes	Somewhat	No
Technology	Spoke about words on screen and did not just read them	Yes	Sometimes	No
	Talked to audience, not to screen/laptop	Yes	Sometimes	No
	Used animations only to explain points	Yes—just enough	Too many	

Record Yourself Speaking

While rehearsing with others and hearing their feedback is very useful, there is nothing like listening to and watching yourself talk. If you give many talks, then you need to record yourself every year and see what habits you have started that add or distract from your presentation. Recording yourself is very easy now with the new cameras and phones. We all carry images and ideas of how we sound and look. For many people, watching themselves is a pleasant surprise. They make comments like, "I look better than I thought I would" or "I don't look or sound as nervous as I felt" or "I sound like I know what I'm talking about." I always record my clients, even if they are only doing an audio call. Why? Because if you are only doing an audio call, you still need to use your hands, vary your facial expressions, and utilize your body movements to convey your enthusiasm and command of the subject. You just can't sit in the chair and not move.

POWERPOINT TIP

Audiotape Yourself in PowerPoint—you can also Record a Narration for Your Talk

Here is a tip from Ellen Finkelstein, author of many books on PowerPoint: When preparing for your presentation, it helps to hear what your presentation will sound like. One secret is to record narration for your entire presentation as if you were presenting. Then run your presentation and sit back and listen. You get an entirely different perspective when you pretend to be the audience. Listening to your presentation enables you to pick up awkward moments, unclear passages, and boring spots much more easily. This is fun to do and very easy to set up.

To record narration, follow these steps:

1. Attach a microphone to the proper connector on your computer.
2. Go to *Slide Show > Record Narration* and click OK.
3. Start narrating each slide.

When you are finished with the slide show and escape, you will see "The narrations have been saved with each slide. Do you want to save the slide timings as well?" Say yes.

Now to hear yourself go to: *Slide Show > Rehearse Timings*. You will hear your voice and you can click through the slides. You must click through the slides. The slides will not change automatically.

When you prepare to give your actual presentation, be sure to go to *Slide Show > Set up Show > Check > Show Options > Show Without Narration* and also check *Advance Slides > Manually*.

PowerPoint 2007: Just the same.

Continue to Consider Changes to Your Presentation

After practicing by yourself and with others, you may find yourself asking: "Do I really need all these slides?" or "Every time I go through this slide, I lose my focus. How can I change it?" or "I need a story here to explain what I mean. I am really not making this point very well." You may also now be better at making your words go along with your animations. Some people forget about the animations, even if they are the ones who prepared the slides. They will start talking ahead of the sequenced animations. All of a sudden, they realize that they have covered all the points, but have yet to unveil them. This looks like they have not practiced. Since you will have practiced, you will not have this issue.

You may also discover that you have too many animations and some of your hyperlinks do not work as desired. And you may see a word that spell check just did not catch. These are the reasons you practice out loud and have others listen as well. Of course, as you are practicing, you want to feel and look confident. The next section provides you the specific tips and exercises you will want to do so you do look and sound professional.

PRESENT WITH CONFIDENCE

Your confidence as you speak has to do with many factors. This section provides you with suggestions in many different areas. First, you can consider your verbal and non-verbal behaviors when speaking. Second, you can think about how your clothes can add to your confidence. Third, you can examine how your internal dialogue and feelings can increase or decrease your professional demeanor. Remember that audiences want to be engaged by a speaker. You are center stage, not the screen. So how do you keep the audience interested in you? One way is to change the pace as you talk. You can change the pace by having slides that do not look all the same. You change the pace and energy in the room by moving around so you are not standing in one spot for longer than ten to fifteen minutes. You change the pace by telling stories and providing examples that capture your audience's emotions. Change the pace by your voice, tone, volume, and speed, plus word emphasis.

When you want to capture the attention of your audience, tell them something they don't see on your slides. Then they will pay attention to you. When you are rehearsing as you create your slides or during your real rehearsal, do not read all the words on your slides and think that this is your presentation. People really dislike listening to someone who just reads the slides. It is one of their big complaints about presenters. You will sound wooden and your presentation will be inflexible. People will be bored and will tune out. If you do not add anything to your slides as you talk, people will view you as the "reader of words." They will start to think that you really don't know that much about the subject. For if you did, you would not have to put your whole talk on the slide. You are in front of your audience because you have some expertise in an area that your audience wants or needs to know about.

Non-Verbal Behaviors to Look Credible

You need to practice not only your presentation, but also where you will stand and how you will look at and relate with the material on the screen. The following are several considerations to take into account during your practice.

1. Position Yourself *Stand so you can see your notes and the screen.* When you stand next to the screen, then you are forced to gesture and speak about the points and images on the screen. The advantage is that everyone's eyes are looking at the same thing. The disadvantage is that you may speak to the screen rather than to the audience. Point your feet straight toward your audience so that your body is straight. If you don't, you will be talking to only part of the room.

An effective presenter also mentions the points and images on the screen so the audience can easily follow along. Don't pretend the image isn't up on the screen. Actively look at the image with the audience, then discuss what it means. Your audience is looking at the image, so look with them. However, it may be impossible to stand by the screen because you will be too far from the audience. Presenters rarely stand by the screen when presenting to hundreds of people, since gesturing toward a gigantic screen just isn't effective. These are types of behaviors that you need to include in your practice, particularly if you have someone watching and helping you. If you think that you are weak in one area, then you can ask your helper to work with you on that particular area. For example, if you think that you may be looking at the screen at the end of the sentence, then have the person watching coach you to change as you speak.

Stand to the left of the screen. People will see you and then your information. This makes it easier for your audience who read, usually, from left to right. Alternatively, some presenters put the screen off to the side so they can stand in the middle of the stage area.

Stand by the laptop. Some presenters position the laptop in front of them so they can use the screen as a prompt. Then they are able to watch the eyes of the audience more easily. It is an advantage to be close to the audience. The disadvantage is that presenters tend to speak to the laptop screen, ending every sentence looking at the laptop rather than at someone in the audience. Do not stare at the laptop while speaking. In Figure 7.2 you see the speaker behind the podium. The screen is off to the side. The speaker is using his hands, not holding onto the podium. His eyes are focused on the audience.

Sit to the side of the laptop. Limit the number of viewers to no more than three if they are going to look at your laptop screen. Make sure that your laptop screen can be clearly viewed at an angle. Use a remote so you don't have to be sitting so close to the laptop. Don't sit in front of the screen. Put your audience in front of the laptop screen. See Figure 7.3.

If you're going to present while sitting, you will probably arrive in the office and boot up with the prospect sitting there watching the screen. Make sure you have nothing offensive or proprietary on your desktop. Files named "inside information on Company X" or "inappropriate pictures" aren't the best images

Figure 7.2
Speaking from the Laptop

Figure 7.3
Sitting by the Laptop

for a prospect to see. A practice run using just your laptop can be useful, as we are sometimes not aware of what is on our active desktops.

Presenting at a podium. When possible, don't stand behind the podium and hold on for dear life. Walk out from behind it and talk so that people can see your whole body. Your movement will help you engage with the audience. Don't glue yourself to a microphone on the podium; wear a wireless microphone. If you are small, find a box or something that you can stand on. You want people to see more of your body than just your head. I am not a big fan of podiums unless you are speaking to hundreds of people. Then you do need to be on a raised platform or they cannot see you.

Prepare for a one-on-one talk. Don't treat a presentation as not important or think that you can be informal and improvise simply because you are presenting to only one person. Follow the same rules as if you had thirty people in the room, except that you will probably be sitting down. Show the presentation in slide show mode. Minimize the amount of text and maximize the graphics. When you want to blank out the screen, just hit the "B" key while in slide show mode. This tells your listener that you just want to speak to him or her.

2. End Sentences Looking at Someone   End a sentence looking at someone, not at the screen, the laptop, or up toward the ceiling. Linger a moment on the person's face. Don't instantly dart your eyes away. Only look at your screen when you need to see the next point or when you want to point out something on a diagram. Your audience will feel that you are really communicating when you look at each person. I was just told, "Love your audience with your eyes."

During rehearsal, practice looking at empty seats or at different parts of the room. In your practice, notice the parts of your slides that detract from your looking at the audience. When you tape yourself, you may surprised to discover that, if you don't look at each person, you won't really appear to be that interested in your audience. You will appear more interested in getting your speech over with and sitting down.

You may discover you have trouble ending a sentence looking at someone because you have turned your back to the audience in order to read the visuals. There are other problems with this behavior besides not making eye contact with your audience. First, your voice will probably become quiet and hard to hear. Second, when you are speaking to an audience in a language that is not their native language, their inability to see the speaker's mouth makes understanding words more difficult. This is very important when doing cross-cultural presentations. Your audience can understand better if they see your mouth as you talk.

> **Looking at Someone:** As you move further and further up the corporate ladder, you will notice how successful people actually look at you when they talk. They engage you with their whole beings. They have learned that, to influence, one needs to connect and have a dialogue—even if that dialogue is only with the eyes.

3. Move Deliberately   Don't shuffle or sway from foot to foot. Don't constantly walk from one side of the room to the other. If you want to move, then take two or three steps and stand still. Watching a presenter who spends an hour shuffling from one foot to the other can make an audience feel anxious. Pick several spots in the room and walk to them. Just be sure that people can see you.

4. Don't Leave the Visual Up When You Aren't Talking About It   As soon as the visual comes up, you have to talk about it, as people are looking at it. But when you are done talking about it, either go to the next one or blank out the screen.

5. Pause Between Your Sentences   Using pauses is the key to avoiding being monotone. But keep in mind: it is almost impossible not to be monotone with a slide containing sentences that you read. (So avoid using sentences on your slides!) Also, pause between your thoughts so you can start a new sentence strongly. Know your key messages so you can emphasize them. End your sentences and pause. Have some silence between your thoughts. Don't always be speaking. Isn't that a very strange hint to give to a presenter who is supposed to speak? But remember that too much food, too much activity, or too much of almost anything overwhelms both you and the others around you. That's true with speaking as well. Well-placed pauses allow both you and your audience to have a chance to think. The audience needs quiet time to digest your information. If you pause following an important element of your talk, they will take time to consider that element. You need time to listen to the audience and sense their reaction to the speech. You also need quiet time that allows you to check in and find out: "How am I feeling? Am I heading in the right direction?" Both you and your audience need time to feel and listen to each other. If there is no quiet time between sentences and important points, the audience stops listening due to information overload.

For your next formal presentation, talk in a meeting, or even phone conversation, first listen and truly process the words you say. Second, listen for the feelings in the room. Then, speak based on your assessment of what your audience really wants and needs to hear. You will probably find you are more comfortable with the group when you actually present what you "sense" they are interested in hearing.

6. Hold the Remote by Your Side   Practice how to hold the remote, since it is sometimes easy to forget during the actual presentation and mishandling the remote can distract your audience. Hold your remote by your side and gesture with the other hand. It is fine to gesture with both hands as you hold the remote, but don't just gesture with the hand holding the remote and keep the other hand by your side.

When you buy a remote, practice with it before you use it. John told us that, when he first used a remote, he practiced by sitting down and forwarding the slides. The day of the speech, he stood up by the screen. Quite often during that speech, he would turn around and notice that his slides had moved forward. He was convinced something was wrong with the computer. But he was just pressing the mouse's forward button without being aware of it. If he had done a real rehearsal and stood up, he would have discovered that his finger moves more than he knows and pushes the forward button. Then during the rehearsal he could have practiced keeping his finger off the forward button when he was speaking.

7. Practice with the Laser Pointer   When you use a laser pointer, you must hold it still on one point on the screen. And you must leave it in one place long enough for your audience to focus their eyes on the spot you are pointing to. Never wave it in your audience's eyes. Practice using the pointer, and have someone watch you and tell you whether you are using it effectively. In your rehearsal, decide on the points that you want to emphasize with the laser pointer. Don't overuse the pointer. Don't use it to point to text phrases on a slide.

Verbal Behaviors to Capture Your Audience
1. Speak So That Everyone Can Hear You   Don't ask, "Can you hear me?" People will be polite and say yes. Ask, "Shall I speak a little louder?" Better yet,

have a person in the audience cue you to let you know whether your voice volume is loud enough. You might have a colleague sit forward in his or her chair to signal that you need to raise your volume.

2. Go into Fewer Details and Ask the Audience Whether They Want More   Don't keep talking until your audience's eyes glaze over. Many times speakers do that, as they want to be sure the audience understands. But you can't ask your audience, "Do you understand?" They will probably say yes. Instead ask, "Shall I say some more about this now?" If the audience says no, go on. Don't bore them. In your rehearsal, ask your colleague to be honest with you about the quantity of the information and your pace as you present. The rehearsal is the best time to cut back on your information.

3. Ask Questions of Your Audience   For many presentations you want to create a dialogue, not a monologue. To do this, I suggest you involve your audience in the first three minutes of your talk. Ask them a question. Ask them for comments. Find some way to show them that this presentation will be one where they talk as well. As you practice with a colleague, find out which parts of the presentation will be most conducive to audience involvement.

4. Graciously Answer All Questions   Suppose that, as you start your presentation, someone asks you a simple question. You realize that you should have included that information in your talk, but didn't. You decide the person is hostile and out to make you look incompetent. Be careful not to go down this path. Your audience will sense your negativity, and the mood and dynamics of the room will become negative. Be positive with your answers. You can be as prepared as possible, but realize that some questions may surprise you. In your rehearsal you may prepare for this by having your colleague interrupt you with a few questions. Find ways to answer them and then get back into the flow. When you answer, practice looking directly at the person asking the question, but then finish the answer looking at someone else. This will not encourage the same person to ask another question.

In some companies, people see it as their jobs to question every detail. For example, Ph.D.s in a biomedical research company listen to a colleague's research and then ask questions to be sure the researcher followed certain procedures and arrived at the most logical result. The Ph.D. believes it's his or her job to make sure the research meets the high standards of the company. But that does not mean you as the presenter in this environment must take all the pointed questions as a sign of your incompetence or lack of preparation. This is the nature of the work people do. The less you take offence, the better you will be at answering the questions and moving on with your presentation.

5. Practice Speaking Better in the Language in Which You Will Give the Presentation I am now giving my course in my version of Spanish, meaning I have a lot to learn. This experience has helped me teach people who are speaking English in my classes. I can see they want to get better but are frustrated. If you are one of those people, then take some accent reduction classes. In the meantime, here are my key suggestions for speaking English more clearly.

Open your mouth more. Many languages are spoken with the mouth more closed. Look in a mirror and practice really using your mouth.

Say the last letter in a word. The lack of understanding happens when the person speaking English leaves off the last letter. In English many times you really emphasize that letter. This takes time, so you will find you speak more slowly. Here are some examples of words you want to really say the end of: talk, went, information.

Stop between sentences so you don't say "uh" or "e." You want someone to tell you if you have this habit; it takes practice to eliminate it. Don't connect your sentences with filler sounds or words such as "and" or "so." Do not say a filler word as you think about how you want to convey a complex idea. Just be quiet.

Be silent sometimes. Your audience needs time to digest the information and you need time to relax. Count to two or three between many of your sentences. Be careful to not run all your words and sentences together just to get it over with.

Slow down and breathe deeply. Keep telling yourself that you have time.

Only put words on slides you can say. This is crucial. If you have to put words up on the slide that are difficult, then don't say them unless you have to.

Say your sentence differently, or use another word to clarify. When you see that someone did not understand you, don't say the exact same sentence again. Say it another way. He or she probably did not understand some of your words.

Ask for feedback. Don't ask, "Do you understand me?" for the person will not want to hurt your feelings. Ask, "What are the words I say that I could say more clearly? Do you remember some of them?" In fact, you can ask someone to write those words down for you as he or she listens to your talk.

Purchase Pimsleur tapes. These are wonderful tapes you can listen to in your car. Even if you speak English fairly well, you can improve your pronunciation by speaking with the tapes. For example, I have clients who speak English at work, but Chinese at home. Consequently, they don't get enough practice speaking. One of them purchased *Pinsleur English for Mandarin Chinese Speakers.* By just speaking for fifteen minutes back and forth to work, he improved his English.

Business Wear Tips

Practice in the actual clothing you will wear. You may have to climb up and down a platform, so don't wear anything too tight that won't let you take big steps. If you have gained or lost weight, be sure the clothes aren't so loose that they bag or so tight that seams will rip open or the zipper pop. (Not a pleasant experience when you are presenting in front of a hundred people! This happened to one of my male colleagues. He did not move for the rest of his presentation.) Women, don't wear bracelets with loose jangling pieces, or every time you push the remote button your jewelry will make a noise against the remote. This is really important when you are attending a teleconference. Every noise is exaggerated. Businesses have different dress standards, so ask what type of clothing people wear and, more importantly, what they expect you to wear. Don't assume that "business casual" dress means khakis and a knit shirt. You must ask, "Tell me, what specifically do people wear?"

You want people to look at you and, in particular, look at your face. Wear something that highlights your face. Look at your complexion and wear a color that sets it off.

I asked Ginger Burr, of Total Image Consultants (www.totalimageconsultants. com), to give you some key hints about dressing appropriately for business. Here they are.

Know What Colors Look Best on You. Stick to them when adding to your wardrobe. You will find that you have an easier time mixing and matching, and you will always look and feel pulled together and professional. A color analysis consultation provides you with a customized color palette of seventy to one hundred colors that will go with your complexion and hair. You will then be able to purchase suits and shirts of the best color combinations for you. Also, everything in your wardrobe will go with everything else.

If You Haven't Worn It in Two Years, You Never Will. If your closet is filled with clothes you don't wear for any reason (dressy clothes are an exception to this rule), you'll feel frustrated and irritated every time you get dressed. Consign, donate, give to friends, pack away, or discard anything you haven't worn in two years. You'll feel happier every time you need to select something to wear, and you'll have room to add new, appropriate attire.

Buy (and Wear) Something Only If You Love It. There is no exception to this rule. Make it your shopping mantra!

Top ten rules for successful business dressing:

1. **Know what's acceptable and what is not.** Don't assume anything.

2. **Look for (and be) a role model.** If you're not impressed with how your manager dresses, do not follow his or her lead—look elsewhere.

3. **Make sure your clothes say what you want about you.** Too often we dress on autopilot. Are you sure you are making the impression you want to make? If not, ask someone whose opinion you value.

4. **Replace clothing and shoes and purses when they fade, lose their shape, or become pilled** (an often-overlooked concern).

5. **When in doubt, don't wear it to the office**—this includes flip-flops (especially if they make that flip-flop noise), tennis shoes, and crocs.

6. **If it doesn't fit properly, have it tailored or just don't buy it**. Be sure that your jacket fits properly, your skirt or trousers are the right length for you, and your sleeve ends in the appropriate place. It is obvious when you "make do." A tailor can help you add the right finishing touches and polish to your image.

7. **Beware the double standard.** Women are still kept to a different standard than men when it comes to dressing for work and are sometimes seen as less authoritative when they dress casually.

8. **Women, own several pantsuits.** A great pantsuit offers versatility as a pivotal piece in your wardrobe. Wear the pieces separately or together, using your jacket to bridge the formal and casual business worlds. This is a more professional look than pants and a sweater set.

9. **Hair and makeup require the same attention to detail** whether you are dressing in traditional corporate or business casual wear. Men sometimes forget to keep their hair under control.

10. **Last, dress for the job you want, not the job you have.**

And last I, Claudyne, want to add one more rule. Always be prepared to meet someone higher up in the organization. Look the part. I know women who always have a neutral-colored jacket in the office. If they have to go speak to someone higher up, they put it on and then go to the meeting. Why? Here is some information from John T. Malloy's book *New Women's Dress for Success*. His firm used photographs of a man and a woman dressed professionally—the woman in a skirted suit and the man in a traditional suit. "When we showed the pictures to businesspeople and asked which person was the vice president and which was the assistant, a slight but not overwhelming majority labeled the man the VP. But when we showed respondents pictures of the same man and woman *without* their jackets, 80 to 90 percent of those questioned identified the man as more senior." They also discovered that when dressing casually without a jacket, men lose some of their authority. Women lose most of theirs. In my classes, I often bring a jacket and have a woman put it on over her blouse. To a person, everyone in the room says she looks more confident and professional.

These clothing rules become extremely important in the presentation context since the focus of the audience will now be on you. As part of your preparation for your presentation, select and try on the clothes and accessories that you are going to wear for your presentation.

Clothes and the Power Suit Client's Story: One time I went to see a client who had been hiring me for years. I wore a gorgeous flowered dress in honor of summer. I showed up and he said, "Oh, what happened to your power suit?" I was taken aback. Then he said, "I'd like you to meet our new head of marketing." I understood. The head of marketing was going to look at me and think, "We send her out to clients. She doesn't look professional for our clients." The next time I stopped by, I wore my suit. He said, "You wore your power suit." This was at least five months after the summer day flowered dress experience. He remembered.

Control Your Inner Monologue and Feelings

Some monologues that go on inside your head before you speak will not make you a better presenter. "I wish I didn't have to do this presentation. I don't know enough. I'll probably trip when I walk up front. I hate the way my voice sounds. I look terrible today. I just want to get it over with as fast as possible." Contrast that monologue with this one. "I feel great today. I practiced yesterday and feel confident. I look good. I'm ready to handle those difficult objections about my product. I can do this. I will enjoy each moment and not wish I wasn't giving the presentation. I want my audience to know I'm glad to be speaking to them."

Your inner monologue, positive or negative, sets the tone for your speech and sends messages to the audience. Which audience would you prefer to be in?

How do you begin to change a negative monologue? First, notice what you say to yourself now. Then begin to tell yourself positive, empowering thoughts. No one else can do this for you—you're the only one inside your head. When you change your monologue to a positive one, your body will feel relaxed and energized at the same time, your mind will be clear, and, most importantly, you will project a confidence that makes your audience glad to be listening to you.

For a week before a presentation, just before you go to sleep every night, tell yourself three positive outcomes you expect from your presentation. You can use the same outcomes every night or select different ones. Here are a few ideas:

- "I expect to have three new clients as a result of my presentation."
- "I expect to sell the audience on my product."
- "I expect upper management to agree to my proposed project."
- "I expect to feel calm and confident while giving my presentation."

Another way to calm that inner monologue is to be sure you have prepared well enough. I notice my clients have more negative self-talk when they have not adequately prepared. Take away this anxiety by doing the preparation work.

To relax, some people get massages. Some people exercise. I am learning to breathe more slowly. Here's the tape I have been using: Respire 1 at www.coherence.com. Also, say positive comments to yourself to encourage relaxation. Be your own best friend. Believe it or not, this too is an important part of your presentation preparation, so take the time as part of your "rehearsal"!

Before some presentations you may be nervous. In fact, for some of you, days before a presentation you may feel nervous. How do you not let your feelings take over? You have to let them out in a safe manner. Some people sing in their cars. Some people exercise to release their tensions. You need to have a method that works for you. Some people listen to a relaxing meditation tape.

You also need to understand that sometimes your feelings will just be there. For example, a friend may have recently died. Someone you know may be very ill. You may be ill. Usually people manage to present, even if their feelings of sadness and grief are very raw and on the surface. What they don't do well is prepare for the speech. If you find yourself very upset, ask people to help you prepare for the speech effectively. You probably won't be able to do it by yourself. Remember, there is nothing wrong with asking for help. Even seasoned presenters have coaches and rely on others to assist them.

A professional speaker was giving a speech at a company's annual meeting. He knew his subject. He had given the same type of speech many times. His father had just died a few months ago. He could not get motivated and organized enough to redo his slides and create new content for the speech. He just couldn't do it. And he didn't ask anyone for help. When he arrived to give the speech, about a half-hour before he was to speak, by sheer coincidence, someone started speaking about how her mother had just died. Suddenly his heart was racing, tears almost came to his eyes, and he wondered how he would give his speech. He gave the speech, but he knew he was on auto-pilot and that he didn't connect to the audience in his usual manner. He also looked as his slides and realized he should have had someone redesign them. From that experience he promised himself that, from then on, he would pay attention to his emotional state and ask for help when he felt he could not prepare well by himself.

Practice Even When Not "Formally" Presenting

What has happened to practice? People attend presentation seminars and learn about some of their presenting issues. For example, they say, "I say 'um' too much," "I speak too fast," and "I get so nervous feeling everyone's eyes on me." The question for them is, "What are you doing on a daily basis to change that?"

Any presentation seminar is a jump-start to changing your behavior, but you have to work on change every day. You can't say "um" all day, speak too fast most of the time, or be uncomfortable speaking in a meeting—and expect those habits and feelings to disappear in front of a group. If only it were that easy. Instead, you need to practice every day.

For example, Terry is a high-energy personality, a little on the nervous side. She tends to get more like that when presenting. Her behavior won't magically change in front of a group. If anything, it will intensify if she doesn't know how to control it. So what does she do every day in order to be more prepared when she's presenting? First, she doesn't eat sugar—she has energy enough without it. Second, she meditates to calm her nervous system. And third, she exercises. Gradually, over time, she has become calmer and calmer in front of a group. That didn't just happen because of a two-day seminar. The seminars and workshops she attended pointed out issues, but she had to practice every day. Here are some unusual strategies to take you out of your comfort zone.

- "I say 'um' all the time." Force yourself to organize your voice-mail messages before you actually say anything. If the voice mail system allows you to hear the message you left, listen to the message to make sure that there are no "ums." Practice a presentation with a friend and have him or her make a noise such as bang a can or snap fingers every time you say an "um."

- "I don't like being the center of attention." Dress up and walk down a busy street where people will look at you. You will begin to see that nothing bad happens just because people are looking at you.

- "I'm scared to be or act stupid." Go into a store and ask dumb questions. Notice that no matter how stupid you sound, the world doesn't cave in.

- "I'm so rushed all the time." Make yourself do one task at a time for an hour. For another hour speak more slowly, end your sentences, and pause for a moment.

Some of these are ideas you can practice on a daily basis. You will notice a tremendous difference in your next formal presentation once you begin to practice changing behaviors and thoughts that get in the way of your effectiveness.

If you still feel you want some more presentation-type training, but have taken several presentation programs, take a theater course. There are many theater or improvisational movement/acting classes. You practice improvising on the stage. How can this help you when presenting? You learn to listen better to everyone because your next line depends on what was just said. You learn to enjoy the anticipation of not knowing what will come next. You may have had a plan for what was to happen next, but frequently had to give up that plan when the scene didn't go in that direction. You begin to appreciate your ability to flow with whatever is happening. Don't these all sound like skills you need as a presenter? Take a course. It will help you become a more relaxed, energetic presenter. Plus, you will have fun at the same time. One of the courses I took that I loved was an Acting Improvisation class. I really learned to listen to people around me, to be open to whatever the next moment had to offer and to enjoy each moment. For more information, see Acting Improvisation in the Resources section of this book.

DO A MINI-REHEARSAL JUST BEFORE YOUR TALK

You want to do a quick run through, if possible, before your actual talk. But first, let's be sure you arrive at the right place at the right time. Confirm the date and time in writing. You may not think it is necessary. Here are several stories from people who didn't confirm the plans in writing. "I didn't confirm my presentation time and they had me speaking in the morning and I had it listed for the afternoon." "After much discussion, I thought we agreed on a day. No memos were sent. I had the wrong day on my calendar and was teaching elsewhere that day. Imagine my shock when I heard on my voice mail, 'Where are you? We expected you at 9 A.M.'" You also want to confirm any equipment needs you have. See the Preparation Checklist at the end of this chapter for details that you should have discussed before your arrival.

Always try to get into the room as early as possible (if it is a very important presentation, then the day before is best) to set everything up and test everything: the PowerPoint presentation, sound, and lighting. It is horrible to be embarrassed in front of the audience when something doesn't work right, particularly if the problem could have been avoided. Based on my experience, everything goes wrong or fails to work at some stage in the life of a presenter. The best approach to dealing with all conceivable eventualities is to invest time up-front in contingency planning and meticulous checking of details. One presenter has this to say: "I am careful, redundant, cautious. I have low expectations. I haven't had a 'fatality' in years." First, you need to work with the people who are setting up the room and in charge of the equipment. Don't just discuss the details with the conference organizer. Speak with the people in charge of the equipment. Frequently, the equipment requirements list doesn't make it to the actual people in charge of setting up the equipment. Speak to them yourself, if you can.

These days, it's fairly likely that the site at which you're presenting will have the necessary equipment. But with different versions of PowerPoint being used,

I would bring my computer to be sure my PowerPoint will work the way I set it up. If you are working in PowerPoint 2007, and someone tells you he or she can just load your CD on a computer, you'd really better be sure they have PowerPoint 2007, not PowerPoint 2003.

BE YOURSELF WHILE ENGAGING THE AUDIENCE

In the final analysis, what people appreciate the most is the presenter's authenticity. How much was the presenter actually in the room "being there" with the group? How much attention did the audience members feel the presenter actually paid to them? Some professional presenters break many of the rules we have suggested. They get away with it because they come across as passionate, full of energy, and totally engaged in their subject. Dare to be the best of yourself when you speak. Some suggestions are listed below.

- *Know yourself versus your act.* You must know the difference between being "you" and just doing your "act"—"Joe the jokester" or "Mary the nice person." When you stop long enough to reflect, you will begin to understand the difference.

- *Take inventory.* Sit down and make a two-column list. Title the first column, "Times when I've been myself" and the second, "Times when I do my act." There's nothing intrinsically wrong with doing your act, but it may limit your ability to be spontaneous, connect with your audience, and discover new parts of yourself. For example, some people smile all the time, even when speaking about bad news. This is a one-act play. When they come to class and stop smiling every moment, they come across as more authentic. People always say, "You seem more real now. I feel I can trust you more."

- *Take a risk.* In the next month do something that takes you out of your element. You will be less able to rely on old behavior patterns, and it is likely that you will enjoy the adventure.

Let's say you have done everything we suggest. You are totally prepared, and still something goes wrong. "What could go wrong?" you ask. The electricity in the hotel goes off. The company has a fire drill. Someone walks by and spills coffee all over your laptop. No matter what occurs, have a sense of humor. Get your audience to laugh with you. No one who laughs becomes or stays upset. Laughter gets everyone on your side.

CONCLUSION

This chapter is based on the truth that to be good at something you have to practice. We started with the motto: Practice out loud to create your ability to look, sound, and feel confident.

Properly rehearsing is an essential part of your presentation preparation. And, as you have read, the rehearsal doesn't just begin with the practice of a particular presentation. When you actually take time to consistently practice and follow the ideas you have just read, you will find yourself enjoying your talks. You will discover that the audience really wants to learn and listen. They want you to be energetic and enthusiastic so they can pay attention. They want to feel comfortable as you talk. Give them that opportunity by doing your necessary real rehearsals. When you can be your best self, all of you, in front of an audience, the people will love you. And remember again, the more you practice everything in this chapter, the more you can adjust to the interests and questions of your audience. After all, the audience is the whole reason you put your talk together. The checklists that follow will lead you on your way.

The next chapter takes you a step further. I call it the graduate-level chapter, since it demands that you have mastered the elements in this and the other earlier chapters and are now ready to flow with your audience's direction during the actual presentation. It is for those of you who really want to be noticed and who desire to move up into an executive position in your company. You first have to demonstrate executive presence and the ability to connect to your executive audience. Then that career you desire may become open to you. Read on to find out what executive presence is about.

The Rehearsal Checklist in Exhibit 7.2 will ensure that you've taken all the necessary steps for an effective rehearsal. The Preparation Checklist in Exhibit 7.3 covers all the items you should be aware of prior to, during, and even after your presentation. The Equipment Checklist in Exhibit 7.4 will help you to remember equipment-related issues for your presentation.

Exhibit 7.2
Rehearsal Checklist

	Yes	Not Necessary or Appropriate
Practiced the Timing: I have done a real rehearsal practicing the timing of my talk.		
Listened to Self: I have actually audiotaped or videotaped myself practicing this presentation out loud.		
Someone Else Listened: I have had someone listen and fill out the rehearsal critique sheet. The person listened to be sure I paused at the end of my sentences and did not say "um" or some variation such as "and, um."		
Tried on Clothes: I have tried on the exact clothes I am going to wear, including underwear. I know I will look appropriate and impress my audience.		
Done Relaxation Techniques: I have practiced ways to calm myself down so I can do that when in front of a group.		
Pep Talk: One of my biggest supporters has heard my talk and given me excellent feedback.		

Exhibit 7.3
Preparation Checklist

Advance Preparation

- ☐ **Back up** laptop's hard drive and presentation.
- ☐ **Carry plan B** in case laptop does not work.
- ☐ **Take other materials.** If you're selling, you may need product spec sheets, price lists, product photos, etc.
- ☐ **Store key information.** Put all key information in one place: access numbers, credit card numbers, other remote-access information, laptop emergency help number. Some people pre-program it on their laptops.
- ☐ **Confirm logistics:** date, time, room layout, rehearsal space (room access), technology needs, wireless microphone available, contact on arrival.
- ☐ **Set up shortcuts on desktop.** Create a shortcut on the desktop so it's easy to access a presentation.

General Preparation on Arrival

- ☐ **Test equipment.** Be sure power cords are working. Don't use battery. Make sure lights don't shine directly on the screen. Make sure everyone will be able to see the screen. Test your sound, if using. Hide and/or tape all the equipments' cords.
- ☐ **Rehearse with the projector.** Rehearse with the projector and the screen size you will use so you can view the color combinations and video clips on the projector.
- ☐ **Turn off screen saver.** Check to be sure the screen saver is also turned off on the projector.
- ☐ **Cords.** Be sure they are taped down and out of the way.
- ☐ **Redo the room layout.** No matter what you send people, it seems you have to rearrange the room. Allow time for that. Try not to have a lot of extra chairs that no one will be sitting in.
- ☐ **Check wireless microphone.** Be sure the sound works well. Use a wireless microphone.
- ☐ **Check the lighting.** Make sure you know how to make the lighting work the best for the room.
- ☐ **Find the restrooms and fire exits.** This is important for you, but also in case someone in your audience asks for directions.
- ☐ **Have water handy.** Put a glass of water where you will be speaking, just not too close to the laptop.
- ☐ **Check clothing.** Be sure everything is buttoned, zipped, etc. Who knows what may have occurred as you set up the equipment.
- ☐ **Ask people.** Find people to be in charge of the room temperature, the lighting, and the backup plan implementation.

During the Speech

☐ **Reboot.** When you are presenting all day, reboot during breaks or as often as possible to clear memory.

☐ **Use remote mouse.** Keep the remote in your hand by your side and gesture with the other hand.

☐ **Drink water.** Keep yourself hydrated and energized by drinking water.

After the Speech

☐ **Take out everything you brought in.** You may be tired. Double-check to be sure you have collected everything. There is nothing worse than leaving your power cord in some company's conference room and having to go back hours later trying to convince the cleaning people to let you in. Worse yet, at 11 P.M. I remember explaining to the cleaning people why I had to get into a training room to find my laptop.

Here is a list of equipment that some people take with them. You will know what you want to take and what is not necessary.

Exhibit 7.4
Equipment Checklist

Need	Don't Need	
_____	_____	1. Laptop with power cord and user's manual—at least the pages you might need
_____	_____	2. Extra battery for laptop
_____	_____	3. Remote
_____	_____	4. LCD projector with power cord, lens cap, and cable for connecting to the laptop and direction booklet
_____	_____	5. Extra bulb for LCD projector
_____	_____	6. Pointer with extra batteries
_____	_____	7. Power strip with long extension cord
_____	_____	8. Duct or electrical tape to tape down cords
_____	_____	9. Screen
_____	_____	10. Phone and phone cord, PalmPilot, printer
_____	_____	11. USB with a copy of your presentation and associated files
_____	_____	12. Adapters, surge protector, etc., for international travel

Demonstrate Executive Presence

Situation today: You have been working on an important project for your company. Although you feel that this is going to help you with your career advancement, in your last performance review your boss told you that he had not been happy with the project updates that you have been giving at the management committee meetings. You told your boss, "I give them all the information I have. They should be happy."

Key problems: People need to be coached on how to talk in management committee meetings. Upper management is really not interested in knowing all the details. Not enough people receive coaching regarding the type of information or the style one needs to have when presenting to upper management.

Key opportunities: Advance your career. Be given more opportunities to speak to key accounts. Be given more chances to attend management level meetings and offer your expertise.

Solution: Learn how to demonstrate executive presence when speaking to the vice presidents and directors in your company or in other companies. Once you understand the behaviors they appreciate, you will be in a position to advance your career.

Story: Joyce was asked to give an update of her customer research during her company's two-day management-level yearly meeting. She prepared her talk and gave it. She thought she did fine. Her audience asked a lot of questions and she gave them all the details. Several days later her boss invited her into her office

211

and said, "You really gave too many details in your talk. You almost sounded like you were rambling. I suggest you find a coach to help you change your style. This style won't work when you speak to the directors." Joyce and I worked together for many months. She learned to give the executive summary of her information. She realized that the president only wanted limited information. She changed her dress to a business-style pants suit rather than a sweater set. She practiced speaking in short, concise sentences. The next time she spoke at the management-level meeting, her boss was very pleased.

Chapter Motto: *Be energetic, take charge, and engage in dialogue with your audience.*

Here are the topics we'll cover in this chapter:

- Choose Your Presence Behaviors
- Plan What to Say About the Data
- Use Entertainment and Drama—When Appropriate
- Do Make a Recommendation
- Be Optimistic
- Consider Your Best Path to Persuasion
- Advice from Executives

Now that you have come to this point in the book and have practiced the suggestions and gone through and done the checklists, you are well on your way to making effective and convincing presentations. By now you will have mastered the art of knowing what key messages you need to present, how to structure your talk for a desired effect, and how to tailor your presentations depending on your audience. You will have incorporated storytelling and other personalization techniques into your talk in order to connect with your audience. Using PowerPoint will no longer be as daunting or time-consuming, since you will have recognized the importance of simplifying your slides and using pre-existing slide designs that you have in a slide library file. And you will have recognized the importance of preparation, whether it be practicing your presentation in front of others, making sure that you are a master of the space where you will be presenting, or having others ask you questions so that you can be relaxed when your audience does the same. You will have recognized the importance of finding time to sit and simply relax before the talk so that the real "you" can be present before your audience. There is no magic in this; all of the foregoing are skills that, with practice, you can learn. And these skills will no doubt make you an excellent presenter. This chapter, however, is about taking the next quantitative step—attaining "executive presence." You will read comments from some leading executives about what they think constitutes "executive presence" and how individuals can demonstrate it.

More and more I am asked to coach people on presenting in meetings or in front of a group because they lack what people term as "executive presence." Managers have told me, "Sara is presenting in front of the board, and she is not convincing them of her views" or "I can't send Majad to meet our top account clients. First, he needs to look more in charge" or "Max is now on the executive management team and he just doesn't seem to be able to make his points" or "I want to give Maria a promotion, but I'm not sure she can handle speaking at our company meetings."

Before we begin to consider what all of these people need in order to fill the role that is being offered to them, let's think about what executives do when they communicate to others. Generally speaking, they involve themselves in planning, negotiating, reporting, and justifying action. Among the variety of things that executives do, they make decisions, report to boards of directors or executive management committees, understand risk and manage it, build relationships so that work will get done, work together with others within an organization so that it functions smoothly, and negotiate deals with other organizations. For our purposes, executives are vice presidents or their equivalent and above. They are the leaders of a particular organization or of a particular function within an organization.

Now let's imagine we follow, for a moment, Alvaro's career. He has just been told by his boss, "You know you have done so well working with our key accounts that now I want to have you talk to the senior management. I suggest you find someone to coach you on how to do that. Our senior management can be tough on people. They ask a lot of difficult questions, are sometimes pressed for time and lack patience, and occasionally become upset or angry. I think that you have great potential and I want you to come across as just the kind of new executive our company needs."

Alvaro has read the rest of the chapters in this book and has taken affirmative steps to work on his communication and presentation skills. He thinks that he is prepared; and in fact, he is. However, he still needs to take one final step in order to transform himself into executive material. This chapter is for the Alvaros of the world. The techniques that follow are transformational. You will explore two key areas. First, the executive behaviors you need to demonstrate when talking and, second, the paths to persuasion and how to analyze the type of information different executives want to hear. This analysis will be very important as you work to influence certain decision makers.

CHOOSE YOUR PRESENCE BEHAVIORS

In a general sense, an individual communicates by using three different presence behaviors. At any given moment, a person can present himself as opinionated, factual, or emotional. The presenter's choices will depend on the audience's expectations and what the presenter believes to be the most appropriate presence behavior for that particular moment. This requires an ongoing assessment of the audience and demands that a presenter be continually aware of the impact that the content and his or her delivery of the presentation is having on the audience. As you try on particular behavior modes, please keep in mind that none of them are "bad" or "good." The behaviors are simply tools that a presenter can choose to use in order to achieve a desired result. Moreover, these behaviors can vary even during the course of a single presentation, depending on the presenter's assessment of the audience's "mood."

Opinionated Behaviors

This is a very difficult behavioral style to adopt when making presentations to executives because it carries with it the risk that you may provoke individuals in your audience to become argumentative or more opinionated in response, even if you are, in some absolute sense, right about what you are saying. If someone is truly operating from an opinionated stance, the person comes across as having the only right answer. When he or she listens, it is mostly to find holes in what someone is saying. Only take this style when you perceive that the audience is asking for strong guidance or when you are truly being asked for your expert opinion and you really know a lot more than anyone else in the room. Become aware of when your audience is exhibiting some of these types of behaviors so that you can adjust your presentation style accordingly.

Exhibit 8.1 provides a list of "opinionated" behaviors.

Exhibit 8.1
Opinionated Behaviors

Voice	Loud Judgmental sounding Clear and strong ending Dominating by tone Commanding: Do what I suggest
Gestures	Finger points with chopping action of the hand Steeple hands Hands on hips Arms crossed Banging on the table
Facial expressions	Lips firmly together Not smiling Stern look Head tilted up
Posture	Forward Stand over people Lean forward to convince
Eye contact	Look into the distance
Words	Interrogative questioning such as, "You just told me that . . ." "Obviously, this is the only path to take."
Position	State your position and the rules to back it up
Negotiating Style	Stance of trying to defeat other person Should, must, have to, no other way Put person on defensive by voice and word choice Distill facts into an opinion State conclusions Ask a closed question
Solutions	One answer/solution

When you are trying to sound "opinionated," you will probably speak in a loud and authoritative voice. Your posture is upright and a bit forward in order to command and to influence others. Your eye contact can be strong and dominating. You may believe it is not necessary to engage others and invite them to disagree. Your opinion stands by itself. Sometimes you may be pointing at the audience or just standing there rock solid.

The purpose of using this opinionated, authoritative manner is to be considered the expert. Someone has asked your opinion and you are stating your expert view on the matter. By the way you present yourself, you are not inviting others in the room to disagree. You are taking a firm stance based on an unshakeable opinion. Your choice of words can be important. You may even say words like, "In my opinion . . ." or "Based on all the relevant information, I believe we will want to . . ." or "This is an obvious decision. The law says we must do. . . ." You might even use words like: should, must, have to, obviously, and no other way.

When you are really the expert in an area such as law, financial obligations, medical matters, or technological issues, among many others, you will be called on to give your viewpoint. You don't want to sound like you don't know what you are talking about. After all, this is what you do for a living. And since you do this for a living, you don't have to give many facts, or any for that matter. You have distilled the facts into an opinion. You are giving the conclusion of that distillation. Then if others want to know how you came to this decision, you will provide some facts. Many times, managers get into trouble because they feel obliged to provide all the details about their opinions, even though they are acknowledged as experts in the area. For the executive listening, this can translate into lack of confidence. The executive may think, "Why is this person trying to convince me with all this detail? Perhaps he doesn't really believe what he says." Other executives may be thinking, "Just get to the point. If I need all this detail, I'll ask. After all, I pay you to do this job. I don't have the time to listen to all of this." And in reality, in some situations, executives will be interested about the facts behind your recommendation and will interrogate you. This can be the moment when some presenters falter. Do not take the questions personally. Be careful when you are being questioned; you do not want to start answering in long paragraphs or mix one fact with another because pressure is being applied. This is where you practice your breathing and calming techniques.

Using opinionated behavior styles can be a useful approach when you are expected to be the expert. The group wants one answer or one solution. You may feel uncomfortable when you are making your judgments based on certain facts and leaving out other facts, either consciously or unconsciously. However, if you are being asked for an opinion based on your position as an expert, it is wise not to be wishy-washy with your view or subject your view to a dozen qualifications (as lawyers, who can get away with this, do!). An audience that expects you to be the expert needs to know that you have absolute confidence in what you are saying and they are looking for all the cues that indicate to them that you possess this confidence and that your opinion is right. You are the expert, and you are presenting in a style that makes them most comfortable and which will give them the confidence that they need in order to make a decision. In order to do that you need to appear confident about what you say.

Experts get into trouble when working with executives, since they sometimes confuse being an expert with being the approver. Their voice tones and words convey what the real approvers in the room "should" do. But the real approvers may dislike what they are hearing and believe there must be a way around this situation or another way of looking at it. In addition, the expert's view may be only one component of what is in reality a more complex situation. If the presenter stays opinionated and *stuck* in this decision, the audience may see him or her as an obstructionist and not really on the side of the company. In other words, repeating over and over that this is the only decision that can be made will not entice people to see you as on their side. Lawyers are often criticized as being impediments to deal-making. The reason is that a lawyer is often charged with finding ways to minimize risk and frequently will insist on inserting "protective" clauses that may shift risk to the other side. While theoretically this may sound fine, in many situations, the underlying structure of the deal, which is based on allocation of risk, may be profoundly affected. Thus, lawyers, for example, when giving an executive a summary of the issues that may need to be resolved, should avoid being overly opinionated and instead approach the presentation with recommendations and options that actually move the deal forward.

Factual Behaviors

The opinionated behavior styles are not useful when you are talking to someone who resents people telling him or her what to do. He or she says, "I don't want anyone telling me what to do or how to think. I want the facts and nothing else." If you are presenting before that type of person or group, then you can use a different behavior style. It will be one in which you use a more factual demeanor and state your views as recommendations, logically explaining the positive and negative consequences of carrying out that recommendation. In this situation, it is prudent that you not force your opinion onto the group. Clearly, in giving the factual content, you don't say all the facts you know—just the most relevant ones. The idea here is that you are acting as a guide in assisting the decision-makers to make the decision that you believe to be the best. In effect, you are presenting in the manner so they can assimilate the information and arrive at their decision.

So how do you sound different when you are factual? The factual style will get you into fewer confrontations when speaking. You do not push any "emotional buttons" by just stating the facts. Your voice is calm and you come across as dispassionate. This tone is excellent when speaking with executives. But you can't use it the whole time because this style lacks emotion or excitement. It is certainly appropriate when presenting facts and figures, advantages and disadvantages of different possibilities, and recommendations for future actions. Exhibit 8.2 provides a list of factual behaviors.

Exhibit 8.2 Factual Behaviors	
Voice	Normal even tone Matter-of-fact End sentences, but not with emphasis
Gestures	Open hand One hand Use hands when talking Count on fingers No gestures
Facial expressions	Open eyes Neutral look Head straight ahead
Posture	Back on heels Upright—head up
Eye contact	Look, but just long enough—two seconds
Words	Now that I know what you want to accomplish, let me explain how to get there within the law. Maybe another way to consider your question is. . . .
Position	Fact based
Negotiating Style	Collaborate, compromise, open to mutual agreement To clarify, here are some key points. . . . The risks and consequences of taking this action are. . . . To sum up our areas of agreement, I hear you saying x. Here is what I would add.
Solutions	Options/several solutions with the risks/consequences of each

A factual voice is more "matter of fact." You end your sentences calmly, not emphatically. You can avoid being monotone by using inflections. Your posture is upright, but usually not the forward and ready-to-take-charge image. Your hands are open and you use them to talk. Your whole demeanor is open and calm since, in effect, you are just stating the facts. You are looking at each person—maybe not for a long time, but you are really looking at each person's face. Your try to convey honesty and a sense of emotional tranquility. You are level-headed and open to problem solving, discussion, and brainstorming. You are there to "assist" with the facts and recommendations that are within your control. You are competent and reasonable since, before this type of group, you will not be attempting to force them into a decision by the strength of your opinion. You will not directly challenge the group when they disagree with you, regardless of your belief that you are the ultimate authority on what you are stating.

You may still be an expert when using the factual behavior style, but you will come across as collaborative and open to mutual agreement. You are listening to the problem or question and, rather than sitting across from your audience, you are sitting with them looking at the problem and discussing it. You may restate the business goal and then discuss the risks and consequences of taking a particular action. You may also look behind the question that was asked and clarify it or restate it in order to see whether there might be another approach. In this mode, you are acting more as the contributor to the issue being discussed. You realize that you are not the approver and you let your audience clearly know that your job is to help them, the approvers, come to a sound decision.

As the person with the facts, you have to be careful not to be carried away with sharing more information than the approvers need to know. For example, in a legal situation your audience may not want to hear all the state codes, the cases, the precedents, and the assumptions about the law. If you go into too much detail, you will lose your executive presence and probably your audience as well. If there is one thing that needs to be emphasized over and over again, it is the following: *If you present too much data, it will sound like you are still doing all the grunt work and not involved in fashioning the big picture.*

For example, you have been asked to give a summary of an analysis of a potential acquisition. You know a lot of facts. Which ones do you share? The executives are considering how this acquisition will fit in with the company's business objectives, culture, and future direction. They need some facts, but not all the ones you have accumulated during your research. Your facts are supporting the big picture that the executives are considering. Remember, this is not a performance appraisal in which you tell them everything you found out. They pay you to do your job. They really don't want to hear all about it.

I remember coaching a manager who was presenting his department's goals to the executives. His slides were filled with technical words in size 12-point font as well as amazingly complicated flow charts. But his explanation was done very clearly and succinctly. I suggested that he cut most of the words and images on the slides and just talk. He did. Someone came up after his talk and said, "Now I know what you are doing. I never have understood all those slides you used to use. They were very confusing." What is interesting is that he never got that feedback until he did something his colleague liked.

If you are prone to present too much data, it is sometimes better to start with the end result by asking of your audience: "What do you really want to accomplish here?" (Asking them what they hope to achieve establishes them as the decision-makers, but it places you in a good position to make your recommendations as to the ways in which to reach their goal.) You could also ask, "What are the results we hope to achieve?" This type of introduction will communicate to the group that your role is to assist in making a decision. As you may note, it is done in such a manner that the group will almost be forced to consider that you are going to be engaged as an integral part of the process and not just someone presenting information.

As the factual provider of information, you are more likely to suggest options or several solutions along with their attendant risks and consequences. There are many pitfalls with this approach. While on the one hand, you want to demonstrate the presence of a "take charge" person, you also need to sound logical and open to mutual agreement and not yield to the temptation to give a strong opinion. The type of audience that wants to actively make decisions on its own will see your "factual" behavior as demonstrating executive presence if you effectively guide the members of your audience to a satisfactory decision.

When you are mostly in the factual behavior mode, it is entirely acceptable to go between being opinionated and factual, again, depending on the situation. For example, if you see some wavering on a point that you truly feel to be critical, then marshal your forces and move your behavior style on that point to being more opinionated. You will find that, if you are using behaviors that are based in the factual mode, it will be much easier to switch behaviors than if you tend to sound and act more opinionated. Again, please keep in mind that factual behavior styles are tools to achieve your presentation objectives—they are not necessarily the best behaviors to use all the time.

Emotional Behaviors

Sometimes it is important to be emotional and make your case with passion, enthusiasm, and energy and then back it up with facts. Many executives love to see a presenter who is passionate about the presentation. There is something compelling and human in sharing emotion with others. I've actually been hired to teach an assistant vice president how to be more energetic when making recommendations to the executive committee. Enthusiasm, emotionality, and compelling excitement all play a large role in business and in many other forms of organization. This style lets your audience know that you are standing behind your recommendations. I was told by one executive, "I like my managers to really show they are behind a new deal. If they don't act excited, then I figure it's not that great a deal."

However, if you let your emotions run rampant and out of control, you will have trouble being seen as a business partner. You may be viewed as being hysterical, overly passionate, or a person not to be taken seriously. You may not be trusted to make sound business decisions since your "emotions" are controlling you. The idea is to be able to choose when and how to use emotion and then switch back to other behavior modes.

Exhibit 8.3 lists a variety of "emotional" behaviors.

When you present with emotion, you will have an excitement in your voice that is perceptible to others. Your voice will have an "edge." If you want to share a passion, you will probably speak loudly and strongly accentuate certain emotional words. If you are sharing something sad or sobering, you may want to lower your voice and modulate accordingly. You will be leaning forward more toward the audience because you want to connect to your audience and have them experience what you are experiencing. You will be looking at each person to find an emotional connection. You will be using your hands to gesture as you speak.

Your passion about the subject matter will infect others to have passion as well. This encourages connection and brainstorming as well as other possibilities. You may state your opinion but then say, "I'm thinking there is another way to look at this situation and, off the top of my head, here are some different ways

Exhibit 8.3
Emotional Behaviors

Voice	Loud or soft, filled with emotion End of sentence may trail off as thinking of another thought End sentences with excitement
Gestures	Open arms and hands Hold hands in front
Facial expression	Smile Laugh Open, expressive eyes Head more forward
Posture	Leaning forward to connect Stand to the side of a person Look less formal
Eye contact	Don't look or look a long time Look in an exciting, enthused manner Look to find connection—three to four seconds
Words	Our last quarter was fabulous. This is a very exciting project for us. It's going to grow our business!
Position	State party's desired position and discuss how to achieve it
Negotiating Style	Accommodate Brainstorm creatively "Let's figure this out together. . ." "How do we solve this?" Tell stories, experiences, examples Broaden picture
Solutions	Creatively offer alternative ways of addressing the situation

to analyze this problem." You are creatively offering alternative ways to address the issue. You are inviting discussion. You are broadening the landscape by using your creativity and intuition. You might say things like, "Maybe another way to consider your question is . . . " or "When I see the underlying issue as. . . , then another approach is. . . ." You are offering out-of-the-box solutions. You are thinking laterally, not linearly. You want to give time for others to talk so you do not find yourself so excited that you take up all the talking space.

Frequently. presenters are told to smile more. The smile has to come from the content. A smile can come when the presenter is telling an emotional story or reporting on positive news or sharing a future vision that is exciting. Be sure to put in phrases and stories that enable you to easily smile.

Just as the emotional executive presence behavior can really help you, it can also hinder you if you go overboard, particularly in your expressions of passion. For example, when you are presenting a recommendation you might start with emotion, you might say, "This is the best deal I have seen in years!" or "This new marketing plan will move us light years beyond our competitors. They won't have a chance! I'm very excited about it." With the right group, this approach can be very engaging. With the wrong audience, it would be a recipe for disaster. A more conservative way to present that uses passion would be to build your presentation in the factual mode with a series of recommendations and then move the behavior to passion after you have established your "factual" credentials. For example, after presenting several recommendations you could say, "As you can see, with the changes that I have recommended, we will increase our production by 15 percent, our market share by 35 percent, and our revenues by 70 percent. There is no doubt that this will once again put us in the number one spot for the next five to ten years! I am very excited about this vision." By using emotion you establish your credibility, show the audience that you care about the result, and share a vision of a brilliant future. This will motivate your audience.

Selecting Appropriate Behaviors

How do you know what executive presence is needed at which moment?

The expectations of your behaviors will be based on your function and the role your audience puts you in. So first, know your true role in the situation. Naturally, you will have evaluated your audience by asking people. Second, know your audience and how they communicate with each other and also with those who come to give presentations. What behaviors do they value? Third, consider what to do with a global audience. How will your global audience be different? You will find out the answers to this information when you ask several people. You can also read books and/or information on the Internet about different cultures' expectations of how a presenter is to share information. When you have managed to make a good assessment of your audience, you can certainly plan your behavioral style ahead of time.

The secret to executive presence is becoming aware of how the audience is reacting to your presentation as you give it and then changing your presentation's content and style to adapt accordingly. This will demand a high level of sensitivity and connectivity on your part.

Here are examples of how people have changed. A newly appointed information technology manager had to learn how to sound more confident and emotional when presenting information. He had to bring more non-verbal emotion into the presentation, use more inviting hand gestures, move around with a little more energy, and engage visually with members of the audience. A newly promoted female vice president had to learn how to sound opinionated. She was working with a very loud, argumentative group of individuals and her soft factual voice got lost. She began to lean forward, point her finger at someone, and state her position with a strong voice. Much to her amazement, everyone liked her new way of acting. A newly promoted talkative senior vice president had to learn to give his opinion and stop going on about all the details. A soon-to-be CEO of a company had to learn to sit up tall in his chair in order to look more in charge. There is very little executive presence in slouching. He had to begin to pay attention to his posture and how he was sitting in the board meetings. His new posture and demeanor impressed his board. Every situation is a bit different, and it is your job to evaluate the audience and adapt your behaviors accordingly for you to capture and keep your audience's attention.

When considering which behavior or behaviors to use, you might determine that one particular behavior is appropriate for the entire presentation. You may, however, decide that more than one behavior is appropriate. In that case, there are many ways you can move through these three behaviors.

Opinions>Facts>Emotion   State your opinions, give several facts, and end with a feeling of excitement. For example, if you are presenting some bad news:

Opinion: "Based on all the information, it is certain and undeniable that we will be 10 percent behind last year in our revenues. I know we have six months left in the year, but in my opinion we won't make our projections."

Facts: "This is due to the entrance of a new competitor in the market as well as the reduction in price that we have implemented in order to meet that competition.

We have worked hard to improve our product, and our team has just patented an accessory that will make our product not only unique but highly desirable."

Emotion: "There is a silver lining in all of this! I am pleased to say that in two years we project our revenues will have doubled from what they are now."

Facts > Opinions > Emotion   State the facts, then make a recommendation, and end with an emotional vision of what this means for the future. This could be a similar version of the example shown above, but in a different order.

Emotion>Facts>Opinions   State an emotion, back it up with facts, and then suggest one action to take. The same example:

Emotion: "I am pleased to tell you about a product that will change our industry. Our product development team has just patented an accessory that will cause our revenues to double in two years!" (excited tone of voice)

Fact: "We did the numbers, and here on the slide are our projections."

Opinion: "We need to do all we can *now* to begin marketing our accessory. I have some opinions on how to go about this."

Your ability to recognize when and how to use these behavior modes and adapt them to your presentation will give you "executive presence." There are additional things that you can do as well.

PLAN WHAT TO SAY ABOUT THE DATA

Don't talk too much or try to oversell your position. Your credibility can diminish when you talk too much. This is the opposite of what you might believe. Many people think that the more you talk, the smarter everyone will think you are. In fact, many executives think that a person is smart if he or she can distill a lot of information into a handful of succinct and important points and convey them well. One way to take charge and gain respect is to say only what is necessary. Three well-said sentences are better than ten rambling ones. If you follow this advice, you will never have to face a wrathful executive who has had enough of the rambling and stops you before you get to your main point.

Length of time: First, ask how long you are expected to talk. Based on the situation, consider making your talk about ten minutes shorter, unless someone tells you differently. Shorter is almost always better. Your audience can always ask questions. Executives pride themselves on grasping information quickly and believe they don't need all the details. You will run the risk of not being asked back if you decide to include all the details in order to sound convincing. A long-winded list of facts will lead your audience to looking at their watches and thinking of pressing matters they have to attend to. Oh, and while we are at it, pause as you talk. Do not create a twenty-minute talk and then decide to say it all in ten minutes. This is very common. Better you say less, pause, and let your audience digest your concepts. If you give them time to digest, they will stay more engaged and open to listening.

Time: Speak for less time. Say only the important points. Then stop talking.

Type of information: Your presentation focus needs to be in the context of the company's strategic business objectives, external resources, and the company's overall mission. You can save all the details for the people who need them. Executives want the big picture. As you read in Chapter 1, present an executive summary and wait to hear whether they want more details. You want to be working at the top of the Communication Pyramid (see Figure 2.1). You might have a one-slide executive summary and then go into more details on certain key points. That's it.

Visuals: Don't use clip art. Only use visuals that help you make your point. Charts can either be useful or totally overwhelming with too much data. Make them simple and clear. Make sure your chart type is the one that is best suited to convey your data in terms of the decision that needs to be made. Once again, don't use too many slides. Don't use animation except to make a point. Don't use sound. If you have too many bells and whistles, your audience may say to themselves, "How does he have time for all this? Isn't he supposed to be doing the real work of the business?"

Recently, I was told a story about a woman who wanted an academic position. She presented her study to the heads of several departments in her area of interest. She did not get the job. One of the deans told me, "She had these awful animations throughout her presentation. Photos and words were flying in from everywhere. She went on and on and the presentation seemed very chaotic.

I would never want to work with someone like that. I couldn't understand the point of what she was trying to tell us. She is too much of a lightweight." What happened here? While this woman could have been very intellectually capable, she lacked the presentation skills to communicate her ideas. The decision not to hire her was based on the negative impact that her presentation had on the department heads. She may never know that her downfall was the quality of her presentation slides.

Answering questions: Be in charge when answering questions. Treat a question with respect, not as an interrogation. Keep in mind that executives are balancing many different points of view when considering options and their questions may not necessarily make sense to you from your point of view. Answer the question with confidence. If you don't know the specific information, say so and promise to get the information as soon as the presentation is over. Use the questions to reinforce the bottom line of what you are presenting. Don't use a question as an opportunity to drown your audience with detail. Keep your responses brief.

USE ENTERTAINMENT AND DRAMA—WHEN APPROPRIATE

Consider this: You are the sixth person to stand in front of the executive management committee. They have been sitting for hours listening to a variety of long-winded and badly presented talks. They are trying to pay attention, but they are tired, have just eaten lunch, and the last thing that they really want to hear is a boring presentation. They do not want to be seen dozing and yet all they are thinking about is how nice it would be to just close their eyes for a minute or so. Obviously, you can't get them to stand up and do a round of calisthenics! So what are your alternatives to get this group going? Engage them by using your energy. Tell an appropriate story, move around, use hand gestures, increase your modulation, propose questions, and get the group talking to you.

As you also read in Chapter 1, anecdotes and stories many times give a better vision and really do break up the onslaught of data that executives experience on an ongoing basis. If you think you are going to keep the executives' attention by going over slide after slide of data, you are wrong. You will surely put them to sleep. They may be looking at you, but I guarantee that they will not be listening to a word you say. Breaking up the facts by entertaining and educating with a story and/or vision may do more for your cause than five pie charts.

When you actually take time to tell a story that is directly related to your point, you will come across as relaxed and in charge. This is because, in order to tell a good story that is relevant to the point of your presentation, you actually need to be fully in charge of the underlying material. People love to hear real-life examples of other people and other companies. Collect them and then incorporate them, as appropriate, into your talk. If you are in business, read *Forbes, The Wall Street Journal,* and other business publications to look for good examples you can use to support your point. Keep a file of these stories and make sure that they are recent so that the group can relate to them and connect with you. Your group will appreciate you and remember your point as well as be impressed by your presentation style and your knowledge of what is going on in the business world.

If you have the type of personality that can use humor effectively, then do so with care. People like to laugh. Do not use canned jokes or jokes that can be insulting to a particular person or group. Your humor should arise from the context of the talk itself. It is best if it arises spontaneously. The best opportunities for this arise, ironically, when something goes wrong. For example, if the electricity goes out and your screen goes blank, you could say, "Well, now the presentation really gets interesting since even I don't know what comes next" or, even better, try to relate the problem to the subject of your presentation: "Since my talk is on contingency planning, I had the electricity turned out to make my point. We really do need to come up with a better plan in the next several weeks." There are as many examples as there are situations that allow for you to be creative.

If you are pitching a cause, it doesn't hurt to be a bit dramatic in your words and voice tone when stating your recommendation. For example, "This is *the best plan* [slowing down those words for emphasis] for our product growth that I've seen in years" or "We should buy this company. *It fits in perfectly* [leaning forward and looking around the table] with our business objectives."

DO MAKE A RECOMMENDATION

One of the comments I frequently hear when asked to coach a manager is: "He just doesn't come across as being sure of himself. He never seems to really make a recommendation. He just presents lots of information. The board is getting tired of this."

In order to succeed, you need to take a risk. Really, it is not that big a risk. It is highly unlikely that you will be fired for making a recommendation. In fact, someone may believe that it is brilliant. Keep in mind that, as a presenter, you are probably the one with the most expertise in the area that you are going to cover. Your audience not only wants to hear a recommendation from you (unless they specifically ask you not to give one), but they need one so that they can succeed. Go ahead, walk out on the limb of life and make a recommendation. It is better to give voice to your ideas and make a mistake than to come across as not having the backbone to state your beliefs. You will be respected more for having stood for some point of view. And, surprise, it is more likely that your recommendations will be followed and you will achieve the purpose of your talk.

I recently coached someone who was supposed to be advising the board on the possible acquisition of a particular company. Her job was to do the due diligence work on potential acquisitions and then report her findings and thoughts. After she had studied the company, she came to the conclusion that it was not something that she could recommend. However, in her presentation she spent too much time telling them about the company and the positive and negative aspects the acquisition. She thought that if they had all the facts, both positive and negative, they, rather than she, could arrive at a conclusion. Indeed, in her presentation, she never really took a stand. After we worked together and redid her presentation, I asked her to practice saying the following for an opening: "I do not believe this is a company we want to acquire. There are three main reasons for my decision. The first reason is. . . ." She kept her reasons short. She stated them with power and confidence. Then she waited to hear the types of questions the committee asked and responded to them based on the data and information that she had collected and evaluated. The board members now had someone with whom they could engage in making their decisions. After the first success, she developed this as a presentation style. After she started talking like this, the board members perked up whenever she began her reports. They liked hearing her viewpoint. They liked having someone to push against. There were several really aggressive committee members, and their questions no longer intimidated her. She even learned to say with utter confidence, "I'm not sure. Let me find that out" or "I don't think that number will matter in terms of our decision here." She actually pushed back and made her own suggestion about what numbers should be considered in making a decision. They were no longer frustrated as she talked. She took a stand.

BE OPTIMISTIC

Executives are in their jobs partly because they see opportunities in situations when others only see failures. Their job is to grow the company, see the possibilities, and make them happen. When you are speaking, don't be pessimistic. Don't say, "We can't do that." Instead, you can say, "Well, let's see what other ways we have of getting to that objective. I believe that another approach might be. . . ." Rather than say "no," offer another alternative. Begin the brainstorming process. Of course, sometimes you just have to say no, but use those moments wisely and maybe even qualify the "no" with statements about existing conditions, the state of technology, the budget, and so forth. You want to be seen as a can-do person. Why is optimism so important? First, people like optimistic people and like to be around them. More importantly, they like people who take their ideas and build on them. Here is a fact from the book *Learned Optimism: How to Change Your Mind and Your Life* to consider the next time you are at the point of disagreeing with someone's idea. "In the twenty-two presidential elections from 1900 through 1984, Americans chose the more optimistic-sounding candidate eighteen times. In all elections in which an underdog pulled off an upset, he was the more optimistic candidate" (Seligman, 2006, p. 192). Not only in elections, but in situation after situation, Seligman proves that the optimistic person or team comes out ahead. He gives this caveat: "We can learn to choose optimism for the most part, but also to heed pessimism when it is warranted" (2006, p. 115). This is your job when presenting to executives. Know exactly when to speak the reality that you see and when to ignore a bit of it and move into envisioning a different future. More often than not, you will not be appreciated for the "negative" reality that you see, and in fact, it may not be shared by anyone to whom you are presenting. Build a vision with your group; don't dismantle the dream.

CONSIDER YOUR BEST PATH TO PERSUASION

You have learned how to demonstrate executive presence. The second key when speaking to executives is to be able to analyze the particular way they want the information presented to them. Of course, this is important with anyone, but with executives you can make or break your career or a deal by the persuasion path you use to "sell" your recommendation. That's why this information is in this chapter. You really must know your audience. You won't get many second chances at this level.

I highly recommend the book *The 5 Paths to Persuasion* by Gary Williams and Robert Miller (2004). They share with you how information should be presented to persuade the decision-maker. The authors surveyed 1,700 executives and describe five decision-making styles—thinkers, charismatics, skeptics, followers, and controllers. I am going to share their information on what is the best way to present to each particular style, plus give you ideas about the slides that each type prefers. I have summarized the information to put on the slides. Depending on the topic and decision-making style of the executive, you may choose to create two to three additional slides for each slide you see here in this chapter. I hope you will also use images and pictures as well as some text.

Thinkers

Thinkers are careful and methodical. They like hard facts based on research—that's what convinces them. Guarded and cautious, they explore every advantage and disadvantage. They are open to new ideas, but only when you have the facts backing up the idea. They are very rational and use numbers to make their decisions. This is why they might not have the best social skills, practically interrogating you about the information. At least you may experience it that way, but they aren't interrogating. They're just looking for more information. While they are proactive and do want to win, thinkers use logic and comprehensive analysis to make decisions. In Miller and Williams' (2004) survey of executives, 11 percent were thinkers.

Format: Thinkers like specific outlines for the presentation of information. For example, a strategy recommendation outline can force you to logically present several strategies and, based on research, choose the most successful one. Thinkers would not be as happy if you presented just one strategy; you cannot assume they would understand that you did your research on other options.

Executive summary: Provide a brief executive summary of your talk and then say, "Now let me take you through our analysis, including some customer research, past production figures, and future predictions."

Interaction: Set up your slides to encourage interaction. When showing charts, be sure they are clear and focused. Put the summary point of the data on the slide, but be prepared for thinkers to want to discuss the numbers in the charts. Make sure the numbers are big enough for them to read. You can ask during your talk, "What other information do you know or want to know that will fill in any gaps you see?"

How to fail: You'll fail to persuade thinkers if you:

- Show them slides with unclear information.

- Don't explain your transitions from one slide to the next so that they hear and see your logic.

- Don't send them any materials ahead of time and then surprise them with a presentation, pushing for an answer right away. Thinkers like time to make a decision so they can consider all the issues involved.

- Put wrong numbers on your slides or say something incorrect, then fail to correct it. Thinkers won't make a decision on the spot but will spend time analyzing and processing the information you provided, so an incorrect data point or misstatement of fact can be fatal.

- Don't really do your homework, instead laboring under the false idea or hope that your enthusiasm will convince them.

Slides Designed for Thinkers

- Show the step-by-step process on how you arrived at your conclusion.

- Prepare clear slides with informative headings and systematically organized content.

- Use a simple background so the information stands out.

- Limit yourself to an interesting graphic only in the title area of the slide.

- Show multiple data points compared on a single chart.

Begin your presentation with a slide like the one shown in Figure 8.1. State the present situation and the desired outcome. List the key analysis pieces you will show. Show a timeline if appropriate to help the thinker understand the events in an order. It may be best not to state your recommended solution at the beginning: A thinker wants to hear your logic and reasoning process, then your recommendation.

The slide in Figure 8.2 shows some potential next steps. Thinkers do not want to see a slide with start dates. Instead, they want time to digest the information, consider what else is important, find holes in your process, and then decide on some next steps.

Figure 8.1
Executive Summary for Thinkers

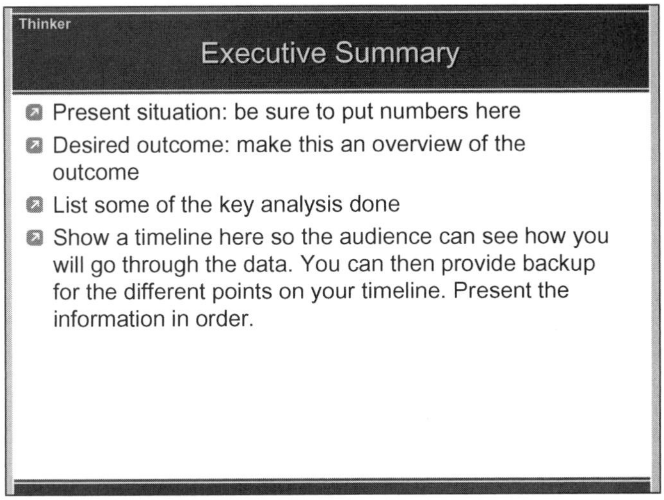

> **Thinker**
> ### Executive Summary
>
> - Present situation: be sure to put numbers here
> - Desired outcome: make this an overview of the outcome
> - List some of the key analysis done
> - Show a timeline here so the audience can see how you will go through the data. You can then provide backup for the different points on your timeline. Present the information in order.

Figure 8.2
Next Steps for Thinkers

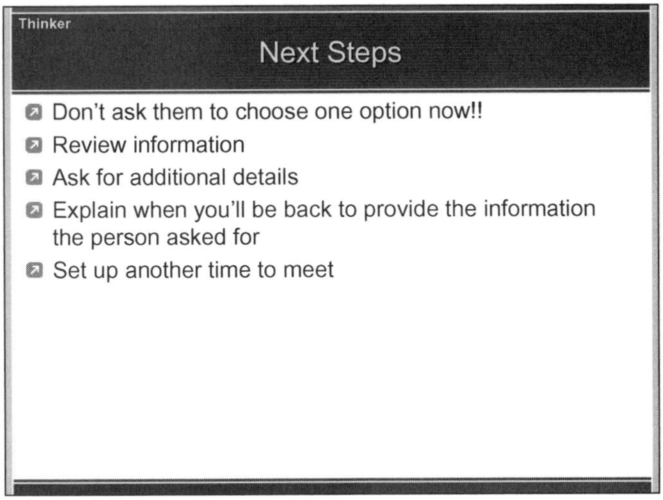

> **Thinker**
> ### Next Steps
>
> - Don't ask them to choose one option now!!
> - Review information
> - Ask for additional details
> - Explain when you'll be back to provide the information the person asked for
> - Set up another time to meet

Charismatics

Charismatic decision-makers are open to new ideas and enthusiastic when you present a new opportunity. They seem very excited about what you are discussing. They like new, out-of-the-box ideas. They don't want to listen to a whole PowerPoint talk—they just want to hear the bottom-line results, not all the details leading up to it. You must engage charismatics immediately, before they lose interest. But don't be lulled into thinking that you don't really have to follow up or present detailed information. You do need to present the risks and how to minimize them. From the way charismatics talk, you think the decision is imminent, but they will give all the details to others to examine. Then they'll decide. Although charismatics might not seem interested in the analysis, others will. In Miller and Williams' (2004) survey, 25 percent were charismatics.

> **Emotion and enthusiasm:** You must, and I mean must, sound interested, enthused, and passionate about your subject. When you do, you may gain the interest, enthusiasm, and passion of your audience. No one wants to listen to someone who sounds bored. You want emotion in your voice, body, and demeanor. (Spoken by a charismatic leader)

Although they do not ask you for every detail, they do expect someone else to go through your recommendations to make sure all the data are logically organized and make sense. They also need to feel comfortable that your ideas are built on solid information, so be enthusiastic, but also present some of your due-diligence work.

Format: Charismatics want to know the end result first. You will basically create two presentations: The first "talking" presentation should be short and to the point. Plan for time to interact, perhaps writing on a flip chart. You do need an organized structure when talking, but only present the highest level of your information. The "second," detailed presentation is one you can hand out. It should include more detailed data and back-up charts. The charismatic will probably not read this version, but will hand it off to managers who will follow up and meticulously check all the facts and recommendations. In the first presentation you persuade through enthusiasm and sharing the overall vision. In the second one, you influence through details. Don't confuse the two when talking to a charismatic.

Executive summary: Provide a brief executive summary of your talk and then say, "How does this unique idea strike you?"

Interaction: Don't use too many slides. Let them talk. But be sure, when you are interacting, that you make your key points. Have those key points on your slides, in your mind, or on a piece of paper. No matter how enthusiastic the audience is, make all your points.

How to fail: You'll fail to persuade charismatics if you:

- Try to tell the story from start to finish with lots of numbers and industry jargon. They want to hear the bottom line first.

- Present a pre-planned talk that you have obviously given many times before.

- Talk without giving them an opportunity to interact with you.

- Don't make your points even as they are discussing side issues and other opportunities that come into their minds.

- Assume that when your presentation is over, you don't have any more work to do but wait to hear a decision. In other words, you don't provide the detailed due diligence presentation for others to look through.

Slides Designed for Charismatics

- Make at least one slide your vision slide.

- Begin with the problems.

- Explain the risks or obstacles that might arise and suggestions for handling them.

Figures 8.3 and 8.4 show some sample slides appropriate for charismatics.

Skeptics

Skeptics have a certain worldview and are distrustful of information that does not fit. To a skeptic, everyone is suspect. Make sure you can quote someone from their inner circle as to why you're there in the first place. If you don't, you will

Figure 8.3
Executive Summary for Charismatics

Start with a visionary slide. Offer opportunities to imagine a better future and visually show results. Charismatics really want to know this is a new idea or concept. Be sure you say this soon in your presentation.

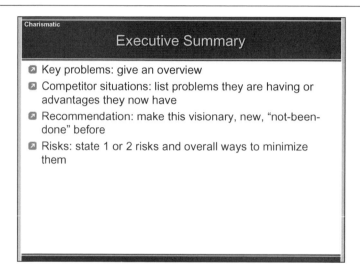

Figure 8.4
Next Steps for Charismatics

Give charismatics the "picture" of the idea on your next steps slide. Make sure it "shows" the true uniqueness of your idea. Be sure you find out who will be your contacts in the organization.

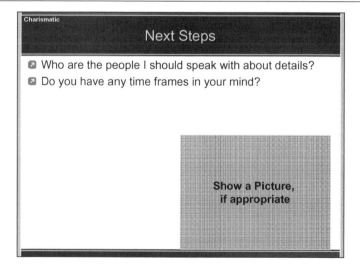

probably fail. When you start presenting, they will question you right away. You have to be credible in their eyes before they listen to you. Skeptics say what they think without regard to your reaction. While thinkers take in the data to make a decision, skeptics look through the data to find what supports the vision. Don't get defensive, and don't rush a skeptic. Because they're unafraid of being wrong, they make bold, risky decisions. Fully 20 percent of the survey respondents were skeptics (Williams & Miller, 2004).

Recently, I was talking to someone on the phone about slides I had created. Before I even started, she asked, "But how do you know they are effective?" Several days before that, I was coaching a vice president on his slides and he said to me, "How did you decide on this font size? I like mine better." Then there was the day I was telling my friend about foods that were important to eat. Her first question was, "Where did you read that?" Followed by, "Who is this person who wrote that?" All of these people were showing the skeptical side of their decision making. They wanted to test the credibility of my suggestions.

Presentation format: Skeptics are interested in where you got your information, ideas, and recommendations. Your format has to document your information. Present your suggestions, but make footnotes or otherwise present the sources of your data.

Executive summary: On this one-slide summary, include primary sources of information and/or people who agree with the idea and data.

Interaction: Prepare yourself to be questioned and interrogated. For those of you who have been to court or had to give a deposition, remember the grueling questions you were asked to lead you down a path where you didn't want to go? Then there were the questions on which you almost lost your emotional balance. Watch yourself! Although the skeptic is really not, at one level, attacking you, you may feel that way.

How to fail: You'll fail to persuade a skeptic if you:

- Present information without backing up its validity.
- Don't present why, logically and factually, your ideas make sense.
- Lose your emotional balance and begin to get defensive.
- Try to put the skeptics in the corner and show them how they are wrong.
- Take credit for all the ideas discussed and don't give the skeptic any credit.

- Start to believe the skeptic is questioning your identity as a competent professional; make your identity more important in the debate than your data.
- Try to get through your PowerPoint slides without stopping and seriously discussing the questions you are asked.

Slides Designed for Skeptics

- Start the presentation with THEIR world view. They will love it, and since they cannot refute it, you will build some credibility.
- Make sure your first slide(s) uses the controller or the controller's company as a source.
- Show more than one option, with the reasons for or against each option.
- Follow a logical, systematic thought process in your slides.
- List information sources on each slide. Look at the slide and be sure you can answer, "What makes this information credible?"

Figures 8.5 and 8.6 show some sample slides that are appropriate for use with skeptics.

Figure 8.5
Executive Summary for Skeptics

Start with an executive summary and be sure you list your credible sources on this slide. This first slide really has to show you have done your research.

Skeptic
Executive Summary

🗷 Present situation
🗷 Desired situation
 ◆ Credible reason why this situation is desired
🗷 3 options
🗷 Recommended option
 ◆ Credible reason why this option is the best

Figure 8.6
List Option 1

You will be presenting several options to show the skeptic that you have once again done your research. This is an option slide.

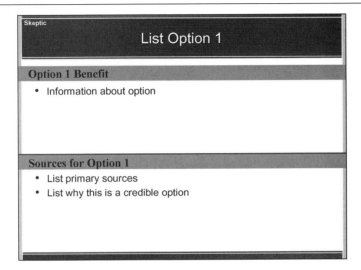

Followers

Sometimes followers come across as open and enthused. But pay attention. Unless you talk about how the process you are describing was successfully implemented elsewhere, they lose interest. They want proof. Followers ask, "Where has this been done before?" That's why they buy well-known brands. Hardly innovators, followers want to protect what the company already has. They are excellent with people, always aware of how their behavior affects others. One last thing: Followers like bargains and enjoy a bit of haggling over prices. Although 36 percent in the survey were followers, only 6 percent of sales presentations are targeted to them (Williams & Miller, 2004).

A colleague of mine is very creative. She has put together some innovative programs, but she'll have a tough time convincing a follower to let her train his employees. They stick to what's been done before and don't want to be the first to try something new. They are very empathic, so when you talk to one, you may "feel" that he is agreeing with you, but that doesn't mean he is going to say yes to your idea. Followers can seem to be skeptics or thinkers by the questions they ask. But when you hear phrases like, "This sounds like what we have been doing" or "Where has this been proven successful?" you'll know you're dealing with a follower. Followers in middle management are more likely to be "yes" people who are unlikely to champion a new idea. They like to follow the path of least resistance.

Format: Followers want to know if, and where, your idea has actually been implemented and worked. In your presentation you need to give examples of how your proposal has been carried out in other situations.

Executive summary: On this one-slide summary, include primary sources of information and a list of places your proposal has been successful. If you are pitching a brand new concept, then make analogies to have it seem less foreign. You can use phrases such as, "This is like what we did. . ." or "This follows the same path as. . . ."

Interaction: Followers ask many questions. You may feel the person does not trust you, but she is attempting to discover how your strategy has played itself out before. The pointed questions about past experience is the follower's way of finding out what happened when someone else implemented this strategy.

How to fail: You'll fail to persuade a follower if you:

- Present information without saying how it is has been successful before.

- Don't put together a solid idea with all the facts and figures. Don't present a partially thought-out idea!

- Pitch your idea with the focus of being the first in the business to do this.

Slides Designed for Followers

- Follow a logical, systematic thought process.

- Show where the successes have occurred and what results were obtained.

- Avoid busy, "avant garde" backgrounds. They will not give the impression of solidity to a follower who wants to keep on the path of what's been done. It would be a very poor choice to use dissolve animations in front of a follower.

Figures 8.7 and 8.8 show slides appropriate for use with followers.

Figure 8.7
Key Facts of Proposal for Followers

You may need several slides for this information for followers. Be sure you don't present only concepts. You must have facts. List the costs and, if possible, show the costs for several options.

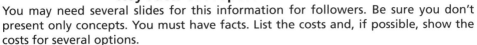

Follower
Key Facts of Proposal

- Be sure to list facts, as well as ideas, about your suggestions
- Include enough information to convince a skeptic or a thinker as well as a follower
  - ◆ Logical thought process
  - ◆ Clear transitions from point to point

Figure 8.8
Past History for Followers

Unless you can list how your idea, process, or strategy was successful elsewhere, you might as well not present. This slide will be crucial in alleviating the fears of the follower.

Follower
Past History

- Include how this idea or process has been successfully implemented somewhere else
  - ◆ List locations and results

Controllers

Controllers are driven by fear and proactively handle that emotion. Highly independent, they like to be in control of the total decision-making process. Controllers don't like to be pushed—you have to get them to believe they made the decisions. Because controllers see information through their own perspectives, it can be difficult to get them to truly take in a piece of data that runs contrary to their view. They are also perfectionists who are not very interested in getting along with people and making them feel comfortable. Controllers run to their own music, so be careful how you present contrary information. They have a tendency to shoot the messenger.

One out of ten executives is a controller (Williams & Miller, 2004). Controllers operate out of fear, often assuming that you do not have their best interests at heart. They read into what you are saying and can be persistent in going over a single point and become aggressive. Stay calm—don't let them provoke you.

Who should give the presentation to a controller? Controllers only want to hear from an expert or a trusted advisor. If you are not one of those, then beware. In fact, if you have to give the presentation, have a trusted advisor with you. Whenever possible, let someone the controller trusts discuss the topic. There seems to only one way to truly "change" a controller's mind. When they are forced by some other entity (government, board), then they change. The most effective way to frame your proposal is as a "must change." Bottom line is that you'll probably never be friends with a controller, but you may still get the deal done if you go this route.

Format: Be sure that controllers have all the information they need—and probably more than you think they need. Do not push them to make a decision. They'll make it in their own time, once they are sure they have the information they need. And they'll only make their decision once they are not afraid of the consequences.

Executive summary: Provide a four-point factual summary of the situation you want to discuss; don't say the decision here.

Interaction: Don't even think about trying to persuade controllers! They will persuade themselves at the right moment for them, which may not be the moment you have in mind. Don't say anything to remind them that they operate out of fear. Remember, when they are attacking, they may be worried about the consequences of certain actions and are looking for reassurance that their fear will not occur.

How to fail: You'll fail to persuade controllers if you:

- Don't give a "must change" reason that forces them to change

- Aggravate their fears.

- Don't let them take credit for the end idea and decision.

- Try to make them see your analysis, rather than discuss their analysis.

Slides Designed for Controllers

- Show them how "the world" is forcing them to change and that they were actually "right" all along. This is not an easy requirement, but a must.

- Follow a logical, systematic thought process.

- Be sure a controller cannot take offense with the words on your slides. Check the words with someone who knows the controller.

- Quote the experts that the controller respects.

Figures 8.9 and 8.10 show some sample slides appropriate for use with controllers.

Figure 8.9
Situation at a Glance for Controllers

Give a quick overview—one that the controller will see as valid. Don't put any assumptions or your own interpretation on this slide. You don't want to start arguing about your views on slide 1 or you may not get past it.

> **Controller**
> ## Situation at a Glance
>
> - This slide shows how you are going to provide the information in a logical and systematic manner
> - Show an overview of the process you will discuss
> - They like to hear rational arguments

Figure 8.10
Possible Options Slides for Controllers

Don't push for one option over the others. Show all the options and let the controller analyze them and come to a decision. Ask the advisors what to include as options. Make sure you avoid hot-button items that will lead you and a controller astray from your topic.

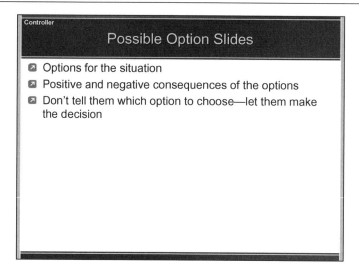

You will serve yourself well when you begin to tailor your message and way of presenting to all of these leaders' styles. It doesn't take that much effort, and your rewards include successful deals, more credibility in the person's eyes, and a presentation that reaches its goal. And remember, if you start to feel disconnected from the decision-maker, stop and think about how to change your pitch. It's never too late to take another path.

ADVICE FROM EXECUTIVES

Several executives were gracious enough to respond to the following question: "When you listen to someone give a presentation, what is the person doing or saying that would induce you to think: 'This person is executive material.' Similarly, what would someone be doing or saying where you would think: 'I wouldn't want this person to present on the company's behalf' or 'I don't think that this person is executive material.'"

I'm sure you will find ways to incorporate their advice into your presentations as you move up in your career. These are the kind of people you will want to impress.

Provide information and an action plan: I am impressed with people who succinctly quantify the information and then recommend action steps. I want to know what the person presenting is thinking. I want to know what the person suggests we do with the information. I do not want to listen to information just to listen to it. Sometimes I see that people who really have not thought out an issue just give me a lot of information. Or they use the information dumping as a way to avoid the real issue. If a twenty-page report is necessary, then give it to me before the meeting. For me, a meeting is a situation in which decisions are to be made. I'm not interested in sitting and listening to someone go on and on about the data.

Present in a very positive way. The energy with which someone presents has an impact on how people hear the presentation. Try to engage people. If you have the personality and it is appropriate, tell a joke.

Respond to questions. Listen to other people in the room and respond appropriately. Be flexible. Go in the direction the audience is moving. Don't present on autopilot. Respond to where the group wants to go. At the same time, do challenge or disagree. Don't be a "yes" person.

Go from simple to complicated explanations. On complicated issues, make sure you have explained the basics first. But explain them in a way that is concise and to the point. Don't ramble.

Don't try to justify things that cannot be justified. Own up to making mistakes. Take responsibility for them and be willing to work harder in order to improve.

—Shari E. Redstone
President of National Amusements
Vice-Chairwoman of CBS Corporation and Viacom
Chairwoman of Midway Games

The first thing I look for is competency. Simply, does the presenter know his/her topic? Do they use specific, concrete examples? Do they know the numbers (and the numbers behind the numbers) they present?

Assuming the presenter is knowledgeable about the presentation's content, the next question concerns executive presence.

Physical presence: It is unfair, but 6-foot 2-inches and in shape beats 5 feet and out of shape. If you are short like me, stand tall, and speak distinctly.

Presentation style: Biggest mistake, being too casual with the audience. While the presenter wants to appear friendly and likeable to connect with his/her audience, it often comes across as disrespecting the audience. Better to be a bit too formal and appear "buttoned up" versus trying to be my new best friend.

Answer the question! Do not dance; it isn't the time or place. "I don't know, but I'll get back to you," stated firmly is fine. It builds credibility. Every other answer does not.

All of the above gives impression of competency and self-confidence. Caution: be self-deprecating enough (but not too self-revelatory) that your self-confidence cannot be interpreted as arrogance or talking down to your audience.

—Drew Staniar
SVP at Supply Chain Risk Intelligence Practice,
Marsh Inc.

Great presenters are credible. They are in the moment. They connect with their audience. There's no spouting of a "canned" presentation . . . their message is clear, crisp, well-rehearsed and on-message. But it seems like a conversation. The verbal message of an effective executive is fully reinforced by all his facial and body expressions . . . and the energy conveyed. You know that such a person KNOWS his subject matter because a great presenter exudes understated self-confidence.

—Michael D. Jeans
President, New Directions, Inc.

As a presenter, you must appear confident and inspire confidence in the audience. This means that you should not look nervous, fidget, slouch, or avoid eye contact. Sit or stand straight and have good posture habits. You will demonstrate executive presence when you speak not by reading notes, but by communicating eye-to-eye with each member of the audience, letting them know that you confident about what you are saying and that you are sincere in your presentation.

Make sure that you are in control of the facts and ready to state them when asked. If there is a single decision-maker present, then pay additional attention to that person. When someone asks a question or makes a comment, wait for the person to finish and answer respectfully by looking at him or her and finding value in whatever has been said. Be courteous and respectful–do not denigrate a person for asking a "dumb" question. You should use questions and comments to further invite audience participation and to build consensus. Don't be afraid to disagree if you have expertise and can back up what you say, but do so in a way that does not put down the person with whom you disagree. Don't talk too much and don't interrupt.

Be yourself; don't be afraid to smile, but make sure that the smile is genuinely felt inside. Most importantly, don't be afraid to honestly state your own opinions when asked. You should speak and act in such a manner as if you were representing the company in its most important decisions.

—Tad Jankowski
Senior Vice President and General Counsel,
National Amusements

The presenter knows the material and doesn't read off the screen. The presenter has good pacing (which suggests both calmness and a strong-enough grasp of the subject to be aware of how he's coming across). He or she is able to engage in dialogue (answer questions, clarify a point, defer a question until later in the presentation). Very importantly, attention is paid to the right people in the audience, making the audience feel included. What presenters do not want to do is appear physically uncomfortable, use verbal crutches to excess, speak using poor grammar, and oversell or undersell a recommendation. This means the presenter really needs to know the audience.

—Ross Elkin
Innovation & Development, Irving Oil

An effective presentation has several components to it. I would note first that the die can be cast before the person walks into the room. When making a presentation, you should be very well prepared. That means to have full command of the subject matter and to think in advance of how you would respond to all questions you can think of. That will also serve to make you at ease when you have to answer a question you didn't think of.

A person who makes me think he or she is "executive material" is someone who obviously knows her stuff and projects confidence. The person should look me in the eye, be animated and engaged, and, very importantly, be succinct and organized. It is not necessary to provide every detail just because you know it. If asked a question, he or she should focus on answering the question, as opposed to reverting back to a pre-planned script.

A person I would not want to present on the company's behalf gets thrown off when asked a question, appears overly nervous, speaks in a droning monotone, or gets into too much unnecessary detail. Any of these can lose the audience and lose the "sale."

In short, be prepared, look and act confident and get to the point.

—*Philippe Dauman*
President and Chief Executive Officer, Viacom

A successful presentation is one delivered by a polished speaker who is well organized, well prepared, brief, informative, interesting, and who interacts with the audience.

Authoritative and knowledgeable: When someone presents, he or she should not stand by the computer clicking from slide to slide. The person should hold a remote in order to transition slides smoothly. He should be able to pitch ideas with his eyes closed and be passionate! When someone presents an idea and you think, "I should have thought of that," that's executive material. The person thinks and presents beyond the observable.

Personality: I am always impressed when a speaker diverts from the structured speech from time to time to interject anecdotes that make the material more interesting.

Exciting: Emphasize but do not rant and rave. Never rush your presentation.

Prepare: The person should have fewer than ten slides, regardless of subject matter. If something requires a longer explanation, handouts are required. A summary handout is also nice, not just a printed copy of the slides.

Know and react to your audience: If possible, walk around; don't get stuck behind a podium during the entire presentation. Size up your audience; the same presentation can be made in more than one way depending on the type of audience being addressed. Explain any technical procedures in layman's terms. Do not assume that the audience knows what you are talking about.

Mention your company's name multiple times: The presenter should not mention the competitor (if one exists). Even if asked about a competitor, the competitor's name should never be uttered by the presenter. The person should have an impressive explanation as to why his or her company is better, of course. But never ever say: "We're better than Yahoo! because. . . ." The presenter should say his company's name as many times as possible throughout the presentation. Why? Cognitively speaking, you want the person listening to that presentation to have heard your company's name multiple times so that it is implanted into long-term rather than short-term memory. Research shows that in the future (even a day later) if the person is asked, "Do you like X or Y (Yahoo) better, they will say X over Y due to the recency effect. A competitor's name is not worth uttering.

Summary: Finally, I always like a short and concise summary of the material that wraps up the important points of the presentation. All too often this last step is forgotten, as is most of the material discussed. The audience should come away knowing and be more interested about your subject than before your presentation.

—Mitchell Rubenstein
Chairman and CEO, Hollywood Media Corp.

CONCLUSION

You have read the graduate course on presenting. It is now your turn to follow the chapter motto: Be energetic, take charge, and engage in dialogue with your audience. To demonstrate executive presence, you must not only take charge of your own behaviors, but seek to understand your audience, size up their way of looking at ideas and present accordingly. Executives don't want to listen too long before they have a dialogue about your information and recommendations.

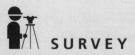

SURVEY

In the survey it became obvious that people do not ask for feedback. When asked, "What would it take for you to be satisfied with your presentation performance?" the survey respondents consistently answered "audience feedback." Presenters want and need feedback from the audience that their message got through, yet they are reluctant to seriously ask for it. The indicators used to assess audience reaction vary greatly from presenter to presenter. Some say they look for smiling faces during the talk or "attaboys" at the conclusion. Others measure success based on closing a sale or gaining acceptance for a new idea. To say the least, these are less than objectives measures.

Let's look at your first opportunity for improvement. How can you obtain accurate, real-time feedback? You have many options. You can attend a presentation class. You can set up individual coaching sessions in person or on the phone. You can give out questionnaires to your audience. In my opinion, you must hand out questionnaires. Real audience feedback is the best way to truly know how your audience perceives you and your message. Use the Executive Presence Behaviors Checklist in this chapter and/or the Rehearsal Checklist in Chapter 7. Be smart; hand them out to all or some of your audience members. Go for it. Be courageous and ask for specific feedback. This will be a challenge for many of you. I dare you to take the risk.

By yourself you can also read over these checklists and start putting these behaviors into your presentations. When you do a little every day in every meeting setting, you will improve dramatically in a short amount of time. You can have a partner in your presentation who gives you feedback about how well you did with one specific behavior you are working on changing. This can be useful if your partner is specific and pays attention to what you want to change.

Why should you take these risks? You really need to understand your strengths and areas for improvement. Don't be delusional, thinking you are worse than you are or better than you are. At this point, some of you really have no idea how people perceive your talks. Get some real feedback. The critique in Exhibit 8.4, when given to the appropriate people, will provide a beginning to your understanding of how others see you. Take a chance and use it. Skyrocket your success. Increase your confidence. Become the presenter of your vision. For the "Ten Keys When Speaking to Executives" go to www.wilderpresentations.com/ten keys/index.html.

Exhibit 8.4
Executive Presence Behaviors Critique

Engaging Opening	Took control from the beginning	Yes	Somewhat	Not enough
	Opening words were strong and engaged the audience	Yes	Somewhat	Not enough
Enthusiastic and In-Charge Manner	Talked with passion and energy; confident, inspiring, charismatic	Yes	Do more	Do less
	Spoke using "in control" words and phrases. Says "I believe," not "I think." Uses precise words, not qualifiers such as maybe, really, really definitely, or perhaps.	Yes	Do more	
	Took a stand. You heard the point of view.	Yes	Do more	Do less
	Really took the time to look at people when talking	Yes	Sometimes	Not enough
	Smiled when appropriate	Just right	Do more	Do less
	Moved toward audience to influence: walked or leaned forward at table	Yes	Do more	Do less
	Emotional	Just right	Too emotional	More emotion
Gives Audience Time to Reflect	Paused for emphasis at the right places	Yes	Too little	Too much
	Stories/examples used	Yes	Do more	Do less
	Stayed on subject: relevant explanations	Yes	Sometimes went off track	

Answers Questions with Style	Spoke in the right amount of detail	Yes	Too much detail	Not enough
	Appeared confident	Yes	Somewhat	Not enough
Motivational Closing	Clear engaging closing words	Yes	Somewhat	No
	Stood still for three seconds before walked off	Yes	Stay a little longer	

General Comments (opening, words to leave out or keep using, closing):

Be the Magic in Your Presentations . . . Be the Wow!

It has been both a challenge and a pleasure writing this third edition of *Point, Click & Wow!* Indeed, much has taken place since the original book was released. In those days the focus was on the technology, the tools, and the special effects for the very reason that much of that was new. The result was that many presenters replaced their own role in the presentation with an undue reliance on gimmickry. To some extent, they have been enslaved by the very tools that have been designed to liberate them! The central message in this book is that we must to some extent turn back the clock in order to move forward. The focus of the presentation should be on the presenter—YOU—who is the master of the tools at hand and can choose to use them in order to maximize the effectiveness of the presentation.

I have been working on this revision during 2007 and 2008, writing from my home in Boston. During that time the Red Sox have won the World Series and the Celtics achieved one of the great team turnarounds in sports history. And I have reflected on what these incredible successes in baseball and basketball mean in the context of making presentations. The superb athletes who participate in these sports do not "wing it" before a game. Nor do they play without thoroughly analyzing and evaluating every aspect of their opposing teams and having a plan that will lead them to success. I suspect that, like all of us, these athletes have concerns about their capabilities or whether or not they will make a mistake during a game when the stress level is so high and the stakes so important. But they deal with them in ways that we all recognize as fundamental to success. Their confidence, skill, and success come from being fully prepared for the "game." This entails training, conditioning, practice, more practice, planning, evaluating the opponents, strategy, and coaching months and years before they are truly ready. And this practice or rehearsal continues even when the athletes are at the peak of their performance so that they can even further refine and improve what they are doing. This is the same thing that you need to do in order to be a superb presenter—and in this sense, not only when you do "formal" presentations, but each and every time you speak with someone. Just as the skills that you need to properly make a no-look pass do not come naturally, so too must you learn and practice those skills that make you an effective communicator. Professional athletes have coaches who exhort them to train harder and to become better. Use this book as your personal presentation coach. Really use the checklists at the end of each chapter; in reality, that is I, your personal presentation coach, guiding and coaching you through every step of the process. If you do even one-fourth (and I hope you do more!) of what I recommend in this book, then I guarantee your presentations will be immeasurably better and you will even surprise yourself.

Now that you have read this book, you know what you need to do to be a successful presenter. First, you need to do the right kind of preparation, which includes understanding what kind of presentation your particular audience needs, organizing the presentation, creating concise slides, and developing stories and other ways to connect with that specific audience in mind. Combine this with adequate "real" rehearsal time using friends and colleagues as your audience so that you can receive accurate feedback. Practice the talk using various types of executive presence behaviors. Look at the members of the audience—connect with them—and try to become aware of what they are thinking or feeling about your presentation. Think about how your audience will want to engage in a dialogue with you and prepare for that as well. Encourage audience participation so that each member becomes "vested" in the topic. Then throughout your presentation, let the audience experience the unique and interesting person that you are as you talk.

Second, in order to keep moving toward excellence, be sure to get professional feedback at least once or twice in your career. You may think that you know what you are doing, but there is nothing better than having a professional coach look at your slides, hear you present, and then tell you what needs to improve. You will be surprised at what you discover. None of us is perfect, and there are always ways to improve. Frequently, we hide our biggest weaknesses from ourselves!

Third, you must remember that your over-arching goal is to make your audience productive. Use your presentation to enable them comfortably to take actions and make decisions. Motivate their productivity by your content and delivery.

Last, always intend the best. You may have your own affirmations that you make in order to give you confidence and drive. Consider adding the following presentation-oriented affirmation to your collection:

> I intend and want to give a presentation that connects with my audience and contains just the right amount of detail to meet their needs and wants. My presentation is informative and interesting and the audience will enjoy the information and stories that I share. I intend that all the members of the audience realize that it is a personal pleasure to be here with them. I intend to enjoy myself and want my audience to know something about who I am. I want them to feel my joy as I present comfortably and confidently. I want to feel and know that each member of the audience is connecting with me and engaging with my topic. And most importantly, I intend to be the focus, the magic, and the WOW of the presentation so that, when I lead them, they will be happy to follow.

WILDER PRESENTATIONS

We offer a range of services from seminars to individual coaching to creatively redoing PowerPoint presentations.

In-House and Public Seminars

Winning Presentations Seminar (one or two days): In this unique seminar, everyone has the opportunity to redo or create a presentation and present a portion of it in class. All presentations are recorded on DVD. Time is spent on providing hints for more effectively using certain PowerPoint features. Save hours creating clear, logical talks that keep your audience's attention. Give presentations that make it easy for people to understand the issues and make decisions based on your talk. The seminar has pre-work questionnaires as well as optional follow-up coaching. Two to three times a year this seminar is open to the public.

Winning Sales Presentations Seminar (one or two days): Turn the boring data presentations into a sales tool. Enhance your salespeople's ability to sell by interacting with their prospects and customers to share the company's message. Frequently for this seminar, we create the ideal presentation before the seminar and then coach the salespeople on how to present it.

Demonstrate Executive Presence Seminar (one day): This high-level seminar is for those who want to become more charismatic, persuasive presenters. Learn how to present to the highest levels in your company. Learn how to give less data-focused presentations and more message-oriented talks geared towards your audience's interests. Learn how to share stories and examples. The seminar shows participants how to practice the executive behaviors discussed in Chapter 8 of this book.

Create PowerPoint Presentations That Get Your Point Across (one day): This seminar covers the chapters in this book on how to develop and design the content for a presentation. A file of effective slide ideas is given to each participant and they practice using the images during the day. Time is spent showing participants how to use certain features in PowerPoint to work faster and smarter. Everyone brings a presentation and spends the day redoing it according to the guidelines taught in class. This seminar is open to all the people in the company who create the presentation slides, but may not actually give the presentation itself.

Coaching, Consulting, and Speeches

Individual coaching: We provide executive coaching to enable clients to demonstrate executive presence when speaking to others. This is sometimes an ongoing process as well as a one-time meeting of several hours. This type of coaching frequently occurs when people are preparing for upper management meetings, investor road shows, and board meetings. The question is: Can you help me speak to upper management in a way that I sound credible and confident?

Conference consulting: Whether it is a sales, investor, or customer conference, we help develop and organize the key messages, design the slides, and coach presenters on their delivery. We equip your company with specific storyboard formats and already designed PowerPoint slides. We show you how to build presentations that incite action. We teach your presenters how to speak with confidence in order to gain the credibility of your audience. You watch each presenter demonstrate success one presentation at a time.

PowerPoint design: We offer all levels of PowerPoint design. We take your special presentation and redesign the slides. We create a set of twenty professional-looking slides for you to use as you create presentations. We reorganize your presentation in a more logical, concise manner and then create the slides to go with it. We are ready to fix one slide for you or help develop the content and create all the necessary slides.

Speeches: Claudyne speaks at company meetings, conferences, and other venues on such topics as: Demonstrate Executive Presence, How an Effective Presentation Is Like a Fabulous Argentine Tango Dance, and Creating PowerPoint Presentations That Get Your Point Across.

Products

Monthly E-Newsletter: The *Presentations Points Bulletin*, a free monthly e-newsletter since 1999. Sign up at www.wilderpresentations.com.

E-Book: This book covers short hints on 12 Habits of Successful Presenters, 12 Keys to Compelling Presentation Content, 12 Ways to Save Hours Creating PowerPoint Slides, 12 Products You Need, 12 Case Studies, and 12 Design Aids to use. Go to www.wilderpresentations.com to download.

Presentations in a Hurry: 26 Formats That Persuade: *Presentations in a Hurry* gives you twenty-six professionally designed PowerPoint slide designs covering most common presentation scenarios, from project updates to communicating bad news. Each PowerPoint file lets you quickly organize your ideas and insert appropriate content for your specific topic. Simply follow the content recommendations and, once you drop in the text, your presentation will be complete. These formats can be downloaded from www.wilderpresentations.com.

Seminar License to Teach the Winning Presentations Seminar or Creating PowerPoint Presentations That Get Your Point Across: Use the expert's materials to become the ultimate presentations coach! Wilder's license gives you all the training materials you need to teach the Winning Presentations Seminar, including teaching modules, PowerPoint presentations, books, and audiotapes. You and your trainers will be able to customize the seminar for specific groups.

Talks You Can Give: Each talk comes complete with PowerPoint slides and speaker notes, ready for you to use. Some of the talks available are Ten Steps to Successful Presentations, Demonstrating Executive Presence, and Creating Effective PowerPoint Slides.

POWERPOINT ADD-IN PROGRAMS

Library of Images to Replace Bulleted Text: Perspector

www.perspector.com/gallery_library.cfm

You can see six of their images on the CD and many, many more at their website. One of the things I like about this program is they have an image in which you can put two slides on one slide. See this and some of their other images on the CD. You can edit the images. You can create, rotate, and animate 3-D shapes. I suggest you try it.

Reduce File Size: NXPOWERLITE

www.nxpowerlite.com

NXPowerLite has a product that will reduce your file size and make it easier to send. I've used it successfully with many files. I've reduced some by two-thirds. A trial version is available from www.nxpowerlite.com.

Screen Captures: SNAGIT

www.techsmith.com/snagit/whatsnew.asp

SnagIt 8.2 makes it easy to print screen captures exactly the way you see them onscreen—the right way, every time. Images and scrolling web pages are readable when printed and retain their original appearance. SnagIt's two new callout styles, plain and glassy, give you more flexibility than ever in customizing your screen capture. With SnagIt's new output accessories you can send your screen capture directly to Word, PowerPoint, Excel, MindManager, or Flickr, with a single click. They also make Camtasia, which is an easy-to-use screen capture and editing video software.

Business Frameworks and Analytical Diagrams: Graphicae

www.graphicae.com

You add this program in to PowerPoint and you can choose from shapes such as funnels, forces, and finance to show your information in the most appropriate and understandable manner. I have used it and like it.

Opazity: Obscure and Then Reveal Images

www.opazity.com

Blurs all or part of the PowerPoint slide and therefore hints at something to be revealed. Helps presenters use the power of curiosity to catch, hold, and maintain an audience's attention. Effects can be created without manipulating the images in some other graphics program and importing them back into PowerPoint.

CRYSTAL GRAPHICS' POWERPOINT ADD-ONS

Crystal Graphics is the #1 provider of tools, templates and content to enhance Microsoft Office. The company offers so many great add-ons to PowerPoint. Here are just some of their great products. Go read about and see demos of all their products at www.crystalgraphics.com.

PowerPlugs: Ultimate Combo: Includes all of Crystal Graphics' most popular graphics and effects products—including Templates, Transitions, Video Backgrounds, and more.

PowerPlugs: Templates for PowerPoint: Thousands of spectacular, award-winning PowerPoint templates. Hundreds of stunning new templates added monthly.

PowerPlugs: Transitions: Transitions add sophisticated television-style 3D slide effects to your presentations. Includes stunning visual effects and realistic, synchronized sounds.

PowerPlugs: Pictures: A diverse, dynamic collection of royalty-free JPEG business photos on CD and/or download. Easily drop them into presentations to make your point with pictures.

PowerPlugs: FlashReady: The easiest way to quickly add the power of Flash to PowerPoint presentations. Includes over ninety Flash animations.

PowerPlugs: PhotoActive FX: Focus your audience's attention on your key visuals with "one-click" photo animation.

PowerPlugs: VideoBackgrounds: Television-quality full-screen moving backgrounds to PowerPoint presentations with just three clicks!

PowerPlugs: Music: Energize your PowerPoint presentations with upbeat background music. Each volume includes twenty-five or more upbeat song soundtracks.

PowerPlugs: Shapes: Direct your audience's attention to your key points with customizable, animated clip art for PowerPoint.

PowerPlugs: Screensaver: Now you can create impressive screen savers, right within Microsoft PowerPoint. Use them to inform, motivate, persuade.

GRAPHIC PROGRAM TO SUPPLEMENT POWERPOINT

www.smartdraw.com

SmartDraw is a program that gives you pre-drawn templates to make it easy to turn your information into brilliant illustrations. The graphics include flowcharts, organizational charts, project timelines, marketing charts, floor plans, and others. This program can give you graphics that you might also put into a report. They are easy to create and help you organize your data.

TIMER FOR POWERPOINT PRESENTATIONS

http://office.microsoft.com/en-us/results.aspx?qu=timer%2bin%2bpowerpoint

Do you need a timer to use during your PowerPoint talk? Microsoft Office has many timers. You can choose from one-minute to fifteen-minute timer slides. It's simple—all you have to do is download the slide and put it in your presentation.

THERMOMETER FOR POWERPOINT FROM INDEZINE

www.indezine.com/addin/thermometer/

This is a nifty little tool to have. You see a thermometer bar in the bottom area of the slide that shows how much of a presentation has progressed and how much more is remaining.

BACKGROUNDS: POWERFINISH

www.powerfinish.com

From single template downloads to complete design collections on CDs, you'll find exactly what you need for a successful presentation. One of the things I like is that they have PowerPoint templates with eighteen matching alternate backgrounds in .jpg format.

"STORY TELLING" BOOKS

Story by Robert McKee is a book about the substance, structure, style, and the principles of screenwriting. It is very useful though when thinking about telling stories during your presentation.

Presenting to Win: The Art of Telling Your Story by Jerry Weissman provides wonderful examples of how to tell a story when you talk. If you are doing an IPO, this is the book to read. If he doesn't convince you to change from data to storytelling, then no one will.

ACTING IMPROVISATION WORKSHOP

http://daenagiardella.com/

Daena Giardella, who works out of Boston, offers weekly and weekend workshops. After learning about improvisation, your presentations in business will be so much easier, creative, and fun to do.

PRESENTATIONS SITES

There are so many presentation sites. I am mentioning these, as I work with these people in some manner.

Geetesh Babaj, author of *Cutting Edge Powerpoint 2007 for Dummies*, provides reviews, interviews, tutorials, templates, a blog, tips, thousands of free templates, and other materials. The site (www.Indezine.com) also has a monthly newsletter that you can sign up for.

Ellen Finkelstein (www.ellenfinkelstein.com) is the author of many presentations books, the latest being *How to Do Everything with Microsoft PowerPoint 2007*. She sends out a monthly newsletter with PowerPoint tips. It is very helpful. You will keep on learning.

AV PRODUCTS

ADTECH Systems in Sudbury, Massachusetts, is a "ProAV" dealer, which is different from a retailer or Internet seller in that the products sold and services offered are geared for business and government. Rather than focusing on box-sales, ADTECH pushes complete solutions. More than just a projector or a Plasma, they do the whole integration, with switching, control and installation. You can reach ADTECH by phone at 800-649-9809 or 508-358-0077, by email at info@theprojectorpros.com, and on the web at www.theprojectorpros.com

PRESENTATION DESIGNERS

Julie Terberg (www.terbergdesign.com) is an amazing designer. She designs for the specific presentation need, not for the design look. She can help you visualize words and ideas into clear, memorable concepts.

Kelly Ellis (www.designendeavors.com) helped with the slides in this book. She also created many of the slide designs for *Presentations in a Hurry: 26 Formats That Persuade.*

BOOKS

Pocket Guide to Technical Presentations & Professional Speaking by Steven Zwickel and William S. Pfeiffer. This is a fabulous book on technical presentations.

Fixing Powerpoint Annoyances: How to Fix the Most Annoying Things About Your Favorite Presentation Program by Echo Swinford. The author talks about going from one version of PowerPoint to another and the problems you will encounter. She sets up the "annoyance question" and then gives an answer in a simple, clear, understandable manner. She has screen shots of PowerPoint so you can see what she means. You will love this book if you have to use PowerPoint.

Cutting Edge PowerPoint 2007 for Dummies by Geetesh Bajaj. This is an excellent book and it has a CD full of templates, textures, images, programs, and more.

How to Do Everything with Microsoft Office PowerPoint 2007 by Ellen Finkelstein. Ellen has written so many books on PowerPoint that she can probably create slides in her sleep. It's an excellent book to have around to look up issues at the last moment.

Perfect Medical Presentations by Terry Irwin and Julie Terberg. This book won the British Medical Association's annual book prize in the Basis of Medicine category. There were 619 entries. This book summarizes everything an enthusiastic presenter needs to know about taking, altering, and presenting medical images for print, PowerPoint, and the web.

Speak Like a CEO by Suzanne Bates. This is a very easy book to read. Suzanne was a top CEO consultant and award-winning television anchor. She has some excellent information on media interviews, toasts, and speeches.

Learned Optimism: How to Change Your Mind and Your Life by Martin Seligman. This is a must if you feel that you need more optimism and an upbeat style when presenting (well, when living as well). I recommend it to many of my clients who berate themselves when things do not go perfectly during a presentation.

The Law of Attraction by Esther and Jerry Hicks. As you move on your journey to being a fabulous presenter, learn how things unwanted and wanted come to you. Understand you want to spend no time talking about the things you don't want to happen in your or other people's presentations. Your presentations will change as you apply these ideas.

Power vs. Force: The Hidden Determinants of Human Behavior by David Hawkins. This book will once again reinforce how you look at and act in your life in order to make your dreams come true. Once you begin to realize you can control more of your life and how you are in front of people, your successes will increase.

The Definitive Book of Body Language by Allan and Barbara Pease. This is a fabulous book that will give you insights into such areas as how to dress, what glasses to wear, how to shake hands, and how to deal with difficult people as you look at them. It is fun to read as well.

Introduction to Internal Family Systems by Robert Schwartz. I can watch a presenter and see that the person is spending a lot of time dealing with internal dialogues that are happening when he or she is talking. This book discusses the family system we all have inside and how to get them all on the same page.

This means that when presenting no one is in your head saying things like, "That was dumb" or "You can't say anything right." I love this little book. Buy it at www.selfleadership.org/store_order_form.asp.

177 Mental Toughness Secrets of the World Class: The Thought Processes, Habits and Philosophies of the Great Ones by Steve Siebold. This is a wonderful book to have you reconsider yourself and how you approach your life and your work. For presentations, it will motivate you to become a world class presenter with beliefs and values to take you to the presentation successes you desire.

CDS
Breathing Practice: *Respire 1*

www.coherence.com

Respire 1 CD promotes the practice of "coherent breathing." Coherent breathing is a breathing modality that directly results in autonomic nervous system balance and cardiopulmonary resonance. This practice will teach you to relax.

www.tomalden.com

Tom Alden has created the most gorgeous CD of combined music and meditation. It includes seven different meditations of about five to ten minutes each. You owe it to yourself to buy one. After you listen to the different segments you will be so much calmer and at peace when presenting. The CD is not about presenting, it is about life and living the full life you intend to live.

REFERENCES

Bajaj, G. *Cutting edge PowerPoint 2007 for Dummies.* Hoboken, NJ: John Wiley & Sons.

Bates, S. (2005). *Speak like a CEO: Secrets for commanding attention and getting results.* New York: McGraw-Hill.

Gladwell, M. (2005). *Blink.* New York: Little, Brown and Company.

Kalyuga, S., Chandler, P., & Sweller, J. (2004). When redundant on-screen text in multimedia technical instruction can interfere with learning. *Human Factors, 46*(3), 567–581.

McKee, R. (1997). *Story: Substance, structure, style and the principles of screenwriting.* New York: HarperCollins.

Miller, R., & Williams, G. (2004). *The 5 paths to persuasion: The art of selling your message.* New York: Warner Business Books.

Seligman, M. (2006). *Learned optimism: How to change your mind and your life.* New York: Vintage Books.

Zwickel, S.B., & Pfeiffer, W.B. (2006). *Pocket guide to technical presentations and professional speaking.* Englewood Cliffs, NJ: Prentice-Hall.

INDEX

Dramatic voice tone, 228
Dress code tips, 198–200
Drop, D., 177–179

E

Electronic handouts, 41–42
Elkin, R., 248
Ellis, K., 148
Emotion-color associations, 123e
Emotional behaviors, 221–223
Emotional connection slides,
    145fig–146fig
Emotions
    color associations with, 123e
    confidence, 190–198
    controlling your inner monologue and,
        201–204
    conveying enthusiasm through
        your, 234
"Empty" content slides
    Change From Present to Future, 105fig
    description and uses of, 100–105, 107
    For a Slide with Key Points and
        Subpoints, 103fig
    Grouping Information for Variety, 103fig
    Harvard Medical International
        Strategic Collaboration Slide, 100fig
    Implementation Timeline, 104fig
    logical presentation of information,
        107fig–110fig
    Mission Statement, 101fig
    Product Summary, 102fig
    Question and Answer Opening, 102fig
    Strategies and Resources Needed, 105fig
    Timeline Slide, 104fig
    title with Subheading, 106fig
    What Are Your Answers?, 106fig
Entertainment, 227–228
Equipment
    avoid using unfamiliar, 179
    bringing your own, 176

laptops, 161–176
LCD protectors, 175
screens, 163, 167
surge protectors, 169
WiFi connections, 178–179
See also Technology issues
Equipment Checklist, 209e
Executive presence
    advice from executives on, 244–250
    benefits of demonstrating, 213–214
    considering best path for persuasion
        context of, 214–244
    emotional behaviors and, 221–223
    using entertainment and drama for,
        227–228
    factual behaviors and, 217–221
    making recommendations for
        improving, 228–230
    opinionated behaviors and, 214–217
    optimistic behavior role in, 230
    plan what to say about the data for,
        225–227
    problems, opportunities, and solution
        for, 211
    selecting appropriate behaviors for,
        223–225
    story on successful, 211–212
Executive Presence Behaviors Critique,
    252e–253e
Executive Summary slides
    appropriated for poster presentation, 73
    CD-ROM examples of, 27fig–29fig
    for charismatics, 235, 236fig
    convincing format, 19fig
    creating an, 25–27
    for followers, 240
    selling and research functions of, 26–27
    selling format, 13fig
    for skeptics, 237, 238fig
    for thinkers, 231, 233fig
Eye contact, 193–194

Key problems (*continued*)
 related to key messages, 1
 related to rehearsing presentations, 181
 related to specific PowerPoint
  features, 77
 related to technology issues, 159
 See also Problems

L

Language issues
 checking the translation, 68
 dramatic voice tone, 228
 using interpreter for, 66–67, 172–173
 Pimsleur tapes to help with, 198
 practice speaking native language of
  audience, 197–198
 slide language and other, 66
 See also Audience
Laptops
 avoid sharing with others, 168
 avoiding accidental damage to,
  168–169, 175–176
 backing up files, 161–163, 171
 check batteries of, 163
 computer crashes, 171, 173, 175
 don't let anyone "fix" your, 163–164
 international presentations and, 172
 learning from other people's stories on,
  173–176
 positioning yourself in relation to,
  191–192*fig*
 practice using remote mouse with,
  164–165
 specific recommendations for using,
  166–168
 theft of, 169–170
 WiFi connections and, 178–179
LCD protectors, 175
*Learning Optimism: How to Change
 Your Mind and Your Life*
 (Seligman), 230

Life After Death by PowerPoint
 (video), 115
Lighting issues, 166
List the Key Benefits of the Product here
 (slide), 15*fig*
Logical information presentation,
 107*fig*–110*fig*

M

Malloy, J. T., 200
Massachusetts General Hospital's
 Leadership Academy, 33
McKee, R., 34
Meeting preparation, 9
Mercury Computer Systems, 60–61
Miller, N., 37
Miller, R., 231, 234, 237, 239
Mini mini-story, 37–38
Mini rehearsals, 204–205
Mini-Talk Meeting Overview, 9*e*
Mission Statement (slide), 101*fig*
Mouse (remote), 164–165
Multiple country presentation tour, 68

N

Narration for talk, 188–189
Nervousness, 126*fig*
New Women's Dress for Success
 (Malloy), 200
Next Steps (slide), 24*fig*
Non-verbal behaviors
 1: position yourself, 190–193*fig*
 2: end sentences looking at someone,
  193–194
 3: move deliberately, 194
 4: don't leave the visual up when you
  aren't talking about it, 194
 5: pause between your sentences, 194
 6: hold the remote by your side, 195
 7: practice with the laser pointer, 195
NxPowerLite, 82

on demonstrating executive presence, 211–212

on designing professional slide looks, 91–92

on increasing credibility, 113–114

on key messages, 2

on rehearsing presentations, 181–182

on using specific PowerPoint features, 77

on technical issues, 159–160

technical lessons from anecdotes of others, 173–178

Story (McKee), 34

Strategies and Resources Needed (slide), 105*fig*

Surge Protectors, 169

Surveys

on excessive length of presentation, 147

on excessive preparation time, 11

on failure to rehearse, 185

on lack of subject-relevant images/ graphs, 107

Sweller, J., 117

T

Tables. *See* Graphs

Technical crew, 165

Technical information preparation, 8–9

Technical presentation, 63–64

Technology Checklist, 180*e*

Technology issues

avoid using unfamiliar equipment, 179

future of technology, 177–179

international presentations and, 172–173

keeping track of your laptop and contents, 168–172

last minute checks before presentation, 165–168

learning lessons from anecdotes of others, 173–178

problems, opportunities, and solution to, 159

recommendations for ensuring success with, 161–165

story on successful use of technology, 159–160

See also Equipment

Templates

appropriate to your corporate image, 120–122

poster presentation, 73

Ten Steps to Your Success, 86*fig*

Terberg Designs, 94

Terberg, J., 94

Theft of laptop, 169–170

Theme ideas, 5

Thinkers

characteristics of, 231

designing presentations to persuade, 231–233*fig*

Timeline Slide, 104*fig*

Titles

background with subheading under, 125*fig*

convincing format slide, 19*fig*

examples of before and after, 132*e*

selection of, 3

selling format slide, 12*fig*

with subheading, 106*fig*

writing informative or action-oriented, 132*e*

Total Image Consultants, 198

Total Visual Checklist, 154*e*–155*e*

Traveling fiascos, 176

Trust, 59

Two-toned background, 124

U

USB drives, 161

Using PowerPoint Checklist, 89*e*

ABOUT THE AUTHOR

Claudyne Wilder is a recognized authority on the art of presentations. As coach to executives, entrepreneurs, and professionals, she helps them develop, design, and deliver presentations that get results. She shows them how to develop and organize with just the right amount of content focused on specific key messages. She teaches them how to design the slides that enhance the message and enable them to communicate confidently and successfully. She coaches them so their delivery is succinct, confident, and engaging to the audience. Her clients learn how to gain commitment by crafting the right message focused on the audience's interests—all with just the appropriate amount of preparation. Her passionate hobby of dancing Argentine Tango gives her additional ways to coach her clients on pace, posture, and creating a connection to the audience.

Her expertise and unique consulting style comes from having worked with such clients as the Gillette Company, Mercury Computer, CVS, Genzyme Corporation, Blue Cross Blue Shield, Arthur D. Little, State Street Global Advisors, The Nature Conservancy, Harvard Medical International, MMA Financial, Avid Technology, and Harvard Medical School, among others.

Some of Claudyne's coaching includes working with executives on preparing for their investor and board meetings; salespeople on how to engage, not just talk to a potential customer; researchers on how sort the data in a way as to make the most important points; fund raisers on how to raise more money by telling stories instead of overwhelming the audience with data; and managers and individual contributors on how to sell themselves and their projects up and down the organization.

Claudyne has been sending out her free monthly *Presentation Points* bulletin since 1999. This bulletin provides her clients and all who sign up with ongoing coaching on effective communication.

You can't judge a book by its cover, but people do judge a business by its communications and formal presentations. Claudyne has been helping her clients transform theirs into the best.

Claudyne can be reached at: claudyne@wilderpresentations.com.

HOW TO USE THE CD-ROM

SYSTEM REQUIREMENTS

PC with Microsoft Windows 98SE or later

Mac with Apple OS version 10.1 or later

USING THE CD WITH WINDOWS

To view the items located on the CD, follow these steps:

1. Insert the CD into your computer's CD-ROM drive.

2. A window appears with the following options:

   Contents: Allows you to view the files included on the CD.

   Software: Allows you to install useful software from the CD.

   Links: Displays a hyperlinked page of websites.

   Author: Displays a page with information about the author(s).

   Contact Us: Displays a page with information on contacting the publisher or author.

   Help: Displays a page with information on using the CD.

   Exit: Closes the interface window.

If you do not have autorun enabled, or if the autorun window does not appear, follow these steps to access the CD:

1. Click Start → Run.

2. In the dialog box that appears, type d:\start.exe, where d is the letter of your CD-ROM drive. This brings up the autorun window described in the preceding set of steps.

3. Choose the desired option from the menu. (See Step 2 in the preceding list for a description of these options.)

IN CASE OF TROUBLE

If you experience difficulty using the CD, please follow these steps:

1. Make sure your hardware and systems configurations conform to the systems requirements noted under "System Requirements" above.

2. Review the installation procedure for your type of hardware and operating system. It is possible to reinstall the software if necessary.

To speak with someone in Product Technical Support, call 800-762-2974 or 317-572-3994 Monday through Friday from 8:30 A.M. to 5:00 P.M. EST. You can also contact Product Technical Support and get support information through our website at www.wiley.com/techsupport.

Before calling or writing, please have the following information available:

• Type of computer and operating system.

• Any error messages displayed.

• Complete description of the problem.

It is best if you are sitting at your computer when making the call.

Pfeiffer Publications Guide

This guide is designed to familiarize you with the various types of Pfeiffer publications. The formats section describes the various types of products that we publish; the methodologies section describes the many different ways that content might be provided within a product. We also provide a list of the topic areas in which we publish.

FORMATS

In addition to its extensive book-publishing program, Pfeiffer offers content in an array of formats, from fieldbooks for the practitioner to complete, ready-to-use training packages that support group learning.

FIELDBOOK Designed to provide information and guidance to practitioners in the midst of action. Most fieldbooks are companions to another, sometimes earlier, work, from which its ideas are derived; the fieldbook makes practical what was theoretical in the original text. Fieldbooks can certainly be read from cover to cover. More likely, though, you'll find yourself bouncing around following a particular theme, or dipping in as the mood, and the situation, dictate.

HANDBOOK A contributed volume of work on a single topic, comprising an eclectic mix of ideas, case studies, and best practices sourced by practitioners and experts in the field.

An editor or team of editors usually is appointed to seek out contributors and to evaluate content for relevance to the topic. Think of a handbook not as a ready-to-eat meal, but as a cookbook of ingredients that enables you to create the most fitting experience for the occasion.

RESOURCE Materials designed to support group learning. They come in many forms: a complete, ready-to-use exercise (such as a game); a comprehensive resource on one topic (such as conflict management) containing a variety of methods and approaches; or a collection of like-minded activities (such as icebreakers) on multiple subjects and situations.

TRAINING PACKAGE An entire, ready-to-use learning program that focuses on a particular topic or skill. All packages comprise a guide for the facilitator/trainer and a workbook for the participants. Some packages are supported with additional media—such as video—or learning aids, instruments, or other devices to help participants understand concepts or practice and develop skills.

- *Facilitator/trainer's guide* Contains an introduction to the program, advice on how to organize and facilitate the learning event, and step-by-step instructor notes.

The guide also contains copies of presentation materials—handouts, presentations, and overhead designs, for example—used in the program.

- *Participant's workbook* Contains exercises and reading materials that support the learning goal and serves as a valuable reference and support guide for participants in the weeks and months that follow the learning event. Typically, each participant will require his or her own workbook.

ELECTRONIC CD-ROMs and web-based products transform static Pfeiffer content into dynamic, interactive experiences. Designed to take advantage of the searchability, automation, and ease-of-use that technology provides, our e-products bring convenience and immediate accessibility to your workspace.

METHODOLOGIES

CASE STUDY A presentation, in narrative form, of an actual event that has occurred inside an organization. Case studies are not prescriptive, nor are they used to prove a point; they are designed to develop critical analysis and decision-making skills. A case study has a specific time frame, specifies a sequence of events, is narrative in structure, and contains a plot structure—an issue (what should be/have been done?). Use case studies when the goal is to enable participants to apply previously learned theories to the circumstances in the case, decide what is pertinent, identify the real issues, decide what should have been done, and develop a plan of action.

ENERGIZER A short activity that develops readiness for the next session or learning event. Energizers are most commonly used after a break or lunch to stimulate or refocus the group. Many involve some form of physical activity, so they are a useful way to counter post-lunch lethargy. Other uses include transitioning from one topic to another, where "mental" distancing is important.

EXPERIENTIAL LEARNING ACTIVITY (ELA) A facilitator-led intervention that moves participants through the learning cycle from experience to application (also known as a Structured Experience). ELAs are carefully thought-out designs in which there is a definite learning purpose and intended outcome. Each step—everything that participants do during the activity—facilitates the accomplishment of the stated goal. Each ELA includes complete instructions for facilitating the intervention and a clear statement of goals, suggested group size and timing, materials required, an explanation of the process, and, where appropriate, possible variations to the activity. (For more detail on Experiential Learning Activities, see the Introduction to the *Reference Guide to Handbooks and Annuals*, 1999 edition, Pfeiffer, San Francisco.)

GAME A group activity that has the purpose of fostering team spirit and togetherness in addition to the achievement of a pre-stated goal. Usually contrived—undertaking a desert expedition, for example—this type of learning method offers an engaging means for participants to demonstrate and practice business and interpersonal skills. Games are effective for team building and personal development mainly because the goal is subordinate to the process—the means through which participants reach decisions, collaborate, communicate, and generate trust and understanding. Games often engage teams in "friendly" competition.

ICEBREAKER A (usually) short activity designed to help participants overcome initial anxiety in a training session and/or to acquaint the participants with one another. An icebreaker can be a fun activity or can be tied to specific topics or training goals. While a useful tool in itself, the icebreaker comes into its own in situations where tension or resistance exists within a group.

INSTRUMENT A device used to assess, appraise, evaluate, describe, classify, and summarize various aspects of human behavior. The term used to describe an instrument depends primarily on its format and purpose. These terms include survey, questionnaire, inventory, diagnostic, survey, and poll. Some uses of instruments include providing instrumental feedback to group members, studying here-and-now processes or functioning within a group, manipulating group composition, and evaluating outcomes of training and other interventions.

Instruments are popular in the training and HR field because, in general, more growth can occur if an individual is provided with a method for focusing specifically on his or her own behavior. Instruments also are used to obtain information that will serve as a basis for change and to assist in workforce planning efforts.

Paper-and-pencil tests still dominate the instrument landscape with a typical package comprising a facilitator's guide, which offers advice on administering the instrument and interpreting the collected data, and an initial set of instruments. Additional instruments are available separately. Pfeiffer, though, is investing heavily in e-instruments. Electronic instrumentation provides effortless distribution and, for larger groups particularly, offers advantages over paper-and-pencil tests in the time it takes to analyze data and provide feedback.

LECTURETTE A short talk that provides an explanation of a principle, model, or process that is pertinent to the participants' current learning needs. A lecturette is intended to establish a common language bond between the trainer and the participants by providing a mutual frame of reference. Use a lecturette as an introduction to a group activity or event, as an interjection during an event, or as a handout.

MODEL A graphic depiction of a system or process and the relationship among its elements. Models provide a frame of reference and something more tangible, and more easily remembered, than a verbal explanation. They also give participants something to "go on," enabling them to track their own progress as they experience the dynamics, processes, and relationships being depicted in the model.

ROLE PLAY A technique in which people assume a role in a situation/scenario: a customer service rep in an angry-customer exchange, for example. The way in which the role is approached is then discussed and feedback is offered. The role play is often repeated using a different approach and/or incorporating changes made based on feedback received. In other words, role playing is a spontaneous interaction involving realistic behavior under artificial (and safe) conditions.

SIMULATION A methodology for understanding the interrelationships among components of a system or process. Simulations differ from games in that they test or use a model that depicts or mirrors some aspect of reality in form, if not necessarily in content. Learning occurs by studying the effects of change on one or more factors of the model. Simulations are commonly used to test hypotheses about what happens in a system—often referred to as "what if?" analysis—or to examine best-case/worst-case scenarios.

THEORY A presentation of an idea from a conjectural perspective. Theories are useful because they encourage us to examine behavior and phenomena through a different lens.

TOPICS

The twin goals of providing effective and practical solutions for workforce training and organization development and meeting the educational needs of training and human resource professionals shape Pfeiffer's publishing program. Core topics include the following:

Leadership & Management

Communication & Presentation

Coaching & Mentoring

Training & Development

E-Learning

Teams & Collaboration

OD & Strategic Planning

Human Resources

Consulting

What will you find on pfeiffer.com?

- The best in workplace performance solutions for training and HR professionals

- Downloadable training tools, exercises, and content

- Web-exclusive offers

- Training tips, articles, and news

- Seamless on-line ordering

- Author guidelines, information on becoming a Pfeiffer Affiliate, and much more

Discover more at www.pfeiffer.com